Ignored

American Society of Missiology Monograph Series

Chair of Series Editorial Committee, James R. Krabill

The ASM Monograph Series provides a forum for publishing quality dissertations and studies in the field of missiology. Collaborating with Pickwick Publications—a division of Wipf and Stock Publishers of Eugene, Oregon—the American Society of Missiology selects high quality dissertations and other monographic studies that offer research materials in mission studies for scholars, mission and church leaders, and the academic community at large. The ASM seeks scholarly work for publication in the series that throws light on issues confronting Christian world mission in its cultural, social, historical, biblical, and theological dimensions.

Missiology is an academic field that brings together scholars whose professional training ranges from doctoral-level preparation in areas such as Scripture, history and sociology of religions, anthropology, theology, international relations, interreligious interchange, mission history, inculturation, and church law. The American Society of Missiology, which sponsors this series, is an ecumenical body drawing members from Independent and Ecumenical Protestant, Catholic, Orthodox, and other traditions. Members of the ASM are united by their commitment to reflect on and do scholarly work relating to both mission history and the present-day mission of the church. The ASM Monograph Series aims to publish works of exceptional merit on specialized topics, with particular attention given to work by younger scholars, the dissemination and publication of which is difficult under the economic pressures of standard publishing models.

Persons seeking information about the ASM or the guidelines for having their dissertations considered for publication in the ASM Monograph Series should consult the Society's website—www.asmweb.org.

Members of the ASM Monograph Committee who approved this book are:

Alison Fitchett Climenhaga, Research Fellow, Institute for Religion and Critical Inquiry, Australian Catholic University

Margaret E. Guider, OSF, Associate Professor of Missiology, Boston College School of Theology and Ministry

RECENTLY PUBLISHED IN THE ASM MONOGRAPH SERIES

Sue Whittaker, *Music and Liturgy, Identity and Formation: A Study of Inculturation in Turkey*

William A. Coppedge, *African Literacies and Western Oralities?: Communication Complexities, the Orality Movement, and the Materialities of Christianity in Uganda*

Ignored

A Practical Theology Inquiry of Korean-Speaking Young Adults in a Transnational Congregational Context

JINNA SIL LO JIN

FOREWORD BY
JUAN FRANCISCO MARTÍNEZ

American Society of Missiology Scholarly Monograph Series 58

☙PICKWICK *Publications* • Eugene, Oregon

IGNORED
A Practical Theology Inquiry of Korean-Speaking Young Adults in a Transnational Congregational Context

American Society of Missiology Scholarly Monograph Series 58

Copyright © 2022 Jinna Sil Lo Jin. All rights reserved. Except for brief quotations in critical publications or reviews, no part of this book may be reproduced in any manner without prior written permission from the publisher. Write: Permissions, Wipf and Stock Publishers, 199 W. 8th Ave., Suite 3, Eugene, OR 97401.

Pickwick Publications
An Imprint of Wipf and Stock Publishers
199 W. 8th Ave., Suite 3
Eugene, OR 97401

www.wipfandstock.com

PAPERBACK ISBN: 978-1-6667-0934-6
HARDCOVER ISBN: 978-1-6667-0935-3
EBOOK ISBN: 978-1-6667-0936-0

Cataloguing-in-Publication data:

Names: Jin, Jinna Sil Lo, author. | Martínez, Juan Francisco, foreword

Title: Ignored : a practical theology inquiry of Korean-speaking young adults in a transnational congregational context / by Jinna Sil Lo Jin; foreword by Juan Francisco Martínez.

Description: Eugene, OR: Pickwick Publications, 2022 | American Society of Missiology Scholarly Monograph Series 58 | **Includes bibliographical references.**

Identifiers: ISBN 978-1-6667-0934-6 (paperback) | ISBN 978-1-6667-0935-3 (hardcover) | ISBN 978-1-6667-0936-0 (ebook)

Subjects: LCSH: Korean American churches. | Young adults—United States—Religious life. | Church work with Korean Americans.

Classification: BR563.K67 J56 2022 (print) | BR563.K67 (ebook)

03/01/22

To all Korean-Speaking young people in America
who have been ignored

Content

List of Figures and Tables | viii
Foreword by Juan Francisco Martínez | xi
Acknowledgments | xiii

    Introduction | 1

1. Research Methodology | 12

2. Descriptive Task | 33
   Emerging Adulthood and Korean-Speaking Young Adults in the States

3. Interpretive Task | 64
   Who Are the Korean-Speaking Young Adults in Korean Immigrant Churches?

4. Normative Task | 98
   Migration Theology and Korean Immigrant Churches

5. Pragmatic Task | 126
   Changes for Korean Immigrant Churches

    Conclusion | 151

Appendices | 163
Bibliography | 191

List of Figures and Tables

FIGURES

Figure 2.1   Generational Replacement Drives Growth of Unaffiliated | 44

Figure 2.2   The Number of Korean Immigrant Churches in North America | 60

Figure 3.1   Age of Members in Korean-Speaking Young Adult Department | 66

Figure 3.2   Visa Status | 69

Figure 3.3   Numbers of Changing Visa | 69

Figure 3.4   Arriving Age | 71

Figure 3.5   Close Family Members in Korea | 72

Figure 3.6   Visits to Korea after Coming to America | 72

Figure 3.7   Number of Times Visiting Korea | 73

Figure 3.8   Close Family Members in America | 73

Figure 3.9   Church Affiliation Experience in Korea | 78

Figure 3.10   Duration of Attendance in the Current Church | 89

Figure 5.1   Missional Change Model | 141

TABLES

Table 1.1   Gender of Pastor Interviews | 21

Table 1.2   Denomination of Pastor Interviewees | 22

List of Figures and Tables

Table 1.3	Occupational Status of Pastor Interviewees	22
Table 1.4	Size of the Congregations	22
Table 1.5	Size of the Korean-Speaking Young Adult Department	23
Table 1.6	Gender of Korean-Speaking Young Adult Interviewees	23
Table 1.7	Age of Young Adult Interviewees	23
Table 1.8	Occupational Status of Young Adult Interviewees	24
Table 1.9	Role in the Church of Young Adult Interviewees	24
Table 1.10	Arriving Age in America of Young Adult Interviewees	24
Table 1.11	Visa Status of Young Adult Interviewees	25

Foreword

WE ARE LIVING IN the age of migration. Hundreds of millions of people migrate all over the world. This international migration brings changes throughout the whole world including America. Within this phenomenon, the United States is the largest receiving country for migrants. As America gets more racially and ethnically diverse, it brings changes and challenges to local communities and churches. Although there is a growing number of studies on immigrants and their churches, there is still a lot of missing research on how the immigrant experience informs the American church community and vice versa. Jinna Sil Lo Jin's work is about a group of young people who have long been ignored.

Dr. Jin's study sheds light on an overlooked yet significant population in the study of Korean American Christianity: Korean-speaking young adults in immigrant churches. Although these young people play a crucial role in the community, they have not yet gotten enough attention academically nor ministerially. Most studies on young people in immigrant churches have been about the so-called second generation who are typically English-speaking church members. Little to no studies have been done on primarily Korean-speaking church members so far. Jinna's study provides basic demographic information (age, gender, job, educational background) as well as immigration information (arrival age, purpose of immigration, visa status). It also highlights transnational ties with Korea, the immigrant church experience, and the experience of emerging adults in the United States. The study is based on a survey with over four hundred young people. It also provides important analysis on the current praxis of young Korean-speaking people in forty in-depth interviews.

Foreword

Jinna's work also applies a transnational approach as it displays previously unheard voices within immigrant studies. Traditionally, immigrant studies have been framed by a classical assimilation approach. The assimilation perspective tends to merely focus on how immigrants assimilate into a host country rather than the full immigrant experience. This study goes beyond the mere assimilation perspective in that it further examines immigrant ties to their home countries as they adapt to their new lives in the U.S. While assimilating into American culture, young Korean-speaking migrants typically maintain strong ties with Korea. This book helps us hear their side of the story: how young people hold ties with their homeland and how those ties impact hosting countries.

Not only does Jinna's work share information and data about young Korean-speaking people. Based on practical theology, this study provides concrete measures that Korean immigrant churches can take so that they can better serve young Korean-speaking adults. The four changes that she proposes are establishing intergenerational connections, an adoptive family of siblings, a missional church leadership culture, and a globally connected community in a transnational context. These are practical steps that are informed by her research. They provide meaningful points of discussion and discernment for church leaders and members as they seek to move forward in better caring for this population. Furthermore, these steps may be helpful for other immigrant churches trying to incorporate other homeland languages (Spanish, Chinese, Arabic, and other languages).

This is not just academic research. This is a living story that must be told. Jinna has actively worked with young Korean-speaking people in a Korean immigrant church. She has seen their struggles and heard their stories. When I met Jinna at Fuller Theological Seminary, she passionately showed the impact that sharing these voices could make on the immigrant church community. Her research compellingly and sympathetically gives a voice to this marginalized group and advocates a new vision for immigrant churches. This work is relevant not only to Korean immigrant churches but also other communities with unheard immigrant voices. I am sure this book will bring new ways of conceiving the structure of immigrant churches and missions all across America.

Juan Francisco Martínez, President
Centro Hispano de Estudios Teológicos

Acknowledgments

THE COMPLETION OF THIS research has been a journey undertaken with many people's support and help. Most of all, I want to acknowledge my parents Sang Hee Lee and Yong Sik Jin for their constant prayer and endless support. They have sacrificed in many ways so that I can finish this long journey. Unlike many traditional Korean parents, they respect my decision to pursue theological education and to be unmarried during my PhD studies.

I cannot adequately express my gratitude for my mentors: Chap Clark, Juan Martinez, and Mark Lau Branson. These three mentors have not only shaped my scholarship as a practical theologian who cares deeply about young people and migrants, but they have also fostered my emotional and spiritual growth. They have believed in me even when I wrestled with my own doubts about my gender and ethnicity. Their love, encouragement, and grace helped me face my fears and finally finish my research. Because of them, I am a better human being before God and his people.

I am also grateful for the Korean-speaking young adults and their pastors who did the surveys and in-depth interviews. Their honesty and willingness to share painful but beautiful stories made this study possible. I will never forget their smiles, tears, and warm-hearted openness toward an unfamiliar researcher.

I cannot neglect to mention Nina Lau Branson here. As my spiritual director, she is the person I go to whenever I need to cry or laugh. Her presence in my life, especially throughout my PhD studies, has been one of God's greatest gifts. Her patience, hospitality, and grace have held me

Acknowledgments

strong whenever I wanted to quit. From her, I have learned to receive the deep love and peace of God.

Also, I would like to acknowledge my husband, David Hyosung Han for his love and care. With his unique experience in three different cultures—Korean, American and Paraguayan—and his perspective stemming from outside the theological academy, he brings me so much insight and teaches me how theologians with humble hearts and eyes can learn about God everywhere and from everyone.

Lastly, I greatly appreciate the American Society of Missiology and its Chair James R. Krabill for their willingness to publish this study, which deals with a group of people to whom attention is rarely paid. With ASM's bold decision, this work becomes the first scholarly research of Korean-speaking young people in the US.

Introduction

BACKGROUND

THE SECOND-LARGEST POPULATION OF the Korean diaspora lives in the United States, with China hosting the largest population. According to the United States Census Bureau's American Community Survey (ACS), there were nearly 1.26 million adult Korean Americans living in the States as of 2010.[1] However, according to the Republic of Korea Ministry of Foreign Affairs, which includes temporary visa holders such as international students in its count, the population of Korean diaspora is more than two million adults as of 2015.[2] Data from the ACS also shows that an overwhelming 30 percent of Korean immigrants have settled in the state of California, with the Los Angeles metropolitan area boasting the largest population.[3] In sum, the population of Korean immigrants living within the United States is massive, and the Los Angeles metropolitan area serves as an important gathering place for the Korean diaspora.

Additionally, according to statistics published by the Pew Research Center in 2012, more than 70 percent of Korean Americans identify themselves as being Christian.[4] As one might imagine, given the significant number of Korean Christian residents, there are also over four thousand Korean

---

1. Hoeffel et al., "The Asian Population," 14.

2. According to the ministry of foreign affairs, as 2015, the number of Korean diasporas in the States is 2,238,989 (Citizens: 1,414,875; Green Card holders: 426,838; Student visa holders: 99,562; other temporary visa holders: 297,714).

3. Hoeffel et al., "The Asian Population," 14.

4. See "The Rise of Asian Americans."

immigrant churches[5] in the United States; these comprise more than 70 percent of all Korean immigrant churches in the world outside of Korea. Considering the fact that only 29 percent of the South Korean population identified as being Christian 2010,[6] it is clear that the role and influence of Christianity and church is *even more* significant for the Korean population in the United States than for Koreans living in Korea.

The history of Korean immigration is itself deeply related to the history of the Korean immigrant church in America. Records show that shortly after Korean immigrants settled in the United States in 1903, they began establishing churches.[7] Alongside Korean immigration, the Korean immigrant church has become a crucial part of Korean immigrant life. Korean immigrant churches have functioned not only as places for religious worship, but also as major social networks that provide fellowship for Korean immigrants, maintain Korean cultural traditions, offer social services for church members and the Korean American community, and supply social status and position for Korean American immigrants.[8]

Although the Korean immigrant church has been growing as a crucial part of Korean immigrant life, its future has become a great concern for Korean American church leaders over the last decade. This anxiety stems both from the general, global trend of young people becoming less involved in church, as well as the particular development of young people leaving Korean immigrant churches. Helen Lee coined the term "Silent Exodus" to illustrate the phenomenon of "young believers who have grown up in these Asian congregations . . . choosing to leave not only their home churches, but possibly their Christian faith as well."[9] Once Lee introduced this term, Korean immigrant churches and scholars have subsequently popularized it in their examination of younger generations of Koreans leaving behind their parents' churches and faith.[10]

However, some scholars argue that the silent exodus claims are exaggerated.[11] Pyong Gap Min and Dae Young Kim insist based on their field

---

5. Shu, "4,233 교회 됐다 [4,323 Korean Churches]."
6. Connor, "6 Facts."
7. See "A Chronicle of the Last 100 Years."
8. Min, "Comparison," 76.
9. Lee, "Silent Exodus."
10. Choi, "Distinctiveness," 157–79.
11. Kim, *Second-Generation Spirituality*, 54; Min and Kim, "Intergenerational Transmission," 268–69.

research that younger generations in the Korean immigrant church are not leaving their faith completely, but rather are rejecting their parents' conservative, traditional, and Confucianized Christianity.[12] Based on these findings, Min and Kim offer the assessment that Korean Protestant immigrants have not failed to transmit their religion to their children, but instead have failed to transmit Korean cultural traditions to their children through religion.[13] In the same light, Sharon Kim demonstrates that many representatives of the second generation of Korean Americans have created their own independent religious space apart from their parents' churches.[14]

Regardless of whether the next generations of Korean immigrants are leaving their faith altogether or forging their own religious spaces, the literature conclusively indicates that the next generation of Korean Americans is leaving Korean immigrant churches. This reality, combined with a decreasing global Christian population, implies that the future of Korean immigrant churches is at risk, because most studies assume that the so-called second generation of Korean Americans—those who were born and raised in the United States—is the generation of Korean Americans that would need to sustain the Korean immigrant church. However, English-speaking Korean Americans are not the only younger generation in Korean immigrant church. There is another group of young people who have been ignored and forgotten both in scholarly research and ministry practice. This study is about the hidden younger generation of Korean immigrant church: Korean-speaking young adults.

PROBLEM STATEMENT

Korean immigrant churches are struggling to understand their future as their younger generation continues to depart. However, the research attending to this issue has primarily focused on the so-called second generation, or English-speaking young people. This emphasis remains even though there is a significant group of Korean-speaking young people that play important roles within the Korean immigrant church. Unfortunately, there have been no in-depth studies devoted to examining the relationship of this particular population with Korean immigrant church.

---

12. Min and Kim, "Intergenerational Transmission," 268.
13. Min and Kim, "Intergenerational Transmission," 279.
14. Kim, *Second-Generation Spirituality*; Kim, "Hybrid Spiritualties," 225–38.

Ignored

GOAL

The goal of this research is to bring awareness to the hidden younger generation of the Korean immigrant church—Korean-speaking young adults—and to propose a discernment process as a faithful practice for Korean immigrant churches to serve them.

MAIN RESEARCH QUESTION

How should the Korean immigrant church as a community understand and serve Korean-speaking young adults?

Sub research questions

1. Who are the Korean-speaking young adults in Korean immigrant churches?
2. What are the current practices of Korean immigrant churches in regard to Korean-speaking young adults?
3. What are the narratives of Korean-speaking young adults to which the Korean immigrant church should pay attention?
4. What is an ecclesiology that the Korean immigrant church should seek, accounting for Korean-speaking young adults as part of the community?
5. How should the Korean immigrant church as a community move forward to discern a faithful practice to serve Korean-speaking young adults?

SIGNIFICANCE

This study is significant in four ways. First, it broadens an understanding of migrants. Traditional approaches to migrants have involved treating them as people who assimilate into their host country and/or demonstrating how they sustain their lives as minority persons. However, this study seeks to provide insight into how this group of Korean-speaking emerging adults simultaneously experiences assimilation into the culture of the host country and retains transnational ties with their home country. Furthermore, this study demonstrates the great potential of Korean-speaking young adults to impact their immediate Korean immigrant church communities, the broader American society, their home country, and finally (with their transnational links) the global Korean diaspora community.

Second, this study seeks to contribute to the academic field of transnationalism and spirituality. So far, many migrant studies have been conducted to explore transnational ties and religious force. Most of these studies have focused primarily on the social function of religious communities in migrant studies. Although this study values and highlights the social function of religious communities as it pertains to migrant studies, it also moves beyond this factor to provide further insight about migrants and their spirituality. This study conveys how transnationality plays an integral role in the spirituality of Korean-speaking young adults.

Third, this study seeks to offer data and resources to broaden Korean migrant and diaspora studies. Most social science studies of Korean immigrants have been conducted by analyzing their culture, assimilation, settlement, and business trends. Only recently have Korean immigrant studies started to adopt a transnational perspective. Furthermore, most of the research looking at younger or emerging generations of Korean immigrants has been conducted by looking at the so-called second generation, namely those who were born and raised in their host countries. With a unique and distinctive approach and target group, this study offers an important contribution to the field of Korean immigrant studies by exploring a hidden population of Korean-speaking adults within the younger generation.

Fourth, this study seeks to contribute to the cause of Korean immigrant churches by anticipating future generations of Korean immigrants. Korean immigrant churches, like many churches in North America, are struggling to discern their futures as younger generations are leaving their churches. By identifying a distinct and often overlooked group of people in Korean immigrant churches, and exploring their profound potential impacts with transnationality, this study will help Korean immigrant churches to think about their futures in different ways. Furthermore, this study could also help Korean churches in Korea and globally by seeking to understand the next generations of Koreans through transnationalism, and by encouraging creative ideas and ministry practices.

TERMINOLOGY

Korean immigrant churches in the United States: Korean churches with dominant Korean-speaking congregations and services in the United States. Although Korean-speaking churches are not limited to the term "Korean immigrant church," this term is used throughout the study because it is the term which is used in academic and ministerial fields. Furthermore, I intentionally do not use the term "Korean-American church" because there are English-speaking Korean churches in the United States.

Korean-speaking young adults in Korean immigrant church in the United States: young adults who belong to Korean-speaking young adult departments. Korean-speaking young adult ministry is different from EM (English Ministry) mainly because they use Korean as their primary language. Korean-speaking young adult departments serve young people that are single and who are beyond high school age up to those in their forties. Although they all use Korean as their primary language, their arrival ages vary from newborns to those who arrived in the States very recently.

Practice: a repeated action that carries out an idea or theory.

Praxis: theory-laden action; "continual movement from experience to reflection and study, and then on to new actions and experience."[15]

ASSUMPTIONS

This study is based on the following assumptions.

- It is assumed that immigrants are maintaining both the cultures of host country and homeland. Thus, although these immigrants are physically distant, their homeland culture still retains significant influence.
- It is assumed that there are different ways to approach and understand migrants. For example, the typical (and simplistic) approach toward immigrants had been typed as first, "1.5"[16] or second generation, depending on their arrival time and condition of assimilation to the hosting country. This study assumes that there are additional ways to define immigrants.

---

15. Branson and Martínez, *Leadership*, 40.

16. 1.5 generation refers to people who immigrated to hosting country as children. Different than their parents who are defined as first generation, and second generation who were born in the hosting country, they speak both languages, have been exposed to both their hosting and home culture, and often go through difficult times regarding their ethnic identity. For more information, see Danico, *1.5 Generation*.

Introduction

- This study assumes that church has a role for human society, not only spiritually but also in many other ways that contribute to the holistic growth of human beings.
- This study assumes that God exists and is working with and among people to fulfill his redemptive work.
- Although its specifics are different than a simplistic, hierarchical cultural understanding, this study assumes human dignity (every human being, regardless of his or her gender, age, or ethnicity, is precious), human subjectivity (human beings are not objects but subjects who are persons and able to feel, think and reflect), and human agency (every human being are important and able to contribute to his or her community and society).

LIMITATIONS AND DELIMITATIONS

This study is limited to the population of Korean immigrants in the United States. Thus, this study may not be generalizable to all other immigrant groups in America. This research is also delimited in terms of its geographical scope. The data has been collected throughout Southern California. As a result, different results may occur when researching Korean immigrants in a different area where the population of Korean immigrants and the number of Korean immigrant churches is not as large. Finally, this research is delimited to Korean-speaking young people who are attending Korean immigrant churches. I acknowledge that there are significant groups of Korean immigrants that do not attend church, and others that attend different types of churches that are not identified as Korean immigrant churches. Among various different types of Korean immigrants or Korean Americans, this study does not account for those who are English-speaking emerging adults or Korean-speaking emerging adults that do not attend church.

RESEARCHER'S STORY, HISTORY, AND EXPERIENCE

I was one of the Korean-speaking young adults in a Korean immigrant church who is bilingual and has a transnational background. In other words, church, young adulthood, and transnationality—three significant topics of this dissertation—are central to my life as well.

For a long time, I was a person on the margins searching to find where to fit in, and I assumed my voice might not be worthwhile.

Ignored

I was born in the family of a pastor who planted three churches. Experiences associated with my upbringing gave me a rich spiritual background of Christianity and great relationships with my peers and also with those from all different generations in church. At the same time, growing up in a poor pastor's family brought about difficult times. As my father planted a church three times in three different cities in Korea without any financial support from outside, our family always worried about rent and living expenses. Although my parents were always grateful for the ways in which God helped and provided for us during difficult times, such financial struggles created anxiety and instability. Furthermore, during those times, my family couldn't think about anything else except the church, and I was forced to share my parents with church. However, as a pastor's kid, I could not share these pains with anyone in or outside of the church due to the expectation of being a good pastor's kid. In that shame-honor culture, I was afraid to share these pains with anyone in the church for fear that I couldn't or shouldn't be like other kids in or out of the church because I was carrying my father's name with me. Looking back, I did not fit in either outside or inside of the church as the pastor's kid who was supposed to be different.

Although I appreciated church was a place where I learned, played, and interacted with great people, at the same time, it was a place where I could not fully fit. This caused me pains of feeling marginalized with financial difficulties and insufficient familial support.

After entering college, I moved to Toronto, Canada to learn English. At that time (and even still now) many Korean young people are encouraged to go abroad to explore and learn English. I thought I would simply stay a couple of years to learn English and return to Korea. However, leaving Korea to study in a foreign country meant more than just obtaining language skills. I attended a language school program, finished my bachelor's degree, and entered a master's program in Canada before transferring into a master's degree program at Fuller Seminary in Pasadena California. I earned my MDiv and completed PhD.

Throughout the journey from Canada to America, I've experienced assimilation to North American culture as my English skills improved; at the same time, I have held strongly my Korean-ness as well. Often, living with these two coexisting cultures has brought confusion and pain. After spending several years in North America, I learned that I am not considered a Korean in Korea anymore. My family and friends started to call me American, and it was not a joke but a serious comment that reflected their newfound recognition of the different culture and behavior I brought with me. I did not recognize until later that I had gone through a process of adopting and assimilating to a new culture, which caused me to assume a different lifestyle, thought processes, and behaviors. However, these changes do not necessarily mean that I became American. In America, I have never been viewed by others as an American. Furthermore, I have not been considered to be Korean-American by Korean-Americans either. Because of my accent, skin color, and visa status, I am always considered a foreigner. Even among Korean young people, I have often been categorized as a so-called "first generation" Korean immigrant, one who is assumed to have conservative and somewhat barbarian manners without adopting more "noble" Western manners. It was not so difficult, although painful, to accept the fact that I am an outsider in American society, but I struggled to fit in within the Korean immigrant community as one who was neither born in the United States nor had I arrived early or come with green card[17] to America. This confusion was only compounded with the loneliness and pain of being alone in a foreign place without family and friends. I had to struggle to find out who I am and where I fit. In the midst of identity discernment and struggling to belong between two cultures, my gender as a female added additional challenges to my painful but meaningful journey. As I studied theology throughout my MDiv and PhD programs and also served in a Korean immigrant church, I started to recognize various distorted views towards women. All told, it has not been an easy journey to finally accept and celebrate myself and my ethnicity, family background, gender and personal history before God.

    Looking back at my young adult years, they mark a journey of finding my identity and calling as one living between cultures, and having experienced life as a female theologian and pastor's kid. With God's grace my studies, ministry, and personal life, along with the support of great teachers, mentors, and friends, have been greatly helpful for discerning and understanding my painful but meaningful journey. I was able to find peace by allowing and accepting my two cultures, gender, and struggles as a poor pastor's kid. Furthermore, I was able even to appreciate and celebrate my gender, transnationality between cultures, and experience as pastor's kid, as I was discerning my calling before God.

---

17. A permit which allows a foreign national to live and work permanently in the United States.

Ignored

In particular, this study helped me to learn that my journey was the journey of one who was marginalized and ignored. The experiences and stories as a poor church planter's kid, a young adult who struggled between two cultures, and a female pastor and theologian have shaped who I am and how I see. With this identity and background, I resolved to research one of the marginalized and ignored populations within my community—Korean-speaking young adults. Throughout surveys and in-depth interviews, I met precious Korean-speaking young adults. They were not just a research population (objects) to be studied. They were real human beings with authentic stories and lives. They are precious children of God who have great potential to contribute to America, Korea and the world. It is also true that they carry deep sorrows and wounds as those who are marginalized.

I am so grateful that my journey was helpful as I listened and learned from Korean-speaking young adults who have been, and continue to be, hidden and ignored.

OVERVIEW OF THE FOLLOWING CHAPTERS

Chapter 1 presents a methodology for this study. First, this chapter establishes practical theology as the overarching method for the study with its definition and importance. Secondly, it establishes the qualitative method based on grounded theory as the study's approach for field research, which includes surveys and in-depth interviews. Lastly, this chapter provides a road map for field research that outlines the process from recruitment to analysis.

Chapter 2 provides a description of Korean-speaking young adults with support from literature reviews. Since there are limited resources pertaining to this particular research population, this chapter presents information that is both gathered and compared, pertaining to young adults in America, in Korea, and English-speaking Korean young adults in Korean immigrant communities, based on existing literature.

Chapter 3 provides an interpretation of the current praxis on Korean-speaking young adults. Based on the current literature on Korean-speaking young adults, this chapter offers field researches this study conducted. As a result of the fact that there is no supporting research on Korean-speaking young adults in Korean immigrant churches or within the Korean immigrant community in general, this study provides 404 surveys to present basic background information about Korean-speaking young adults. In addition to the surveys, this study also offers forty in-depth interviews, including with Korean-speaking young adults and their pastors, to shape a deeper understanding of the young people and the current practices within their churches. From the surveys and in-depth interviews, this chapter provides research findings and interpretations.

Chapter 4 surveys the theological norm for Korean immigrant churches with respect to their younger generations. This chapter engages Scripture as a theological framework for understanding Korean emerging adults and immigrant churches to seek a holistic ecclesiology for Korean-speaking young adults and the Korean immigrant church. In order to present a holistic ecclesiology, this chapter starts with the current ecclesiology for Korean-speaking young adults based on migrant theologies and Korean immigrant theology. The chapter then moves to discuss three theological concepts, which provide the framework for building an ecclesiology for Korean immigrants and their young people.

Chapter 5 develops a pragmatic way to move forward for Korean young adult ministries in Korean immigrant churches. It offers potential changes Korean immigrant churches could make as a faithful response based on the findings, analysis, and reflection in the previous chapter. Instead of providing a model to apply to every church, this chapter demonstrates a way of processing changes, acknowledging that each church has a different context. This chapter ends by suggesting a simple and helpful way to begin the process of leading change in a local church setting with the Appreciative Inquiry method.

In the concluding chapter, I offer a summary of the entire research and its potential contribution to academic and ministerial fields. The last chapter also provides suggestions for further studies, addressing areas of research pertaining to the Korean immigrant church, Korean immigrant community, and migrant studies in general.

1

Research Methodology

THIS STUDY IS BASED on a practical theological methodology. This chapter first explains the nature of practical theology and the importance of the use of its methodology for this particular study. Secondly, as part of the practical method, this study reports the findings of two types of field research: surveys and in-depth interviews. For those particular parts of the research, this study involves a qualitative method approach. Thus, this chapter states how the qualitative method approach fits with practical theology and the process of field research, including recruitment, procedure, analysis, and challenges and limitations. Finally, this chapter details the cultural sensitivity embodied in this research, the role of the primary researcher, and the study's correlational work with social science.

PRACTICAL THEOLOGY METHOD

> If there is no one ideal strategy or model for all churches, then each particular church, usually in local networks and other associations, must gain competencies and capacities that are specific to its own time and place. In order to do this the leaders of a church need to gain skills in theological reflection—this is what is called practical theology.[1]

For a long time, churches and institutions have tried to find "the" model for ministry, and they have applied different models to their organizations, hoping each one would work. In the same way, Korean churches and organizations have adopted different models and applied each to their

---

1. Branson and Martínez, *Leadership*, 39.

systems; often the models have been Western. The overarching assumption when applying various models has been that, if Korean churches try harder, implement the model in the right way, and work at the model long enough, Korean churches will be successful in the same way that other Western churches and organizations that utilized the model have been. However, the truth is that there is no one perfect model for all churches and organizations. Because every church and organization have a different people, story, space and history—in short, a different context—we need a different way to think about how we engage in ministry based on the particular context in which the church is located. This is the reason why this study uses practical theology as its overarching methodology. In order to demonstrate how and why practical theology can bring a different approach to ministry than one that simply applies a model, I will outline four important aspects of the practical theology method.

First, practical theology moves from praxis to theory and then to praxis, not simply from theory to practice.[2] Although this statement implies many things, there are two implications that are particularly important and agreed upon among practical theology scholars. One implication is that practical theology starts from theory-laden action, not from a theory or model. As Andrew Root notes, "Practical theology, whether it starts with a crisis, established practice, or lived belief, is placed first and foremost on the ground."[3] In other words, practical theology starts from practices in a specific context—a unique place, people, history, and/or story.[4] The other major implication is that practical theology is an ongoing process of moving not only from praxis to theory, but cyclically to praxis again, and so it continues. Mark Lau Branson describes praxis as a "continual movement from experience to reflection and study, and then on to new actions and experience."[5] In other words, practical theology is not a linear, "do it once and you are done" type of task, but rather an ongoing process of reflection and action. These two implications demonstrate

---

2. The term *praxis* is Aristotelian, referring to theory-laden actions. Ray Anderson states, "Praxis is an action that includes the telos, or final meaning and character of truth. It is an action in which the truth is discovered through action, not merely applied or 'practiced.' In praxis one is not only guided in one's actions by the intention of realizing the telos, or purpose, but by discovering and grasping this telos through the action itself." Anderson, *Practical Theology*, 49.

3. Root, *Christopraxis*, 24.

4. Clark, "Youth Ministry," 18.

5. Branson and Martínez, *Leadership*, 40.

that practical theology takes each particular context seriously by starting from and continuously reflecting upon praxis so that a church can discern a particular way to engage in ministry, instead of adopting a model from the outside and applying it artificially.

Second, in order to understand the current praxis, practical theology pays attention to other studies of human culture. Chap Clark states:

> Practical theology is in its essence a correlative relationship between theology and any other data set that can inform and illuminate God's call to his people. Whatever the source of these data sets, anything that speaks into the human condition such that believers can receive a deeper and more thorough understanding of the context in which the Gospel is to be lived out is an important part of practical theology method.[6]

Since practical theology starts from praxis in a particular context, it is crucial to understand and analyze deeply the current praxis, not only with theological tools but also with other studies of human culture. This examination of the current praxis using a correlative approach should lead to a new shape for the praxis; this approach is different than beginning with theory and applying it.

Third, *practical theology is human participation in God's mission*. Although practical theologians respect and carefully examine human behavior and social science, the goal of practical theology is not to find morally appropriate answers or to pursue human interest. Rather, with theological and other resources, practical theology reflects and discerns God's word and ongoing work so that we can participate in his work. Thus, the practical theology process of action and reflection with support from other studies helps people to confess and commit to participate in God's action[7]. The process causes a person to ask, "What is Christ doing in this situation?" instead of "What should we do?" Ray Anderson writes:

> Christ's ministry was the ministry of God working through him by the power of the Spirit of God. Our ministry is the ministry of Christ continuing through us by the presence and power of the Spirit of Christ. Theological praxis means that truths of God are discovered through the encounter with Christ in the world by means of ministry. That is what I call Christopraxis.[8]

6. Clark, "Youth Ministry," 17.
7. Root, "Practical Theology," 62.
8. Anderson, *Ministry*, 29.

In other words, practical theology does not ask how we can choose the best model to apply in our context but seeks to discern what God is doing in our particular context and how we can join his work.

Finally, "practical theology seeks to provide leadership in the process of communal discernment."[9] Practical theology is a communal process and cannot be done by one person or leader. We often see and expect leaders to manage and control situations as the experts. In this way, often only a few leaders make decisions about what kind of model to use to solve the problems facing a community. However, practical theology helps leaders to create an environment for their communities to name, analyze, and reflect on the current praxis, to discern God's calling in the given context, and to help them find a new praxis as a community rather than as individuals. In that way, leadership teams can lead a church to shape an environment in which the people of God participate in the action-reflection cycle as they gain new capacities to discern what God is doing among and around them.[10]

Practical Theology in This Study

Although there are many ways to approach the practical theology method, with the understanding of practical theology offered in the previous section, this study adopts and uses Richard Osmer's four core tasks of practical theology: descriptive-empirical, interpretive, normative, and pragmatic.[11]

First, the descriptive-empirical task is about "gathering information that helps us discern patterns and dynamics in a particular episode, situation, or context."[12] This task leads us to answer questions about what is going on by paying attention to a current praxis in a particular context.

Concerning the descriptive-empirical task, this study explores the current practices of Korean-speaking young adults in Korean immigrant churches. The descriptive-empirical task in this study demonstrates the status of Korean-speaking young adults with in-depth literature reviews. As mentioned previously, Korean-speaking young adults have been ignored and have not received sufficient attention from those in the academic and ministerial fields. Thus, the existing literature and resources are limited. As a result, the descriptive-empirical task presents related literature across a broad spectrum, including research on the topics of

9. Root, "Practical Theology," 62.
10. Branson and Martínez, *Leadership*, 57.
11. Osmer, *Practical Theology*.
12. Osmer, *Practical Theology*, 4.

young adults in American and Korean contexts, as well as Korean American young adults in America.

Second, the interpretive task involves "drawing on theories of the arts and sciences to better understand and explain why these patterns and dynamics are occurring."[13] In order to draw upon theories and evaluate what is happening among Korean-speaking young adults in Korean immigrant churches, this study conducts qualitative surveys with Korean-speaking emerging adults in Korean immigrant churches, as well as with pastors who are currently serving these groups of people. With the findings and results from of the qualitative research data, this task seeks to provide an interpretation. Given the process, this study aims to provide a critical analysis of the current praxis of Korean-speaking emerging adult ministry in Korean immigrant churches.

Third, the normative task is described as "using theological concepts to interpret particular episodes, situation, or contexts, constructing ethical norms to guide our responses, and learning from 'good practice.'"[14] With a depth of theological reflection, this task seeks to answer the question "What ought to be going on?" The normative task not only provides a broad sense of biblical and theological ethics, but also leads us to go deeper with a particular context and issue by inviting us to critically reflect on the current praxis through a theological framework.

In this task, this study seeks to discern a holistic ecclesiology for the Korean immigrant church regarding their Korean-speaking younger generation. By engaging Scripture, Christian history, theology, and existing ecclesiology in migrant contexts, the normative task seeks to identify the church's role for emerging Korean American generations. This theological and critical reflection about the church's role will not only demonstrate what ought to happen in the Korean immigrant church for Korean-speaking emerging adults, but will also lead to reflection of God's ongoing mission from the past to the present and future in churches with emerging generations. Further, this task provides theological discernment of how we can participate in God's ongoing redemptive work within our unique contexts.

Lastly, the pragmatic task is "determining strategies of action that will influence situations in ways that are desirable."[15] This task seeks to answer the question, "How might we respond?" With careful observation and

---

13. Osmer, *Practical Theology*, 4.
14. Osmer, *Practical Theology*, 4.
15. Osmer, *Practical Theology*, 4.

Research Methodology

interpretation of the current praxis and critical engagement of theological reflection, the pragmatic task leads people and their communities to pursue practical ways to participate God's mission.

Regarding the pragmatic task, this study provides practical reflection toward a new way of thinking about Korean-speaking emerging adult ministry in the Korean immigrant church. Instead of providing a model for every church to adopt, the pragmatic task in this study helps and guides leaders to process change as a faithful response to the current reality of Korean-speaking young adults, which this study demonstrates with literature reviews, research findings, analysis, and reflection.

QUALITATIVE METHOD APPROACH

With its practical theological approach, this study begins with the current praxis of ministries on Korean-speaking young adults in Korean immigrant church. In this step, this study requires data that can provide information and understanding of the current praxis. Furthermore, the data needs to be analyzed to provide a better understanding and explain of the current praxis, which is the second task of practical theology in this study—the interpretive task. In this light, this study conducted qualitative-oriented field research, including surveys and in-depth interviews.

Unlike quantitative approach, which pursues generalization and objectivity, qualitative approach is to explore and understand the meaning individuals or groups ascribe to a social or human problem.[16] In the same light, with Bomb and Hartmann's words, Flick states, "To formulate such subject- and situation-related statements, which are empirically well founded, is a goal which can be attained with qualitative research."[17]

In the same vein, this study does not pursue an objective generalization of Korean-speaking young adults in the world. Rather, it seeks to have in-depth understanding of specific population (Korean-speaking young adults) in a specific context (Korean immigrant churches in America). Thus, the qualitative approach can bring helpful tools for understanding the current practices and interpretation of Korean-speaking young adults in the Korean immigrant church.

Although there are many ways to utilize qualitative research, this study is based on particularly surveys and in-depth interviews.

---

16. Creswell, *Research Design*, 4.
17. Flick, *Qualitative Research*, 14.

Ignored

Location of Qualitative Research: Surveys and In-Depth Interviews

The field research was conducted in fifteen different cities in Southern California, including cities from Los Angeles County, San Bernardino County, Orange County, and San Diego County.[18] Southern California holds great importance for Korean immigrant church studies. Although Korean immigrant churches are all over the United States, California is the state with the most Korean immigrant churches (1329 churches, 31.4 percent), according to data from the Korean immigrant church directory listing in 2013.[19] This is more than triple the number of Korean immigrant churches in the second largest state, New York (436 churches, 10.3 percent). Among the over one thousand Korean immigrant churches in California, about 80 percent are located in Southern California.[20] Therefore, even though this study is limited to Southern California, its findings can be relevant for a much larger number of Korean immigrant churches.

Survey: Gathering Demographic Data

CONTENT[21]

Due to the lack of research on Korean-speaking young adults, there is no background data, which directly related to this particular population. Because of this lacuna, I conducted 404 surveys to gather background and demographic data for Korean-speaking young adults. Based on the literature review from relevant areas,[22] the questionnaire included 5 different categories: basic demographic information (age, gender, job, educational background), immigration information (arrival age, purpose of immigration, visa status and its changes), transnational ties with Korea (how often and in what way they are connected to Korea), Korean immigrant church experience (reason to choose the current church, reason to change churches, duration of staying the current church), and emerging adulthood experience (identity, belonging, and autonomy).

---

18. Because Korean immigrant society is narrow and well connected, this study intentionally does not indicate any details and information about the participant churches and people other than what is necessary.

19. Shu, "4,233 교회 됐다 [4,323 Korean Churches]."

20. Shu, "남가주에 1,077개 [1,077 in Southern California]."

21. The entire questionnaire can be found in Appendix A.

22. Please see chapter 2 for the literature review.

Recruitment

As the primary researcher, I intentionally contacted the six main denominations of Korean immigrant churches: Presbyterian, Baptist, Methodist, Independent, Pentecostal, and Holiness.[23] Furthermore, I contacted churches from different demographic settings (urban and suburban) and of different sizes to seek a valid sample group.

By drawing from my own personal network and accessing church websites from the Korean immigrant church directory,[24] I contacted thirty different churches for this survey. Ultimately, 404 Korean-speaking young adults from eight churches participated in the survey.

The eight churches include: each of the top six denominations; four from urban and four from suburban settings; and a variety of different sizes (two having more than two thousand congregation members, two between one thousand and fifteen hundred members, two between five hundred and one thousand members, and two between two hundred and five hundred members). Considering Korean immigrant church network is comparably small and often well connected, this study does not identify any detailed information of the participant churches, including their specific locations.

Procedure

Once the pastor for Korean-speaking young adult department gave permission, I visited each church's Sunday Korean-speaking young adult service. Between the end of the service and the beginning of the small group, I conducted the survey.

Challenges and Limitation

One of main challenges I faced in conducting this survey was contacting small churches. To conduct the survey with various and valid sample sizes, I have contacted churches of different sizes, including small churches with fewer than one hundred members of the entire congregation and fewer than ten members of Korean-speaking young adult department. However, it was extremely difficult to convince pastors of small churches to participate the

---

23. According to Korean immigrant church directory listing data in 2013, the top six denominations of Korean immigrant churches in America are Presbyterian (40.5 percent), Baptist (17.9 percent), Methodist (12.9 percent), Independent (6.9 percent), Pentecostal (6.7 percent), and Holiness (6.6 percent). Shu, "4,233 교회 됐다 [4,323 Korean Churches]"

24. http://www.koreanchurchyp.com.

Ignored

survey. Although further research might be required to assess the Korean pastors' reluctance, I observed a level of defensiveness, a fear of exposing their church, and a deeper shame on the part of small church pastors. Although I explained to them that small churches are important and particularly were looking for small churches of that size, some of the small church pastors even articulated as the reason for their refusal "because we do not have enough people in our department" or asked, "Why don't you find a better church?" as their excuse not to participate. Other pastors said yes in the initial contact, but then never replied to the follow-up emails. Thus, despite my careful efforts, this survey and its findings might not be relevant for small churches (fewer than one hundred congregation members, and ten members of Korean-speaking young adult department).

Another limitation of this survey may be that of its setting. This survey was conducted after the Sunday service and right before the small group began. Although there were some churches where most people who participated the Sunday service participated in small groups, most of the churches had fewer people participating in small groups than in the service. Thus, this survey and its findings are limited to the Korean-speaking young adults who were committed to small groups; it might not be as generally relevant to people who do not come to church on Sunday, or who only participate in Sunday services.

In-Depth Interviews: Gathering Qualitative Data

In order to gain a deeper understanding of Korean-speaking emerging adults in Korean immigrant churches, this study includes forty in-depth interviews: thirteen with pastors who are currently serving in a Korean-speaking young adult department, and twenty-seven with Korean-speaking emerging adults who are attending Korean immigrant churches.

Content

Interviews with pastors:[25] seek to understand what the practices of Korean-speaking young adults ministries are and how pastors understand the Korean-speaking young adults. The questions include a description of the church and the department they are serving, its strengths and value, main programs and ministries, unique ministry compared to adult congregation and English-speaking young adult congregation, the relationship between

25. See Appendix C for the in-depth interview questionnaire with pastors.

Research Methodology

the Korean-speaking young adult department and the entire church, and the top two challenges for their ministry.

Interviews with Korean-speaking emerging adults:[26] seek to gain a deeper understanding of Korean-speaking emerging adults. Based on the review of relevant literature, the questionnaire has four different sections: migration experience,[27] ties with Korea, experience of American culture, and church experience.

Recruitment

Interview with pastors: in order to have legitimate sample group, I defined several dimensions of the sample, including denomination, gender, location, and duration of the pastor's service. In this light, I intentionally contacted pastors who are serving in Korean-speaking young adult departments considering their denomination (in order to represent all of the six major denominations of Korean immigrant churches in North America), their gender (in order to ensure equitable representation and participation of men and women), their location in Southern California, and the duration of their service. To ensure their depth of understanding of ministry and of Korean-speaking young adults, I interviewed pastors who had served in their current church for more than two years. With these dimensions of sample structure, I contacted twenty-two pastors by drawing from my own personal network and by searching church web site through the Korean immigrant church directory. Of those twenty-two pastors, I conducted thirteen interviews. They are from six different denominations, two females and eleven males, six urban and seven suburban areas from eight different cities.

Table 1.1 Gender of Pastor Interviewees

Gender	Number of Participants
Female	2
Male	11

---

26. See Appendix E for the in-depth interview questionnaire with Korean-speaking young adults.

27. The migration experience section is adapted from Sheringham, *Transnational Religious Spaces*.

Table 1.2 Denomination of Pastor Interviewees

Denomination	Number of Participants
Presbyterian	7
Baptist	1
Methodist	1
Independent	2
Pentecostal	1
Holiness	1

Table 1.3 Occupational Status of Pastor Interviewees

Occupational Status	Number of Participants
Full-time pastor only serving in a Korean-speaking young adult ministry	1
Full-time pastor serving in another ministry as well as in a Korean-speaking young adult ministry	4
Part-time pastor only serving in a Korean-speaking young adult ministry	5
Part-time pastor serving in another ministry as well as in a Korean-speaking young adult ministry	3

Table 1.4 Size of the Congregations in Which Pastor Interviewees Are Serving

Number of the entire congregations	Number of Participants
100–200	3
201–500	2
501–1000	2
2001–2000	3
Above 2001	3

Research Methodology

Table 1.5 Size of the Korean-Speaking Young Adult Departments in Which Pastor Interviewees Are Serving

Number of the Korean-Speaking Young Adult Members	Number of Participants
10–30	3
31–90	4
91–150	3
151–200	2
Above 200	1

Interviews with Korean-speaking emerging adults: the main dimensions of this sample group are age, gender, occupational status, visa status, arrival age, and role in Korean immigrant church. With this sample structure, I contacted thirty-nine Korean-speaking emerging adults throughout my personal network and with help from pastors and Korean-speaking emerging adults who had already participated in the interviews. I conducted twenty-seven interviews.

Table 1.6 Gender of Korean-Speaking Young Adult Interviewees

Gender	Number of Participants
Female	12
Male	15

Table 1.7 Age of Korean-Speaking Young Adult Interviewees

Age	Number of Participants
19–24	7
25–30	13
Above 30	7

Table 1.8 Occupational Status of Korean-Speaking Young Adult Interviewees

Occupational Status	Number of Participants
Full-time school only	3
Part-time school only	1
Full-time work only	11
Part-time work only	2
School and work	12

Table 1.9 Role in the Church of Korean-Speaking Young Adult Interviewees

Role in the department	Number of Participants
Lay leadership	12
Member	15

Table 1.10 Arriving Age in America of Korean-Speaking Young Adult Interviewees

Age	Number of Participants
Birth–3	2
4–12	4
13–18	9
19–24	3
24–30	8
Above 30	1

Table 1.11 Visa Status of Korean-Speaking Young Adult Interviewees

Legal status	Number of Participants
Naturalized citizenship or permanent residency	9
Temporary visa holder	16
Undocumented	3

PROCEDURES

Both types of interviews were conducted in places where the interviewee felt comfortable. Most interviews were conducted in a café near interviewee's home or workplace, except for two pastors who requested that the interview be done in their church office. I provided flexible timing, such that the interviews varied in length from forty minutes to two hours.

CHALLENGES AND LIMITATIONS

One of the biggest challenges for the interview with pastors was gender integration. I went through Korean immigrant church directories and Korean immigrant church websites to find female pastors to ensure equitable gender representative. However, it was extremely difficult to find female pastors who are serving Korean-speaking young adults. As a result, only two female pastors were available to be interviewed, while the number of male pastor participants is eleven.

Another challenge for the interview was to find pastors who have served at the same church more than two years. Again, the rationale for the dimension of ministry duration was to ensure their depth of understanding of Korean-speaking emerging adults and ministry in their local setting. However, in the recruiting process, it became quite clear that many of pastors who are currently serving Korean-speaking young adults in Korean immigrant church in Southern California have newly begun their ministry within a year. Given this reality, it was difficult to find pastors who had served at their current church for more than two years. With these challenges, this study made the allowance to include two pastors who had served their church for 1.5 years, provided that they had equivalent ministry experience in another ministry setting.

Ignored

Third, the dynamic of shame in Korean cultures offered another challenge and limitation. Although there were enough people who were willing to open up and go deeper in their experience and stories, several people felt shame in sharing these realities. For example, when the interviewer asked about challenges in their ministry (for pastors) or in their church life (for young adults), some people simply said "no." In other areas related to shame, some people opened up reluctantly. In that light, one of this study's limitations is its heavy reliance on participants' stories that might not represent the full picture of their real life and ministry.

Cultural Sensitivity

Cultural sensitivity is one very important issue in conducting research with people from different cultures.[28] Although this study does not involve a typical cross-cultural research dynamic, in which the researcher and participants are from different cultures,[29] it still requires cultural sensitivity in conducting research with an ethnic minority group in America. Liamputtong states that without appropriate cultural sensitivity, misunderstandings, or even worse, racist attitudes may surface. This will jeopardize the accuracy and progress of research, or at the extreme level, terminate it.[30] Thus the researcher of this study is well aware of the importance of cultural sensitivity throughout the research, even though she is an insider. In particular, there are two main cultural factors that the researcher has paid attention throughout the research: honor-shame culture and social hierarchy.

Korea culture is honor-shame based, rather than guilt based. In an honor-shame culture, it is possible to threaten participants by bringing them shame in any field research. Thus, I tried to create a safe place where participants could share their stories and experience through survey and interviews without bringing shame. In order not to bring any unnecessary shame when conducting my research, I engaged in four particular practices throughout my field research.

First, I provided detailed information about the entire study, and particularly the role of the survey or interview. I provided this information not

---

28. Liamputtong, *Qualitative Cross-Cultural Research*, 86.

29. For more information about cross cultural research and cultural sensitivity, see Weinfurt and Maghaddam, "Culture and Social Distance"; Papadopoulos and Lees, "Competent Researchers"; Walsh-Tapiata, "Maori Research"; Hall and Kulig, "Kanadier Mennonites"; Birman, "Ethical Issues"; Liamputtong, "Cross-Cultural Context."

30. Liamputtong, *Qualitative Cross-Cultural Research*, 86.

only with a written document but also verbally and repeated it when necessary. It was obvious that most of participants were not familiar with such research, so I tried to ensure that all participants sufficiently understood what the entire study is about, what the particular survey is about, and what would happen when they consent the survey. In that way, I tried to set up a safe environment without any unexpected steps during research.

Second, I emphasized the confidentiality and anonymity of the study. I repeated the policy of confidentiality and anonymity in the study from the initial contacts to the end of the survey to make sure participants would feel comfortable to open up. Since Korean culture is communal culture with great value of harmony, if anyone brings different idea—even though it may be a right or good one—it can bring shame. Many times in the interview settings, many participants said, "Maybe other people think differently," or "It might be just my experience." In times of when these concerns arose, the researcher repeated the study's confidentiality and anonymity policy, while affirming the importance of their stories.

Third, I clearly articulated that the purpose of the survey is to gather information, not to critique their ministry or life. During recruiting, participants often expressed that they were not a good sample to interview and gave different reasons, including because their church is small, they do not have a good job, they are undergoing church conflict, etc., expecting me to find so-called successful pastors or people. Thus, I made sure to explain that the goal of the survey and interview is not to expose or judge their personal stories, but to gather information to understand the current practices of Korean-speaking emerging adults in Korean immigrant churches.

Fourth, I stressed participants' right to refuse to answer any questions or the entire survey. When I visited churches to conduct surveys after the Sunday services, the entire Korean-speaking young adult department who attended their small group was encouraged to participate in the survey by their pastors. In that case, I was aware that rejecting the survey could possibly bring shame (i.e., by rejecting their leader's request and by breaking the harmony of the entire group participating). Thus, I explained their right to refuse any question or the entire survey. Furthermore, for in-depth interviews, I ensured that the participants were aware of their right to skip any question or to drop out of the interviews any time without any harm.

Another cultural factor I paid attention to throughout the research concerns social hierarchy. Confucianized social hierarchy based on gender, age, and title is deeply rooted in Korean culture. I was aware of my social

Ignored

status (as female, as younger than most pastors and older than most Korean-speaking emerging adults who participated in this research, and as a PhD student and non-ordained pastor) and how it could be perceived. Interestingly, my social status was somewhat helpful to create non-threatening and safe space to share for pastors because I had lower status compared to the most of pastor participants. Thus, it helped to promote the researcher's intention of learning and gathering the information from them, rather than judging or evaluating their words. However, for Korean-speaking young adult participants, as a pastor, PhD student, and older person, I had to remind them that my role is not that of a pastor, counselor, or someone with seniority ahead of them, but as a researcher who was willing to learn from and listen to them in order to gather the information. Although the Korean-speaking emerging adult participants were very polite and respectful to the researcher by calling me pastor, my ministerial status (a non-ordained pastor currently not involved in any ministry) and gender seemed to helpful to differentiate the researcher from their own authoritative pastors, since most of their pastors are ordained, older, and male.

Data Analysis

Grounded Theory Method and Practical Theology

Grounded theory method is one helpful way to engage in the interpretative task of practical theology. As practical theology moves from praxis to theory, grounded theory is also founded on data rather than beginning from a set theory. Throughout the analytical process, grounded theory coding shapes an analytic frame from which the researcher builds the analysis.[31] In this way, grounded theory helps researchers to understand the participants' views and actions from their perspective,[32] rather than from the researcher's preset views or theory.

Grounded theory research is one of the strategies that Osmer presents for empirical research for the descriptive-empirical task. Osmer demonstrates that this strategy seeks to develop a theory that is closely related to the context of the phenomenon being studied.[33] Grounded theory "leads to

---

31. Charmaz, *Grounded Theory*, 113.
32. Charmaz, *Grounded Theory*, 116.
33. Osmer, *Practical Theology*, 52.

attend to context and data and develop a theory out of the research,"[34] just as practical theology moves from praxis (theory-laden practice) to theory.

Grounded theory is particularly suited for situations in which there exists little research or theory. Considering the significant dearth of research on Korean-speaking young adults and the lack of an emergent theory, grounded theory provides a process to shape a theory from this particular context. Thus, this study uses grounded theory method for data collection and its analysis.

DATA ANALYSIS PROCESS

For surveys with Korean-speaking emerging adults, I used Qualtrics[35] software to collect the data from online surveys. The surveys largely consisted of close-ended demographic questions. However, there were a couple of open-ended questions such as "If you ever moved to another church in the States, what was the reason?" and "What are the top two important criteria for choosing a church?" which I went through thoroughly to collect and analyze the data.

Six basic steps for data collection and analysis were utilized for the in-depth interviews. First, interview audio was recorded and handwritten notes were taken during each interview. Second, the dialogue from each interview was transcribed, either by me or another transcriber. I intentionally chose a transcriber with enough knowledge of Korean culture to understand the interview content, but was an outsider to the community of Korean-speaking emerging adults in Korean immigrant churches. This decision was made to prevent potential dual relationships and any unnecessary assumptions that might overlay on the transcription data.[36] Third, I read through each interview transcript in their entirety to create an initial structure for interpretation. In this stage, I read through all of notes that I took during the interviews and wrote notes of potential themes and interpretations during this initial reading. Fourth, after the initial reading, an initial coding was conducted. The purpose of the initial coding was to explore whatever theoretical possibilities could be used to

---

34. Charmaz, *Grounded Theory*, 3.

35. Qualtrics is one of survey software programs. Please see www.qualtrics.com.

36. The transcriber is a Korean-speaking person who was born in a third country. The transcriber requested anonymity in this study.

understand the data.[37] With the initial coding, I kept in mind the following questions from Charmaz:[38]

- What is the data a study of?
- What do the data suggest? Pronounce? Leave unsaid?
- From whose point of view?
- What theoretical category does this specific datum indicate?

One of most important things that I paid attention to at this stage was to remain open to all analytic possibilities and to create codes that best fit the data.[39] In the initial coding, I created Excel file matrices with all codes that corresponded to quotes from the interview transcripts. I found forty-seven codes during this stage. Fifth, I moved to focused coding. Focused coding is using codes from the initial coding to shift, synthesize, and analyze large amounts of data.[40] During this stage, one is required to make decisions to categorize and reduce codes to finalize the themes that fit the study. Thus, it is up to the researcher's discretion to make key decisions about which codes among the initial codes make the most analytic sense in order to categorize data incisively and completely.[41] To define which codes could serve best as focused codes, I carried these questions from Charmaz during focused coding:[42]

- What do I find when I compare my initial codes with data?
- In what ways might my initial codes reveal patterns?
- Which of these codes best account for the data?
- Have I raised theses codes to focused codes?
- What do my comparisons between codes indicate?

I also consulted with a clinical psychologist and sought supervision from a sociologist to make decisions in selecting important codes, clustering meanings, and finalizing themes. During the focused coding, I utilized

---

37. Charmaz, *Grounded Theory*, 116.
38. Charmaz, *Grounded Theory*, 116.
39. Charmaz, *Grounded Theory*, 117.
40. Charmaz, *Grounded Theory*, 138.
41. Charmaz, *Grounded Theory*, 138.
42. Charmaz, *Grounded Theory*, 140.

horizontalization[43] to reduce codes with content and thematic analysis. Sixth, the final themes emerged and coding was completed. In order to complete the coding process, revisit the data, cluster codes, reduce codes, and finalize themes of content and thematic analysis, the researcher drilled down on certain themes in order to highlight larger themes from smaller sub-themes. It was a discernment process to identify which information seemed to be more important to offer theory versus additional information, which is less relevant to the theory. This was accomplished through an iterative cycle between formulating a theoretical framework and then re-examining the data to see if the data is consistent with the theory. Finally, the final themes were to create a coherent narrative or picture of the occurring phenomena, which will be discussed further in the following chapter.

Role of the Primary Researcher in Data Collection and Analysis

Although I tried to be open and to learn from Korean-speaking young adults and their churches as a researcher, it is impossible for me to perfectly and objectively value-free. I acknowledge this limitation. I am also aware of believe my experiences of pastoring, counseling, teaching, being a Korean-speaking young person in a Korean immigrant church, and training in practical theology can bring a crucial piece as the primary instrument for data collection and analysis. I might have inadvertently influenced the participants of surveys and interviews, which could have skewed the result and conclusion of this study. Yet, my prior experience and training in this field prepared me to pay attention to and highlight this unknown population.

Correlational Work with Social Science

As previously mentioned, one of practical theology's essence is a correlative relationship with social science in order to have deeper understanding of the context. As Swinton and Mowat state, "The social sciences have offered practical theologians vital access to the nature of the human mind, human culture, the wider dimensions of church life and the implications of the social and political dimensions of society for the process of theological reflection."[44] I believe that social science has brought unique assets to reflect

---

43. Horizontalization is one aspect of focused coding, with identifying clusters of meaning and meta-analyses being other aspects of focused coding.

44. Swinton and Mowat, *Practical Theology*, vi.

Ignored

upon Korean-speaking emerging adults by revealing a deeper understanding of its context in this study.

As the primary researcher of this study, I not only appreciate any other studies of human cultures but also social scientists who have been conducting those works. As a practical theologian, I admitted that I had limits in social scientific field research and its data analysis for this study, and that I would need professional help from social scientists to have valid research. Other than the first and second readers of this study, Shin Oak (a PhD candidate in clinical psychology in Fuller Theological Seminary) was a close consultant on the data collection and analysis, and Dr. Sharon Kim (an associate professor of sociology in California State University Fullerton) supervised throughout the qualitative research and its data analysis.

2

Descriptive Task

Emerging Adulthood and Korean-Speaking Young Adults in the States

DEFINING THE DESCRIPTIVE TASK

IN ORDER TO PARTICIPATE in God's work and to serve his people better, we need to first understand our context. Who are the people? What type of history and memories do they share? What are their stories? How and what is God doing with this people and place? These are some questions we need to ask to understand our context, as we seek to create a holistic environment for Korean immigrants and their young people. To do this, we must engage the task of the descriptive process.

Practical theology begins with praxis in a particular context. The practical theology method does not suggest that there is one right model or strategy to apply to every situation and/or organization, yet it does claim that all practice is theory-laden, as Browning states below:

> All our practices, even our religious practices, have theories behind and within them. We may not notice the theories in our practices, take them so much for granted, and view them as so natural and self-evident that we never take time to abstract the theory from the practice and look at it as something in itself.[1]

Thus, practical theology does not start with theory and then apply theory to a particular context, which would be either application or

---

1. Browning, *Practical Theology*, 6.

practice. Rather, practical theology starts from a particular context—a people, culture, and/or current practices—and describes what is going on within this context.

Osmer defines the descriptive-empirical task as "gathering information that helps us discern patterns and dynamics in a particular episode, situation, or context."[2] He emphasizes that the key term of the descriptive task is "attending," or relating to others with openness, attentiveness, and prayerfulness.[3] He warns that this task is challenging in a task-oriented culture, which relates people solely in terms of the function or the job we need to accomplish, and encourages us to pay attention by being present, listening, and praying to find out who people are and what they face without rushing to judgment.[4]

Osmer conceptualizes a continuum of attending with informal attending, semiformal attending, and formal attending.[5] He describes informal attending as "the quality of attending in everyday life with active listening and attentiveness in interpersonal communication."[6] Semiformal attending "involves the use of specific methods and activities that provides structure and regularity to our attending."[7] Lastly, formal attending is "investigating particular episodes, situations, and contexts through empirical research.[8]

Descriptive Task in This Study

The descriptive task in this study seeks to gather substantial information and resources to understand Korean-speaking young adults and their praxis in Korean immigrant churches in the United States. There are two different types of descriptive tasks in this study: the first task is an in-depth literature review of related studies, and the second task is field research, which includes surveys and in-depth interviews.

There has been no research conducted with reference to this particular group of people—Korean-speaking young adults—prior to this study, and as a result a literature review within this study surveys related areas to infer the current praxis of Korean-speaking young adults in Korean immigrant

2. Osmer, *Practical Theology*, 4.
3. Osmer, *Practical Theology*, 34.
4. Osmer, *Practical Theology*, 34.
5. Osmer, *Practical Theology*, 37–39.
6. Osmer, *Practical Theology*, 37.
7. Osmer, *Practical Theology*, 38.
8. Osmer, *Practical Theology*, 38.

Descriptive Task

churches. The literature review starts with young adults in a North American setting and their relationships with churches. The review then goes on to address young adult studies in a Korean setting, and the relationship of Korean young adults with churches. Finally, the literature review surveys Korean immigrants and their young people and addresses their relationships with churches in the United States.

Although a part of the field research relates to the descriptive task, all of the findings and interpretation of those surveys and in-depth interviews are located in chapter 3, in order to provide less confusion and a better layout for readers.

LITERATURE REVIEW

As mentioned, there are no existing studies that have been conducted to look more closely at Korean-speaking young adults in the Korean immigrant church in America. Thus, this literature review starts with research about young people in America and Korea, before moving on to Korean American immigrant studies, which should enable us to infer the current state of Korean-speaking young adults and the practices of Korean immigrant churches related to these young people. There are different terms to refer young people of after high school before marriage in Western literatures (emerging adults, late adolescents, young adults, etc.). Although this study deals with literature on young people regardless of terminology, it pays more attention to emerging adulthood, as a legitimate way to describe Korean-speaking young adults.[9]

Emerging Adulthood

It was Jeffrey Arnett who proposed the term "emerging adulthood," which was used for the first time in 2000.[10] Since then, this concept of emerging adulthood has been used in various disciplines, including sociology, psychology, and theology. Although there are no clear set boundaries for the stage of emerging adulthood (some argue 18–25 years of age, while others extend it to the early thirties), scholars agree that emerging adulthood is a transition period between high school and adulthood, which is

---

9. There is a growing number of literature that confirms emerging adulthood in Korean contexts. This is supported by the results of field research with Korean-speaking young adults. See chapter 3.

10. Arnett, "Emerging Adulthood," 469–80.

prolonged compared to previous generations. Some scholars, like Côté, disagree with using a new term of emerging adulthood as a developmental life stage.[11] Côté points out the methodological flaws of Arnett's research, saying Arnett does not report the analytic strategy and methodology on his study.[12] Although Arnett claims that education and social class background are important factors on young people's experiencing emerging adulthood, he uses it as a general concept for all people, not just for college students.[13] Schoon and Schulenberg also argue that the concept of emerging adulthood offers a psychological model of free choice focusing on the postponement of commitments, although it relates more to the social and economic conditions that have produced extended transitions.[14] These scholars who dissent with Arnett's emerging adult theory claim that gives these above reasons, the concept of emerging adults would be a dangerous myth to young adults if policymakers are misinformed about what is causing the transition to adulthood to be prolonged by marginalizing young people who continue the traditional routes to adult life through early entry into the labor market or who cannot take advantage of higher education opportunities due to personal and family resources.[15] In this light, these scholars disagree with the use of the term emerging adults, and they do not consider emerging adulthood a new stage of life development.

Although critiques about emerging adulthood are worthy of attention, this study seeks to carefully review the literature on emerging adulthood for multiple reasons. First, although some scholars do not agree with using the term "emerging adults" or considering emerging adulthood as a new life stage, all scholars agree that there are growing numbers of young people who experience a prolonged transition to adulthood. This study does not take a side in arguing whether or not the Korean community needs to accept emerging adulthood as a new life stage, but rather focuses on the way in which Korean-speaking young adults experience this prolonged transition. Thus, it is helpful to review the literature on emerging adulthood and to understand its concepts in order to compare and contrast with Korean-speaking young adults. Second, scholars agree

11. Côté, "Emerging Adulthood," 177–88; Hendry and Kloep, "Emerging Adulthood," 169–79; Schoon and Schulenberg, "Adult Roles," 45–57.

12. Côté, "Emerging Adulthood," 178.

13. Côté, "Emerging Adulthood," 179.

14. Schulenberg and Schoon, "Adult Roles," 46.

15. Schulenberg and Schoon, "Adult Roles," 46.

that this prolonged transition is related to the socioeconomic status and educational background of young people.¹⁶ Korean young people share similar levels of socioeconomic and educational background with other North American young people, marked by economic growth and a higher rate of college education, and thus experience a longer transition to adulthood. In this light, reviewing and comprehending emerging adulthood literature is helpful for understanding Korean-speaking young adults, a population that has not been researched.

RISE OF EMERGING ADULTHOOD

Acknowledging that the contemporary median marriage age is much later than it was in past years, Arnett argues that later ages of marriage and parenthood have created a space for the new life stage of emerging adulthood. He goes on to state that "these later ages were not causes of the new life stage in and of themselves. Rather they were reflections of other vast changes taking place in modern societies."¹⁷ Arnett presents four revolutions—the Technology Revolution, the Sexual Revolution, the Women's Movement, and the Youth Movement—as significant contributing factors to the birth of the developmental stage of emerging adulthood.¹⁸

The Technology Revolution is about the rise of manufacturing technologies that transformed the American economy. Arnett considers extraordinary advances in technology that have allowed for society to function with far fewer jobs, and notes that the shift has made America and other developed centuries move from a manufacturing economy to a service economy. He points out that these changes require people, especially young people, to acquire different skills, which also lead them to pursue postsecondary education and training. Arnett adds that nearly 70 percent of the population will now continue their education beyond high school.

The second significant change is the Sexual Revolution, which is connected to the invention of the birth control pill in 1964. This development led to young people feeling that they no longer needed to enter marriage in

---

16. Arnett, *Emerging Adulthood*, 22; Tanner et al., "Emerging Adulthood," 31; Schulenberg and Schoon, "Adult Roles," 46.

17. "In 1960, the median age of marriage in the United State was just 20.3 for women and 22.8 for men. . . . [B]y 2010 the typical age of marriage was over 26 for women and over 28 for men, a six-year rise for both sexes in the span of just four decades and still right every year." Arnett, *Emerging Adulthood*, 3.

18. Arnett, *Emerging Adulthood*, 2–7.

order to have regular sexual relationships. Arnett offers his interpretation about the sexual revolution:

> Today most young people have a series of sexual relationships before entering marriages, and most Americans do not object to this, as long as sex does not begin at an age that is "too early" (whatever that is) and as long as the number of partners does not become "too many" (whatever that is). Although Americans may not be clear, in their own minds, about what the precise rules ought to be for young people's sexual behavior, there is widespread tolerance now for sexual relations between young people in their late teens and twenties in the context of a committed, loving relationship.[19]

The third revolution is the Women's Movement. Most young women in 1960 were under great pressure to find a husband and have children. However, today young women have wider options both in terms of education and occupation. Arnett points out that from grade school through graduate school, girls now surpass boys, and that statistics are mostly equal in terms of women being able to obtain degrees and jobs in various fields. These changes allow women not to hurry toward marriage and to enjoy their freedom during their emerging adult years.

Lastly, the fourth change is the Youth Movement. In the past, young people were eager to enter adulthood and settle down. However, young people today see adulthood and its obligations a little differently. Although some young people still pursue the option to settle down, most young people today do not want to rush this stage of life. Young people see that "[a]dulthood and community offer security and stability, but also represent a closing of doors—the end of independence, the end of spontaneity, the end of a sense of wide-open possibility."[20]

Christian Smith, who has also done significant research on emerging adulthood, points out four macro social changes that contribute to the rise of emerging adulthood, including the dramatic growth of higher education, the delay of marriage, frequent job changes, and the extending of financial and other support from parents.[21] The first two changes of higher education and delaying marriage are similar to two of the changes references by Jeffrey Arnett, while the latter two are somewhat different from Arnett's. Smith argues that not only do jobs require young people

---

19. Arnett, *Emerging Adulthood*, 5.
20. Arnett, *Emerging Adulthood*, 7.
21. Smith et al., *Lost in Transition*, 4–6.

to gain new education and training that delays them from beginning a stable and life-long career, but young people also want to maximize their options and postpone commitments to long-term careers by trying different jobs. Smith also argues that one of the noticeable changes for youth is that parents today seem increasingly willing to extend financial and other support to their children to help them succeed. With Schoeni and Ross' data,[22] Smith notes that American parents spend, on average, $38,340 per child in total material assistance over the seventeen-year period between the ages of eighteen and thirty-four. He continues by pointing out that these recourses help to subsidize the freedom that emerging adults enjoy while taking their time before settling down fully into adulthood, which is culturally defined as the end of schooling, a stable career or job, financial independence, and a new family formation.

Five Features of Emerging Adulthood

Arnett demonstrates five main features of emerging adults, explaining that they are not unique, but rather distinctive to emerging adulthood.[23] They are summarized and quoted as follows:

1. Identity explorations

    Emerging adults develop an identity. That is, they clarify their sense of who they are and what they want out of life, by trying out various life options, especially in love and work. Their questions on love and work are more identity-focused: "What Kind of person am I, and what kind of person would suit me best as a partner through life?" and "What kind of work am I good at? What kind of work would I find satisfying for the long term? What are my chances of getting a job in the field that seems to suit me best?"[24]

2. Instability

    While trying out various life options in love, work, and place of residence, emerging adults go through an unstable period. Trying out different people for dates, different schools, majors, and jobs, and different

---

22. Schoeni and Ross, "Material Assistance," 396–416.
23. Arnett, *Emerging Adulthood*, 8.
24. Arnett, *Emerging Adulthood*, 9–10.

places to live, they revise their plan and learn something about them. In this stage, exploration and instability go hand in hand.[25]

3. Self-focus

Emerging adulthood is a stage when there are few ties that entail daily obligations and commitments to others (while children and adolescents are under parents' supervision, and married adults have commitments to their spouse and children). Thus, emerging adults focus on themselves more than at any other time. By focusing on themselves, emerging adults develop skills of daily living, gain a better understanding of who they are and what they want from life, and begin to build a foundation for their adult lives.[26]

4. Feeling in-between

The exploration and instability of emerging adulthood give it the quality of an in-between period—between adolescence, when most people live in their parents' home and are required to attend secondary school, and young adulthood, when most people have entered marriage and parenthood and have settled into a stable occupational path. In-between the restrictions of adolescence and the responsibilities of adulthood lie the explorations and instability of emerging adulthood.[27]

5. Possibilities/optimism

Emerging adulthood is the age of possibilities, when many different futures remain possible and little about a person's direction in life has been decided for certain. It tends to be an age of high hopes and great expectations, in part because few of their dreams have been tested in the fires of real life. Also, this stage offers the potential for changing dramatically the direction of one's life compared to other stage.[28]

Common Themes in the Literature of Emerging Adults

Although it is only recently that the term "emerging adults" has been used in academic settings, some scholars prefer to use different terms like youth,

---

25. Arnett, *Emerging Adulthood*, 11–13.
26. Arnett, *Emerging Adulthood*, 13–14.
27. Arnett, *Emerging Adulthood*, 14–15.
28. Arnett, *Emerging Adulthood*, 15–16.

young adult, young people etc., there are some common themes about contemporary young people in the literature. First, society, including religious communities, does not know what is happening in lives of young people these days. Most of the researchers themselves began their studies in order to better grasp what was happening in the lives of young people. The representative scholars on emerging adults—Jeffrey Arnett and Christian Smith—indicate that their primary goal is to illuminate the contemporary young person's life and culture, which has been unknown.[29] Furthermore, much of the literature about young people in general, including adolescents and young adults, moves in the same direction as well. With this motivation and intention in mind, these studies demonstrate that young people today face a rapidly changing society that vastly differs from the society that older generations have previously encountered. The studies urge that adults should make serious observations and learn about the particular environments that young people face today, rather than assume that they understand based on their own previous experiences during youth.

Second, the studies indicate that attitudes towards younger generations are quite negative. Referencing the term "quarter life crisis," Arnett states that the interpretation of emerging adulthood by older adults, who did not take as long to reach full adulthood as today's emerging adults do, are mostly negative.[30] More strongly, Smith argues that our culture sees emerging adults as "problems," because we see significant deficits at this life stage.[31] This is not much different from adult society's attitude toward teenagers. Smith and Denton strongly state:

> [A]dults typically frame adolescence in ways defining teenager life per se as *itself* a social problem and adolescents as alien creatures, strange and menacing beings, perhaps even monsters driven by raging hormones, visiting us from another planet.[32]

Instead of treating adolescence and emerging adulthood as "a unique phase of life that must be understood and dealt with on its merits,"[33] society tends to burden young people with negative views, even as problems, without knowing who they are and what is happening in their lives.

---

29. Arnett, *Emerging Adulthood*; Smith, *Lost in Transition*.
30. Arnett, "What Is It?," 70.
31. Smith, *Lost in Transition*, 10.
32. Smith and Denton, *Soul Searching*, 264.
33. Clark, *Hurt*, 27.

Ignored

Third, although emerging adults are supposed to have freedom and opportunity to explore themselves in various ways with less commitment, as Arnett argues, they often have a difficult time going thorough this stage. Affirming Arnett's positive view on emerging adulthood, Smith adds that positive features of emerging adulthood are also often accompanied by large doses of transience, confusion, anxiety, self-obsession, melodrama, conflict, disappointment, and sometimes even emotional devastation.[34] Facing ignorance and often negativity from adult society, emerging adults are trying to figure out this new transition and unstable period that previous generations did not experience with much anxiety.

Fourth, these young people, including teenagers and emerging adults, are isolated and segregated in an adult-centered world. Chap Clark argues that contemporary adolescents have been abandoned systemically and created a safe place of "world beneath" for their own survival in an adult-oriented world.[35] Describing adolescent times to the adult community, Alice Schlegel points out adolescents' segregation from adult community in contemporary society, stating that adults generally believe this is what adolescents themselves prefer.[36] Smith also states that most emerging adults spend most of their time only with their peers and are isolated socially by adult society; whatever problems youth have are entirely *their* problems, and are unrelated to the adults around them.[37] This isolated, negative view of young people has led to inadequate support and care for young people on the part of adults. Elucidating that "the young generation has lost meaningful relationship with adults,"[38] Chap Clark further points out:

> The adolescent is left to discern how to handle the multi-conflicting messages related to home, stable relationships, and internal security—all while trying to figure out how to survive lengthened adolescence. This only adds to the aloneness most feel.[39]

In the same vein, Smith states:

---

34. Smith, *Lost in Transition*, 15. Cf. Twenge, *Generation Me*; Kadison and Digernimo, *College of the Overwhelmed*.

35. Clark, *Hurt*, 43–56.

36. Schlegel, "Adolescent Ties," 141.

37. Smith, *Lost in Transition*, 11, 214.

38. Clark, *Hurt*, 50.

39. Clark, *Hurt*, 34.

> [S]tructurally, most emerging adults live this crucial decade of life surround mostly by their peers—people of the same age and in the same boat—who have no more experience, insight, wisdom, perspective, or balance than they do. It is sociologically a very odd way to help young people come of age, to learn how to be responsible, capable, mature adult.[40]

In other words, today's emerging adults are trying to survive in this new period with insufficient support and guidance, all by themselves, while they are in an important transition to adulthood.

Emerging Adulthood and Religiousness and Spirituality

As Arnett demonstrates, emerging adults seek to create their own set of values, beliefs, and worldviews. Pointing out that emerging adulthood is a crucial time for the development of a world view, he argues that although worldview development begins during early ages, during emerging adulthood people more directly address worldview questions and abstract reasoning about concepts such as God, death, and right and wrong, and reach at least an initial resolution to their worldview questions.[41] Barry and Abo-Zena also reach this conclusion concerning physical development. They state that since adolescents have undergone tremendous pubertal changes in addition to brain maturation, involving synaptic pruning, myelinization of the prefrontal cortex, and limbic system changes, emerging adults are increasingly able to engage in higher levels of metacognition, planning, and abstract thinking—all of which support a more complex understanding of religious and spiritual issues.[42]

Although there are some potential detriments,[43] researches generally agree with potential benefits on religiousness and spirituality for emerging adults.[44] The literature has shown that greater religiousness and spirituality is linked to lower risk behaviors, including drinking

---

40. Smith, *Lost in Transition*, 234.
41. Arnett, *Emerging Adulthood*, 212.
42. Barry and Abo-Zena, "Religious and Spiritual Development," 23.
43. Religious and spiritual struggles with low self-esteem: Bryant and Astin, "The Correlates." With higher levels of depression, anxiety, and even suicide: Exline et al., "Guilt." High risk on sexual transmitted disease and unwanted pregnancy: Lefkowitz et al., "Religiosity."
44. For literature review on potential benefit and risk of religiousness and spirituality for emerging adults, see Magyar-Russell et al., "Potential Benefits."

Ignored

issues, drug use, smoking, deviant behaviors and sexual related problems.[45] Greater religiousness and spirituality are also related to better mental health, including less anxiety and depression.[46] Engagement in religion and spirituality is also related to personal well-being, creating a sense of purpose in life, directives about what is right and wrong, greater perception of bounding in social relationships,[47] and distinctive sets of coping strategies for dealing with life stressors.[48] Furthermore, a religious community can provide belonging in a safe, communal space where young people can establish their worldview and gain access to peers, mentors, and elders.[49] This is a unique intergenerational environment where emerging adults can be in the presence of a wide range of individuals who can offer perspectives from different life stages.[50]

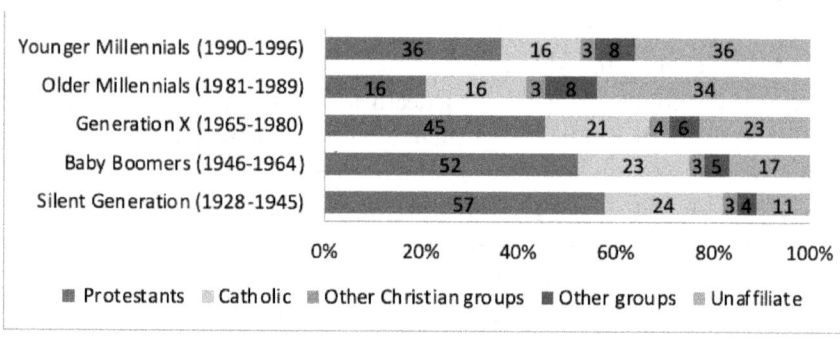

Figure 2.1 Generational Replacement Drives Growth of Unaffiliated

Source: 2014 Religious Landscape Study, Pew Research Center.

Although studies have shown that religiousness and spirituality has important and positive roles in emerging adulthood, younger generations are less involved with religions. According to Pew Research in 2014, 35 percent of adults who were born between 1981 and 1996, and 34 percent of adults who were born between 1981–89 have no religious affiliation. This is double the number of unaffiliated adults who were born between

45. Yonker et al., "The Relationship," 299–314.
46. Smith and Snell, *Souls in Transition*.
47. Smith, *Lost in Transition*; Smith and Snell, *Souls in Transition*.
48. Mahoney et al., "Religious Coping," 341–54.
49. Good et al., "Just Another Club?," 1153–71.
50. Magyar-Russell et al., "Potential Benefits," 42.

1946–64, and three times the number of unaffiliated adults who were born between 1928–45.[51] This shift has been a great challenge for churches as well. Churches have been facing a sharp decrease in membership, with the most serious losses occurring among young people.

Church's Response

As North American churches have become more aware of serious declines in the participation of young people, they have created youth ministries/groups to satisfy young people's felt needs with contemporary music and fun activities. They hire ministers who have energy and fun personalities to take care of young people, and younger generations spend time meeting young peoples' needs. Although this might be attractive to young people, this has created a gap between youth groups and rest of the congregation in churches, as youth ministries have become isolated and segregated. It was Stuart Cumming-Bond who pointed out this issue seriously and called this "The One-Eared Mickey Mouse."[52]

Some decades after the one-eared Mickey Mouse era, churches and scholars started to become aware of the relational gap with young people and began to recognize the importance of developing relationships between young people and adults in the community. Highlighting that meaningful relationships provide a place for people to belong, pursue the truth, and grow to the next level of maturity, churches and scholars have now come into a new era of youth and family ministry from the one–eared Mickey Mouse model. Recently literature and ministries for young people have been focused on building community and relationships in the forms of family ministry, intergenerational ministry, and small group ministry.[53]

Although there are efforts to overcome this gap between younger generations and the church in various ways, the motivation of these efforts seems to be still from an adult-oriented perspective. Reviewing recent research on youth, young adults and religion, Anabel Proffitt critiques churches' commodification and consumerism towards younger generations:

---

51. Lipka, "Millennials."

52. Cummings-Bond, "The One-Eared Mickey Mouse," 76–78.

53. Garland, *Family Ministry*, is more about demonstrating a way of congregational life as a whole and how it shapes and strengthens family relationship. DeVries, *Family-Based Youth Ministry*, focuses on family's value in youth ministry. Joiner et al., *Creating a Lead Small Culture*, provides some models to create a place with small group strategy where the young generation can belong in a local church setting.

Ignored

> As a professor of educational ministry, I was regularly asked by local churches and judicatories to come tell them "how to keep the kids in the church." This was my first hint of the extent to which youth were viewed as a commodity of which the church was either in short supply or was anxious about losing. This made sense of the dearth of substantive books, as the church seemed intent on providing an "entertainment model" of youth ministry that privileged games and gimmicks as ways to attract young people to church. . . . For too long churches have operated with a model of commodifying youth desirable products for congregations to attract in order to how them off to prove their "vitality."[54]

Instead of respecting and paying attention to the lives young people, churches often see young people as a commodity to maintain the church and guarantee its future.

Emerging Adults in Korean Context

Most of the studies on Korean young people, especially of young people in their twenties, agree that contemporary young people are dealing with new times and that this is linked to a prolonged transition to adulthood. These studies are generally in the same vein as the work of Arnett and Smith on emerging adults. Although there are some differences, pursuing further education, depending on parents financially, and delaying marriage are common issues happening in Korea as well as in the United States.

Although it is still developing, there is some research that affirms and uses Arnett's emerging adulthood to understand young people in a Korean context. The Korean Institute for Youth Development did a national research project, including a survey with two thousand young people between the ages of nineteen and twenty-four in 2011, in which they adopted Arnett's survey.[55] The result of the survey in the Korean context affirms Arnett's emerging adulthood in general. Tae Young So interprets the national research of the Korean Institute for Youth Development in 2011 as showing that Korean young people, ages nineteen through thirty, should be seen from a new perspective, i.e., emerging adulthood.[56] He continues by stating that not only external social changes, but also internal identity exploration with work and love (as Arnett demonstrates)

---

54. Proffitt, "Countering Commodification," 3–4.
55. An et al., "청년기에서 성인기 [Transition from Youth to Adulthood]," 1–221.
56. So, "성인 발현기 [Emerging Adulthood]," 4.

Descriptive Task

are present in emerging adulthood for Korean young people.[57] Eunjung Kim conducted qualitative research with female Korean college students in 2010, and also agrees with Arnett's emerging adulthood based on the results.[58] Eunhee Yoo,[59] Hang Sook Park,[60] and Tae Young So also use Arnett's work to describe contemporary young people in Korea. Furthermore, there are many studies about Korean young people that also agree with the notion of young people's prolonged transition to adulthood even though they do not reference the term "emerging adults."

Common Themes in Korean Emerging Adulthood Literature

Korean literature on emerging adulthood is not so different from North American literature. First, Korean society, including religious communities, does not have a depth of understanding about contemporary young people in the same way that North Americans do not. Most of the literature on Korean emerging adults and youth indicate that one of their primary goals is to provide a better understanding of contemporary young people like American studies do. What stands out within Korean literature is a different level of ignorance. One of the main reasons that American society does not understand what is going on in the lives of contemporary young people is the rapid changes of recent years. Korea has also recently undergone rapid changes in many ways; however, Korea has in some ways been through even more intensely rapid changes within a shorter period of time, as compared to the United States. Korea went through intense industrialization and urbanization within only three decades.[61] In the 1960s, Korea was an almost entirely agricultural country; however, by the 1990s, more than 75 percent of the entire population resided in cities with non-farming jobs.[62] Along with industrialization, the Korean economy grew rapidly beginning in the 1960s. In the 1960s, Koreans were surviving on an average of 79 dollars per year, but in 2015, GNI (Gross National Income) per person in Korea is over twenty-seven thousand US dollars.[63] With these changes, most young people in Korea now go to college. By

---

57. So, "성인 발현기 [Emerging Adulthood]," 10.
58. Kim, "성인모색기 [Emerging Adulthood]," 329–72.
59. Yoo, "성품교육 [Character Education]," 283–327.
60. Park, "기독교신앙교육 [Christian Faith Education]."
61. Choi, "청소년 문제 [Youth Issues]," 2.
62. Choi, "청소년 문제 [Youth Issues]," 5.
63. The Bank of Korea, "국민계정 2015 [National Accounts 2015]."

2008, 83.8 percent of young people entered college, while only 33.2 percent entered college in 1991.[64] Young people are also not hurry for marriage. The median age at first marriage was 27.9 for males and 24.8 for females in 1991, but 32.6 for males and 30 for females in 2015.[65]

Although these intense changes in Korean society have brought material wealth, they have also caused serious generational conflicts. Since the gap between older generations and younger generations is so significant, this is often linked to serious generational clashes in many ways. Generational conflicts have been a crucial, sometimes pathological, issue in Korean society.[66] This significant generational gap and conflicts due to intense rapid changes in Korea have made younger generations become unknown or appear incomprehensible for most Korean adults.

Some scholars argue that these generational conflicts are caused not only by a difference between the life experiences of the two generations, but also ignorance about the lives of young people. Eunjung Kim points out that recent major studies only focus on differences between previous generations' twenties and today's twenties, without paying attention to reasons that cause those differences.[67] Ki Ho Um also criticizes adults' negative assumptions, writing, "We just paid no attention to how the twenties actually experienced their world."[68]

Second, contemporary Korean emerging adults are undergoing restlessly intense and continuous competition. Although emerging adulthood itself is an unsettled and unstable period, as previously mentioned, Korean emerging adults experience a more intensified reality of pressure and hardship than their North American counterparts. This generation of Korean emerging adults went through intense competition to get into their colleges, as education is one of the most important values for Korean

---

64. Korean Educational Development Institute, "교육통계연보 [Statistical Year Book of Education]"

65. Statistics Korea, "2015년 혼인 이혼 통계 [Divorce Data 2015],"

66. For information on contemporary emerging adults compared to previous generation, see Lee, 이것은 왜 청춘이 아니란 말인가 [Why This Is Not Young Life]; Kim, 혼돈의 20대 [Confused Twenties]; Song et al., 위기의 청년세대 [Younger Generation in Crisis]; Woo, 88만원 세대 [Generation of 880 Dollars]. For generational conflicts, see Han, "세대갈등 [Generational Conflicts]"; Hong, "세대연구 [Research on Generations]"; Park, "세대 갈등[Generational Conflicts]"; Hong, "세대갈등 [Generational Conflicts]," 154-72.

67. Kim, "성인모색기[Emerging Adulthood]," 331.

68. Lee, "소통의 위기 [Crisis of Communication]," 279.

Descriptive Task

society. In traditional Korean society, education has been one of the few avenues for social mobility, not only for a child but also for one's family. Although there is no longer any visible social hierarchy, an invisible hierarchy is still present in the current social system, and people attempt to raise their status in Korea through education. From kindergarten to high school, getting into a good college is the primary educational goal and the most important duty for Korean young people. Korean families spend a significant amount of money on their children's education, including afterschool programs and tutoring, and abusive private education has been a significant issue for students in Korea.

College, however, is not the end of the story. After college years, young people currently must go through another competitive war to get a job due to Korea's frozen job market. Korean economy experienced such rapid growth up until 1997, but in 1998 Korea faced a serious national financial crisis—the "IMF crisis" (International Monetary Fund). At that time, the IMF issued strict guidelines on credit for debt-ridden chaebols, stopping them from borrowing freely from overly friendly banks with no real collateral to back up loans.[69] After the IMF crisis, there was another financial crisis as well, and Korea has been suffering economic recession since, leading to job market instability. As job markets became unstable, and even froze, getting a full-time job with a contract has become even more competitive. Thus, irregular jobs without security and/or benefits have increased. According to Korean Labor Institute figures, almost two-thirds of the young people who were hired last year became irregular workers with earnings below the minimum wage.[70] Suffering in irregular job conditions, young people put huge amounts of energy and effort into getting a full-time job with security and benefits. Not only are college graduates looking for a job now, but current college students are stressed to achieve a high GPA, further education, certificates, language skills, internships, and often overseas education and work experiences to improve their resumes in order to pursue full-time jobs with security and benefits.

With such a competitive life for young people, Ki Hyung Lee states:

> Youth is no longer a period marked by a heart-throbbing pursuit of ambition, as it was described quite familiarly to the older generation by The Youth Admiration, a popular essay in their high school textbooks. Rather, younger Koreans are marked by unremitting

---

69. Kirk, "What 'Korean Miracle'?"
70. Fifield, "Young South Koreans."

Ignored

agony and anxiety as they routinely endure a fierce, cruel competition for jobs, which has been already too rigidly structured to call it "crisis," and thus normally face the possibility of unemployment. Even after suffering an enormous rivalry to enter so-called "top schools," many of them encounter in college a wall of graded ranks again in order to survive and get picked up in stratified companies driven into relentless conflict and contest.[71]

Third, Korean society is also quite negative towards contemporary younger generations. Like North American society, which sees youth as a social problem instead of understanding and treating them as people who are going through a unique stage of life, Korean society sees youth in a similar way. What stands out for Korean context is that Korean adults often treat young people as failures, comparing their lack of achievement to the stunning economic achievement of the previous generation. Until the 1980s, the twenties was considered to be adulthood in Korea. Most people in their twenties would have had full-time jobs and been engaged in society as responsible adults at that time. Even those who entered college, in their twenties embraced adulthood as an elite group, leading many social movements like the democracy movement, even though they were not yet financially independent.[72]

However, contemporary Korean emerging adults live in very different times. They take longer to assume the full responsibilities of adulthood. Most of them go to college, and it takes them longer to become financially independent. While most young people have left their parents' home in North America, young people in general stay with their parents until they get married in Korea. In a previous century, even after marriage it was normal for people to live with their parents (usually the husband's parents). It is a common courtesy in Korea that parents pay for their children's college tuition, and often for further studies. Living with their parents, young people are fully financially dependent on them not only for tuition but also

---

71. Lee, "소통의 위기 [Crisis of Communication]," 271. Original text: "청년기는 더 이상 기성세대가 고등학교 교과서에서 접했던 자신들에겐 상당히 낯익은 '청춘예찬'에 나오는 가슴이 뛰고, 청운의 꿈을 추구하는 그런 시절이 아니다. 한국의 청년세대는 '위기'라고 말하기엔 이미 강건하게 구조화된 구직과 취업이라는 치열하고 냉정한 관문이 주는 압박과 무한경쟁의 영향 속에서 상존하는 불안과 잠재하는 시련의 상황을 일상적으로 맞닥뜨리고 있는 고뇌하고 불안해하는 주체들이다. 소위 "일류대학"에 들어가기 위해 이미 엄청난 경쟁을 겪어냈다면, 청년세대의 다수는 대학에 진학하면서 또 다시 위계화된 등급의 벽과 만나고, 이들은 서열화 된 직업시장 속에서 살아남고 간택되기 위한 치열한 경주와 경쟁에 다시금 내몰린다."

72. Kim, "성인모색기 [Emerging Adulthood]," 335.

Descriptive Task

living expenses. That being said, the time periods between young people either obtaining a full-time job and/or getting married was not that long in the past. However, with various reasons and an unstable/frozen job market after the IMF crisis, the transition period from fully depending on parents at home to independent adulthood is increasing. Even if emerging adults attempted to obtain part-time work to support themselves financially, they would not be able to spend long amounts of time working at that part time job because of all of the other activities required to prepare and search for full-time jobs. Additionally, the minimum wage is very low in Korea (5,580 Won = $4.70 US dollars), and emerging adults often get paid even less than the low minimum wage with "Passion wages." A "Passion wage" is a new term in Korea referring to the practice of using people's passion for their work as an excuse for paying them little.[73] Research about the current status of Passion wages for young people by the Presidential Committee on the young generation in 2015 reported that seven out of ten of young people have received less than minimum wage or worked for free.[74]

With such limited financial resources, many Korean emerging adults must receive more financial support from their parents to prepare and search for full-time jobs with security and benefits. Research shows that 60 percent of college students took extra curricular activities in 2007, and that the average cost for extracurricular activities per college student, per year was 3,390,000 Won (about $285 US dollars) in 2007; it was 2,670,000 Won (about $225 US dollars) in 2001.[75] These costs are mainly subsidized by parents as financial dependency for emerging adults is increasingly necessary.

Although external factors, such as frozen job markets and serious competition, have caused huge challenges for young people, adults quickly criticize them and assume that they are thinking and acting in ways that are self-oriented and immature, as if young people are totally at fault for the issues they face.[76] This fact has often led Korean adults in society to consider today's Korean emerging adults as failures to fulfill the tasks of adulthood (such as financial independence, completion of education, marriage, having children, etc.) which previous generations completed at that age. For this perspective, Suk Hoon Woo strongly states, "In this structure and system,

---

73. Yoon, "Passion Wages."
74. Yoon, "Passion Wages."
75. Shin and Moon, "스펙경쟁 [Qualification Competition]," 83.
76. Lee, "소통의 위기 [Crisis of Communication]," 278.

Ignored

Korean twenties are scapegoats. Although they are the victim, they are forced to repent of their wrongdoings, as if they caused the problems."[77]

Generally speaking, emerging adulthood in Korea is more about surviving than exploring young people's identity in freedom. With this negative Korean context, many scholars often mention that young people are at risk in Korea.[78]

Emerging Adults and Churches in Korea

The Korean church experienced great growth as the Korean economy grew since 1960s. In fact, the Korean church has been well known not only as a place of rapid proliferation of churches, but also as a place of the emergence of mega-churches.[79] By 1984, Korea was home to the world's largest church (Yoido Full Gospel Church), and by 1992, twenty-three of the fifty largest churches in the world were located in Korea.[80]

However, in the last couple of decades, the Korean church has lost many young members in their teens and twenties.[81] Yoon Sik Choi, a Korean futurist and professor at the State University of New York (Korean campus), predicts that the Korean church will lose all of its young people within the next thirty years. He posits that the Korean church will be reduced to small adult congregations, unless it can do something different for its young people right away.[82] According to Gallup, Korea's research on "The Religion of Koreans" in 2014, 31 percent of Koreans aged 19–29, and 38 percent of Koreans aged 30–39 had a religious affiliation, while 45 percent of 19–29 year-olds and 49 percent of 30–39 year-olds had a religious affiliation in 2004.[83] Similarly, church affiliation among young people has been in decline. Only 18 percent of Koreans aged 19–29, and 20 percent of Koreans aged 30–39 had a church affiliation in 2014, while church affiliation was 23 percent for both 19–29 year-olds and 30–39 year-olds in 2004. What is interesting among this group of young people who have religious affiliation is that only 12 percent of all respondents aged 19–29 started to have religious affiliation during ages

---

77. Woo, 88만원 세대 [Generation of 880 Dollars], 290.
78. Lee, 청춘 [Youth]; Kim, 혼돈의 20대 [Confused Twenties]; Song et al., 청년세대 [Younger Generation]; Woo, 88만원 세대 [Generation of 880 Dollars].
79. Chong, Deliverance, 22.
80. Chong, Deliverance, 22.
81. Yang, 프로테스탄트 [Protestant], 33.
82. Choi, "한국교회 [Korean Church]."
83. Gallup Korea, "한국인의 종교 [The Religion of Koreans]."

of 19–20.⁸⁴ In other words, most young people with a religious affiliation have had their religious affiliation from an early age; only a few gained a new religious affiliation during emerging adulthood.

The Korean church has been aware of a decline in young people, and considers that decline to be the Korean church's crisis. There have been many conferences and ministerial books that offer models or manuals about ministry for younger generations in recent years. Most of the books and resources are (numerical) church growth-oriented with so-called youth ministry experts providing *the* model to apply. Whether these are translated publications from the West or written by Koreans, they focus on how to keep young people in the church without paying careful attention to contemporary young people and their context. It seems that the Korean church treats young people as commodity in the same way that Proffitt critiques American churches for doing: to keep them in the church for its vitality.⁸⁵ As it continues to lose young people, the Korean church is concerned about its future and wants to keep them without doing the difficult work of understanding and genuinely caring about what is really going on in the lives of its young people. Few scholars that research young people in Korean contexts point out the lack of understanding and research with reference to young people. Emphasizing the changes that Korean emerging adults are facing, Hyang Sook Park points out that there is no effort in the field of Korean Christian education to understand emerging adults with their contemporary context.⁸⁶ Tae Young So also points out that although emerging adulthood is an important transition to adulthood, it is hard to find ministries or programs that support and help their transition in Korean churches.⁸⁷

Korean-Speaking Young Adults in the States

Brief History of Korean Immigrants

Korean immigration to the United States began in the early twentieth century, and was motivated by a mix of political, military, and economic factors. There are about 1.1 million Korean immigrants in the United States, as of 2013. Emigration from the Korean peninsula to the United States occurred

---

84. Gallup Korea, "한국인의 종교 [The Religion of Koreans]."
85. Proffitt, "Countering Commodification."
86. Park, "기독교신앙교육, [Christian Faith Education]," 4.
87. So, "성인 발현기[Emerging Adulthood], 21.

Ignored

in three phases, according to the Migration Policy Institute.[88] The first wave (1903–5) brought about seven thousand predominately uneducated male laborers who were employed on sugarcane plantations in Hawaii. The second wave began in 1951 with the outbreak of the Korean War that brought back many US soldiers with Korean brides, orphans, refugees, professionals, and students. The third wave of immigration commenced with the 1965 Immigration Act, which allowed family and employment immigration. After the Immigration Act, the number of Korean immigrants living in the United States grew rapidly, from 11,200 in 1960 to 38,700 in 1970. A high percentage of the third-wave of Korean immigrants were well-educated, immigrating to the States in their prime working age to seek a better life, pursue education, and join their family members. In the late 1960s and early 1970s, Korean immigrants were able to invite their siblings to become permanent residents in the United States, gradually increasing the proportion of Korean family-sponsored immigrants. However, after the Immigration Act of 1990, the number of professional and managerial immigrants increased, while family-sponsored immigrants decreased.[89] In recent years, significant numbers of those considered to be Korean immigrants are actually the result of changes in status rather than new arrivals to the US According to the *yearbook of immigration statistics*, more than 80 percent of the 2009 Korean immigrants were status adjusters from temporary residents status, including international students, visitors for sightseeing, and temporary workers.[90] Among these status adjusters, the largest group was those that were previously international students who finished their degree and wanted to legalize their status to permanent residents through employment-sponsorship.[91] Min points out that this group of people is generally young, fluent in Korean and actively practicing Korean culture, and is also fluent in English. He adds that this group of people has helped the Korean community in the US maintain far more transnational ties with South Korea than before, and is likely to continue to increase in the future.[92]

---

88. Zong and Batalova, "Korean Immigrants."
89. Min, "The Immigration of Koreans," 31.
90. Min, "The Immigration of Koreans," 31.
91. Min, "The Immigration of Koreans," 31.
92. Min, "The Immigration of Koreans," 31.

Korean Immigrants and Their Church

The church has been a crucial and central place for Korean immigrants from the earliest immigrant community until now. About 70 to 80 percent of Korean immigrants were affiliated with Korean churches and about 40 percent converted after immigration, according to Hurh and Kim's study in 1990.[93] Although the numbers declined bit, Korean immigrants in the US still hold strong church affiliations compared to Koreans living in Korea. According to the 2003 New Immigrant Survey, 63 percent and 15 percent of Korean immigrants have an affiliation with Korean Protestant and Catholic churches, respectively, as compared to 18 percent and 11 percent of the population in Korea, based on 2005 data.[94] With such high rates of church affiliation, Korean immigrants also demonstrate high rates of frequency of participation. According to Asian American Survey by Pew Research in 2012, 81.8 percent of Korean immigrants attend church at least once a week (26.2 percent once a week and 55.6 percent more an once a week).[95]

Research on Korean immigrants and their church affiliation demonstrates that Korean immigrants go to church not only for religious reasons but also to fulfill their psychological needs as a result of downward social mobility and to fulfill their practical needs for communal bonds and social services.[96] Pyong Gap Min and Sou Hyun Jang states that the combination of Korean Protestant immigrants' overwhelming affiliation with an ethnic church and their great frequency of religious participation give them the maximum benefits of social services and ethnic attachment from Korean churches.[97] In other words, the Korean immigrant church has not merely been a religious place, but rather a space where their members receive support and resources to survive in a foreign land, and can maintain their ethnic identity and heritage.[98]

---

93. Hurh and Kim. "Religious Participation," 19–34.

94. Min and Jang, "Asian Immigrants' Participation," 261; Min, *Preserving Ethnicity*; Min and Kim, "Intergenerational Transmission," 263–82; Kim and Kim, "The Ethnic Role," 71–94; Hurh and Kim, "Religious Participation," 19–34.

95. Min and Jang, "Asian Immigrants' Participation," 267.

96. Min, *Preserving Ethnicity*, 69.

97. Min and Jang, "Asian Immigrants' Participation," 269.

98. See Min, "The Structure and Social Functions"; Kwon, "Houston Korean Ethnic Church."

Ignored

Younger Generation and Korean Immigrant Church

Almost all Korean church studies on younger generations have been focused on the so-called second generation who were born and raised in the States. Although there are some studies on the so-called 1.5 generation who were born in Korea and came to the United States by age twelve, most studies, especially when dealing with younger generations of the Korean immigrant church, consider both as one group.[99]

Common Themes of Korean American Young People, Especially in Korean Immigrant Churches

Although there is limited research about Korean American youth, research on English-speaking Korean youth has two common themes in church studies. First, younger generations of Korean Americans, both those who were born in the States and those who were born in Korea and came to the United States at an early age, experience assimilation to American culture that often that causes conflicts with their parents' generation. It is not surprising that Korean Americans who receive American education in the US experience assimilation to American culture. The different worldviews, lifestyles, and behaviors stemming from cultural differences often cause generational conflicts in the Korean American context. Many studies have shown that, especially in Korean immigrant churches, younger generations have struggled with older generations due to cultural differences. While older generations of Koreans treat immigrant church not only as a religious space but also a cultural place where they can practice and keep their Korean-ness, the younger generation often refuses to practice Korean Confucianized Christianity. While Korean immigrant congregations emphasize formality and collective experience with sermon-oriented service, English-language congregations maintain an informal style of worship and emphasize each individual member's spiritual connection to God.[100] While the leadership of the immigrant generation aligns rigidly with age (older) and gender (exclusively men), the younger generation, influenced by Western egalitarianism, has rejected the older generation's emphasis on hierarchical authority.[101] Furthermore, while the immigrant generation expresses cultural conservatism and strictness, the younger generation considers evangelical

---

99. Min and Jang, "Asian Immigrants' Participation," 253–74.
100. Min and Jang, "Asian Immigrants' Participation," 253–74.
101. Kim, *A Faith of Our Own*, 30.

Christianity identity to be much more important than Korean cultural virtues.[102] As another example, English-language congregations have refused to follow the immigrant generation's church style, considering the immigrant churches as dysfunctional and hypocritical religious institutions.[103] However, in the Korean immigrant church, where the immigrant generation has held dominant (including financial) power, English-speaking ministries that usually depend on the immigrant generation financially have lacked of ownership and authority. In that context, English-speaking congregations have been treated as second-class citizens.[104]

With these conflicts, some studies believe that English-speaking young people are leaving the Korean immigrant church and possibly leaving their faith, frustrated and discontent with their parents' churches. Using the term of "the silent exodus," one researcher indicates that about 90 percent of post-college Korean Americans are no longer attending church. Another study in the New York City area found that while up to 75 percent of the first generation attend church, only 5 percent of the second generation remains in the church after college.[105] In contrast, however, some scholars argue that the silent exodus claims are exaggerated.[106] Min and Kim argue that about 67 percent of 1.5 and second generation Korean American adults retain their childhood religion, and more than two-thirds of second-generation Korean American Protestants were found to attend an English Ministry (EM) Korean congregation.[107] In this research from 1998, the authors indicate that second-generation Korean Americans refuse their parents' conservative, traditional and Confucianized Christianity in Korean immigrant churches, while they emphasize the gospel in evangelically oriented faith. Min and Kim interpret this to mean that Korean Protestant immigrants have not failed to transmit their religion to their children but have failed to transmit Korean cultural traditions to their children through their religion.[108]

Second, English-speaking Korean Americans are still demonstrating Korean influence in their lives. Although they have refused Korean

102. Choi, "Distinctiveness," 157–79.
103. Kim, *A Faith of Our Own*, 27.
104. Kim, *A Faith of Our Own*, 33.
105. Choi, "Second Generation," 300.
106. Kim, *A Faith of Our Own*, 54.
107. Min and Kim, "Intergenerational Transmission," 268–69.
108. Min and Kim, "Intergenerational Transmission," 279.

Ignored

Confucianized church practices, assimilation to Western culture does not necessarily mean that they are completely disconnected from Korean culture and its influence. A recent study demonstrates that although one of the tasks in emerging adulthood is independence and separation from parents—a widely accepted US social norm—Korean American emerging adults carry on a sense of filial obligation, which is one of the most important Korean Confucian virtues.[109] Raised by Korean immigrant parents, English-speaking Korean Americans have been influenced by Korean culture as well as American culture. One of the common themes within Korean American younger generation literature is an identity crisis between Korean and American cultures. Although they are fluent in English and understand Western culture, studying and working with non-Koreans, they have different needs than mainstream North American young people. Emphasizing the significance of race, Sharon Kim argues that second-generation Korean Americans share a set of distinct experiences growing up as members of a racial minority, and they choose to attend co-ethnic churches where they can be understood and address their needs as an ethnic minority.[110]

Third, expecting a generational transition from Korean-speaking to English-speaking, the studies are focused on how these two differing generations can communicate and work together, especially in a church context. Im states that in the 1990s, several prominent, highly respected Korean senior pastors of Korean immigrant churches, including Dong Sun Lim (Oriental Mission Church), Hee Min Park (Young Nak), and Kwang Shin Kim (Grace Church) publically proclaimed that in the twenty-first century, there would be transition for Korean immigrant churches from Korean-speaking ministries to English-speaking ministries.[111] It has been assumed that in the near future Korean-speaking congregations would be smaller than English-speaking congregations in Korean immigrant churches, which would bring about a leadership transition and result in an increase of English-speaking pastors. With this assumption, studies have primarily focused on how to understand and communicate better with the English-speaking generation for the future of the Korean immigrant church.[112]

109. Kang and Raffaelli, "Personalizing Immigrant Sacrifices."

110. Kim, *A Faith of Our Own*, 64, 80.

111. Im, "The Korean Diaspora," 41.

112. See Hertig, *Cultural Tug*; Goette, "The Transformation," 125–40; Choi, "Distinctiveness," 157–80; Lee et al., "Second Generation," 233–55.

However, this transition from the immigrant church to English-speaking second-generation church has not yet occurred. Im and Oh argue that many of the English-speaking congregations have been leaving Korean immigrant churches due to generational disconnect and lack of leadership transition, but that the English-speaking ministry remains a department within the Korean immigrant churches.[113] As Min and Kim demonstrate, it is not their religion but their Korean cultural traditions that the Korean American younger generation has refused; significant numbers of English-speaking Korean Americans are still involved in church.[114] Yet, as we can assume by the fact that English-speaking ministry remains small, the Korean American younger generation has found different churches than Korean immigrant churches (although, there are undoubtedly some who have left their faith behind altogether). With ten years of field research, Sharon Kim finds that second-generation Korean Americans tend to create a hybrid spiritual space apart from their former generation and seek a healthy and safe environment where they can share and be understood in the totality of their immigrant minority experience.[115]

New Reality of Korean Immigrant Church in Transnational Perspective

DEMOGRAPHIC CHANGES FOR KOREAN IMMIGRANT CHURCH

Whether English-speaking Korean Americans have chosen to go to their own churches or dropped out of church attendance, there are significant numbers of English-speaking Korean Americans who are leaving the Korean immigrant church behind. In other words, it is clear that Korean immigrant churches are not now undergoing the transition to English-speaking Korean American churches, and at least for the near future they will remain Korean-speaking churches.

Although Korean churches are still serving Korean-speaking migrants, the Korean immigrant church is currently facing a new era. After the 1965 Immigration Act, the number of immigrants from Korea increased dramatically, but there was a significant reduction in 1991, and since then the numbers have continued to decline. While the number of

---

113. Im and Oh, "Korean Diaspora," 318.
114. Im and Oh, "Korean Diaspora," 279.
115. Kim, *A Faith of Our Own*, 89.

Ignored

new Korean immigrants in 1985 was over thirty-five thousand, it reached its nadir of 12,840 in 1999.[116]

The decline of Korean immigrant churches in America would be expected, given the significant number of English-speaking Korean Americans leaving and the declining numbers of Korean immigrants; yet Korean immigrant churches have been growing. Although there was a minor decline in 2000, the numbers of Korean immigrant churches have continued to grow. There are more than four thousand Korean immigrant churches in the most recent directory (2014).[117]

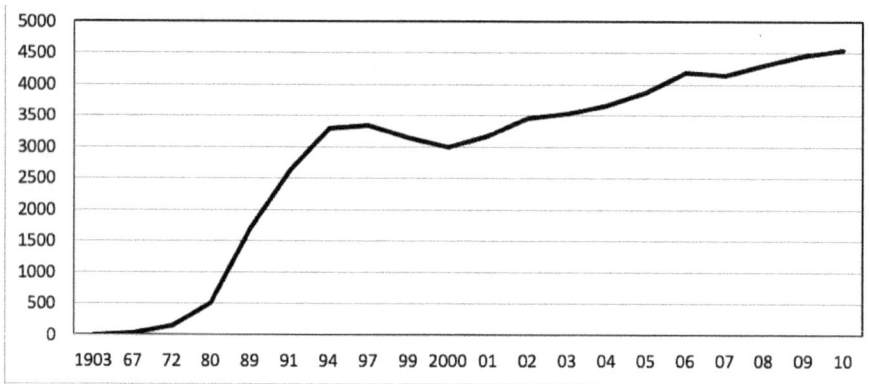

Figure 2.2 The Numbers of Korean Immigrant Churches in North America

Source: Korean Immigrant Church growth, Christian Today

Im and Oh argue that continuous Korean immigrant church growth, even with a decrease in English-speaking Korean Americans and declining numbers of new Korean immigrants, is the result of increasing numbers of nonimmigrant visitors from Korea including pleasure and business travelers, international students, temporary workers and families.[118] According to the Department of Homeland Security, there were 1,946,887 South Korean nonimmigrants admitted in 2015, and these numbers have increased.[119] The number of Korean nonimmigrants visitors to the United States was only 235,000 in 1990, rose to 849,593 in

---

116. Min, "The Immigration of Koreans," 13.
117. Shu, "4,233 교회 됐다 [4,323 Korean Churches]."
118. Im and Oh, "Korean Diaspora," 316.
119. Teke and Navaroo, "Nonimmigrant Admissions."

1996, and now has reached over a million.[120] With this data, Im and Oh argue that the transition the Korean immigrant church is facing is not from Korean-speaking to English-speaking ministry, but to account for a change in membership from legal permanent residents and naturalized citizens to nonimmigrant short-term residents.[121]

Transnationalism and Church

As Korean immigrant churches have a growing number of people with different statuses, it is crucial to understand the nonimmigrant visitors who sustain and even make growth possible for Korean immigrant churches. We can assume that these people would have some differences along with some similarities with immigrants who came and settled in the United States permanently. However, in order to understand this group of people better, there is an important perspective on migration studies that needs to be reviewed: transnationalism.

The term "transnational" appeared in the early 1970s to describe the proliferation of non-state institutions and governance regimes acting across boundaries.[122] Years later, transnationalism began to be used for migration studies by the anthropologists Basch, Glick Schiller, and Blanc-Szanton in 1992.[123] Nina Glick Schiller and her colleagues insisted on significant differences in today's immigrants. They demonstrated that although immigrants of earlier years had broken off all homeland social relations and cultural ties, and thereby relocated themselves solely within the socio-cultural, economic, and political orbit of the receiving society, today's immigrants are composed of those whose networks, activities, and patterns of life encompass both their host and home societies.

After that, transnationalism has become the most prevalent contemporary framework to approach migration studies.[124] It has been integrated with economic, social, political, and even religious fields to understand and analyze migration and cross-cultural activities. Although the

---

120. Im and Oh, "Korean Diaspora," 316.
121. Im and Oh, "Korean Diaspora," 316.
122. Keohane and Nye, *Transnational Relations*.
123. Schiller et al., "Transnationalism."
124. For more information on transnationalism, please see these authors: Faist et al., *Transnational Migration*; Levitt, *Transnational Villagers*; Levitt and Jaworsky, "Transnational Migration," 129–56; Levitt and Schiller, "Conceptualizing Simultaneity," 1002–39; Portes, "Transnationalism," 181–93; Vertovec, "Cheap Calls," 219–24.

transnationalism discussion is vast in many areas, there are four important themes that will help to elucidate this study. First, researchers have highlighted the crucial role of technology development. Although there is some debate as to whether the transnational aspect of migration is a new phenomenon or not, scholars generally agree that technology development, including the internet, accessible international calls, and international trips, reinforce or bring about a different level of transnationality for migrants. Second, the transnational approach brings a different level of understanding on migration and migrants' lives. Compared to a traditional understanding of and approach to migration, which mainly focused on immigrants' assimilation to hosting countries, transnationalism tries to compensate for the limits of micro and macro levels of analysis. It also countervails against one-directional assimilation thinking by demonstrating how migrants carry not only immigrants' culture but also their homeland culture. Third, although there are some transnational elements in the experiences of all migrants, the degree of connectivity between home and host countries—transnationality[125]—can vary depending on an individual's own given context with transnational activities and spaces. Fourth, although there is lack of research, it is clear that religions have played a crucial role in migrants' lives by providing "transnational religious spaces." Transnational religious space is Seringham's term in her recent study of Brazilian migrants in England.[126] She argues that religion's role is crucial not only for migrants themselves, but also for migrants' friends and families that do not migrate, but which send and receive people and remittances.

CONCLUSION: NEW REALITY AND FURTHER

This literature review on demographic changes in Korean immigrant church and transnationalism highlights four things we need to pay attention to. First, Korean immigrant churches in America (and possibly all over the world) have been a crucial transnational place for Korean immigrants. That is why it is so important to keep Korean traditions in the church for the immigrant generations, even when it has caused some trouble with subsequent generations. Second, the growing number of members in Korean immigrant churches is not due to legal permanent residents, but nonimmigrant visitors with temporary visas who have increased transnational ties with their home country, i.e., Korea. That is why this new group of people accepts and often

125. Faist et al., *Transnational Migration* 15.
126. Sheringham, *Transnational Religious Spaces*.

reinforces Korean culture in the immigrant church while English-speaking Korean Americans reject Korean cultural practices. Third, among the huge number of nonimmigrant visitors from Korea, there are significant numbers who are of a younger generation. Research shows that a large group of these nonimmigrant visa holders are international students from Korea, while those that hold temporary working visas also include college graduates seeking more opportunities in the United States.[127] Although there is no research that indicates the age range of nonimmigrant visitors, it is reasonable to infer that there are significant numbers of young people whom we would identify as Korean-speaking young adults.

Fourth, and finally, these Korean-speaking emerging adults in Korean immigrant churches are a crucial piece for understanding Korean immigrant churches' present and immediate future. They are current members of Korean immigrant churches who will have a significant impact on Korean immigrant churches in the future, whether they plan to adjust their visas to stay or not; this is especially true considering the fact that a high percentage of Korean emerging adults that hold temporary visas eventually do immigrate to the United States.[128]

---

127. Min, "The Immigration of Koreans," 25; Im and Oh, "Korean Diaspora," 316.

128. Based on the data from yearbook of immigration statistics, Min states that the portion of status adjusters (who entered America with non-immigrant status and changed their status to permanent residents) among Korean immigrants were only 20 percent in 1967. However, this number has sharply increased, and in 2010, more than 80 percent of Korean immigrants were status adjusters rather than new arrivals. Min interprets that huge portion of status adjusters are previous international students. Min, "The Immigration of Koreans," 25; Im and Oh, "Korean Diaspora," 24.

3

Interpretive Task

Who Are the Korean-Speaking Young Adults in Korean Immigrant Churches?

DEFINING THE INTERPRETIVE TASK

PRACTICAL THEOLOGY IS A process that moves from practice to theory, not from theory to practice. Interpretation of practices is required in order to gain a deeper understanding of theory, which is necessary for describing practices. Osmer defines this interpretive task as "drawing on theories of the arts and sciences to better understand and explain why these patterns and dynamics are occurring."[1] In this stage, the social sciences, history, the humanities, and philosophy are all helpful for understanding the influences and consequences of the current praxis.[2] Osmer states, "[T]heories help us understand and explain certain features of an episode, situation, or context but never provide a complete picture of the 'territory.' Wise interpretive guides, thus, retain a sense of the difference between a theory and the reality it is mapping." It is crucial to understand not only what is going on (descriptive task) but also why it is going on (interpretive task), supported by thoughtful interpretation in concert with theories, cultural studies, and other studies of the humanities to have complete understanding of the "territory."

Osmer uses the term "Sagely Wisdom" as a synonym of the interpretative task, and this sagely wisdom is conceptualized with thoughtfulness,

1. Osmer, *Practical Theology*, 4.
2. Branson and Martinez, *Leadership*, 43.

theoretical interpretation, and wise judgment.³ Interpretation must be thoughtful, kind, and considerate of the practice's circumstances; simultaneously, interpreters must be careful to avoid making imprudent or incorrect assumptions.⁴ The interpretive task also requires an ability to draw on theories of the arts and sciences to understand and respond to particular episodes, situations, or contexts.⁵ Finally, Osmer states that the interpretative task requires capacity to interpret episodes, situations, and contexts in three interrelated ways: (1) recognition of the relevant particulars of specific events and circumstances; (2) discernment of the moral ends at stake; (3) determination of the most effective means to achieve these ends in light of the constraints and possibilities of a particular time and place.⁶

Interpretive Task in This Study

Although there are many ways to approach the interpretive task, a qualitative approach based in grounded theory was utilized for this study. Swinton and Mowat have demonstrated how qualitative methods can be appropriate for practical theology without clashing with its essential theological methodology in their research for five different case studies.⁷ They claim that through mutual correlation, qualitative research can provide helpful insights to interpret context and practices.⁸ Insights drawn from the interviews in this study have been further supported by qualitative research.

As discussed in chapter 1, this study conducted two unique field researches—a survey administered to 404 Korean-speaking young adults from eight different churches, and forty in-depth interviews (with thirteen pastors currently serving Korean-speaking young adults and twenty-seven Korean-speaking young adults in Korean immigrant churches). Based on these two researches, this chapter addresses the interpretative task by answering two main research questions: *(1) Who are Korean-speaking young adults in Korean immigrant churches?* and *(2) What are the current practices of Korean immigrant churches?* Out of these two questions, this study seeks to demonstrate an interpretive analysis supported by a review of related literature and field research in order to listen to and understand

3. Osmer, *Practical Theology*, 82.
4. Osmer, *Practical Theology*, 82.
5. Osmer, *Practical Theology*, 82.
6. Osmer, *Practical Theology*, 82.
7. Swinton and Mowat, *Practical Theology*, 77.
8. Swinton and Mowat, *Practical Theology*, 77.

Ignored

Korean-speaking emerging adults without bringing about premature or imprudent assumptions. This study also aims to offer a theoretical interpretation supported by qualitative field research, analysis, and wise judgment to both recognize context and practices, and to discern moral ends which could eventually lead to determining new practices.

RESULTS AND FINDINGS

Who Are Korean-Speaking Young Adults in Korean Immigrant Churches?

EMERGING ADULTHOOD

The research indicates that Korean-speaking young adults experience a prolonged transition to adulthood as emerging adults. The surveys and interviews demonstrate that Korean-speaking young people share many features in common with the characteristics of North American emerging adults listed in social science research.

Figure 3.1. Age Of Members In Korean-Speaking Young Adult Department

Age Range	Percentage
36-40	12%
31-35	25%
25-30	38%
18-24	25%

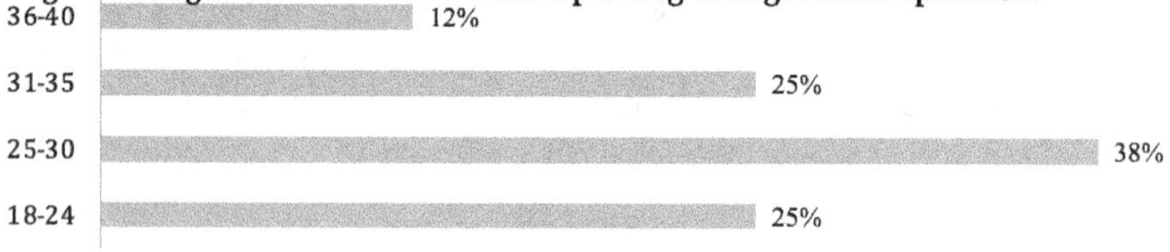

The age range of Korean-speaking emerging adult members of Korean-Speaking young adult departments who participated in this study is eighteen to forty. This group is comprised of recent high school graduates to those transitioning into the adult department. Based on this research, the composition of Korean-speaking young adult departments was: 25 percent college-aged people (18–24 years old), 38 percent people aged 25–30 years old, 24 percent people aged 31–35 years old, and 12 percent people aged 36–40 years old. Although the oldest individual who took this survey was 40 years old, according to some pastors, some people who are even older likely remain in Korean-speaking young adult departments. In other words, this department is made up of individuals from age eighteen (immediately post-high school) to single adults over forty.

Scholars have yet to arrive at a consensus age range for emerging adulthood, as some restrict it from eighteen to twenty-five years, while

Interpretive Task

others extend it to thirty.⁹ Yet it is clear that emerging adulthood is a period that begins sometime after high school and continues until adulthood. Korean-speaking young adult ministries seem to share the same idea about the transitional nature of young adults. These departments are theoretically intended for young people who are beyond high school youth groups but not yet ready to join the adult departments. In Korean culture, marriage is typically viewed as the benchmark life event to enter adulthood; single individuals are not considered to be adults. Marriage also seems to be a necessary benchmark for entering the adult department in Korean immigrant churches.¹⁰ This group of unmarried young people is culturally considered to be at an in-between stage.

Arnett demonstrates that emerging adults are exploring their unique senses of self by exploring different majors, jobs, work, and living conditions in which they revise their life plans and learn more about themselves.¹¹ This research indicates that Korean-speaking young adults are also engaged in introspective exploration in areas of their lives as they extend young adulthood through seeking further education and delaying marriage. In fact, this research shows that most Korean-speaking young adults seem to be pursuing further education at a rate higher than average. Of the 404 respondents to the interview, 93 percent respondents reported that they are currently enrolled in or have graduated from college. This is higher than the American college entrance rate of 80.8 percent and also higher than Korean college entrance rate of 87.1 percent, based on OECD research in 2015.¹²

Pursuing further educations, Korean-speaking young adults explore themselves in different areas. Of the young adults interviewed, 71 percent (ten) stated that they had changed majors in their secondary schools. Most of them tried different jobs as well. There was only one person that had stayed at the same job for more than five years; all of the others had tried different kinds of jobs, or different work environments with the same kind of job, rather than staying in one place. Furthermore, these young adults relocated to explore different geographic areas, and about 20 percent of the interviewees reported having lived in countries other than Korea and

---

9. Concerning the age range of emerging adulthood and further literature, see chapter 2.
10. This is well-known cultural concept in Korean society.
11. Arnett, *Emerging Adulthood*, 11–13.
12. OECD, "Enrolment Rate."

Ignored

the United States. Whether for education, work, or traveling purposes, they resided in other countries for durations that ranged from months to years. More than half of those interviewees with undocumented status, despite their limitations regarding international travel, reported that they had moved around within the country too.

Meanwhile, as Korean-speaking young people explore themselves, they are also delaying entering into marriage. According to the survey with 404 Korean-speaking young adults, the average age of those involved in Korean-speaking young adult ministry departments was twenty-nine years old, and about 37 percent were older than thirty-one. Throughout the in-depth interviews, Korean-speaking young adults expressed that exploration and experiments to understand their life is more important than marriage, and that they were not pressured to hurry into marriage. In other words, Korean-speaking young adults share the same experiences that North American emerging adults do: going on dates with multiple people, trying different schools, changing college majors and jobs, and moving frequently.

Ethnic Minority

The results from the survey and in-depth interviews suggest that Korean-speaking young adults struggle as ethnic minorities. There were many different types of struggles expressed by those interviewed, such as language barriers, financial difficulties, hardship finding employment, discrimination, and rejection from the mainstream culture. Although the difficulties that they expressed varied based on their individual conditions, it is clear that an overwhelming majority of the interviewees experienced hardship as ethnic minorities. Among these hardships, those associated with visa status[13] were one of the most commonly expressed, and most painful issues in the interviews. One young adult interviewee stated,

> One of the unique aspects of the young adult department in the Korean immigrant church, compared to the church in Korea, is the visa issue. In Korea, there are different difficulties like family problems, financial issues, and getting jobs, but here in immigrant churches, we often pray for the visa issues of members. Even in

13. There are different types of status for Korean immigrants. Stable resident status includes permanent residency (or Green Card) and naturalized citizenship; both allow people to stay and travel overseas freely. Temporary visa status includes travel, students, work vistas which allow people to stay for a temporary period of time. Often, temporary vista status restricts overseas travels. Other people are undocumented, staying without visa or other necessary documents.

Interpretive Task

Sunday services, young adult group services, and small groups, we pray for visa issues. This is something that churches in Korea don't have.... When you do not have a stable resident status, it is extremely difficult. Even if your loved one or friend in Korea is sick and about to die, you can't return because of your visa status; it's like being in a prison. It means no freedom. I know I am exaggerating now, but this is how we feel. It is like Korean military service. Yes, there is a life going on, but you have limits in your freedom. At least Korean mandatory military service has its end, but for visa issues, there is no guarantee that you will get out of that.

Another young adult who applied for a green card and was waiting for approval stated, "I am so worried. What if my mom gets really sick before I get the green card? One of my friends has serious nightmares of losing her passport many nights.... Pray for me that my green card[14] gets approve sooner."

The intensity of the struggle and pressure these young adults face seems very high.

Figure 3.2. Visa Status

Figure 3.3. Number of Changing Visas among people who have Green Card or Citizenship

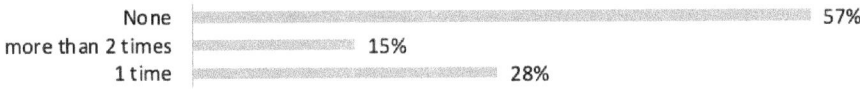

In this study, a significant portion of people included either currently held or have held temporary visas. In the survey, 53 percent of those interviewed had stable resident status and 40 percent had a temporary visa, such as a student, work, or travel visa. There were 7 percent who reported being undocumented.[15] Among the 53 percent who have stable resident

---

14. Green Cards are used to attain permanent residency.
15. Recognizing Korean shame-based culture, the survey provided an option for "Others" instead of "Undocumented."

Ignored

status, 43 percent reported undergoing several status changes before acquiring permanent residency or naturalized citizenship in the US In other words, the survey indicates that 70 percent of the people in Korean-speaking young adult departments have likely experienced the instability and difficulties associated with holding temporary visas.

Although there are people who did not need to worry about their status, due to holding permanent residency or naturalized citizenship at their time of immigration, it seems that visa issues have become a shared burden for the Korean-speaking young adult community.

One lay leader in a Korean-speaking young adult department said this in an interview,

> Visa issues are one of the most difficult things. It is difficult for people whether they have green card or temporary visa. When someone is going through a difficult time because of visa issues, we really care and pray together. We do not look down on people who do not have green cards. Hardship relating to temporary visas and undocumented status is our shared pain. We pay extra attention not to create any shameful situations for these people. We do not ask for a person's visa status unless they share. We try not to do activities that require background checks, such as particular community work because most of us have experienced hardship due to visa issues. Even when you have never experienced visa issues, you know the struggle as a minority.

This shared hardship of visa status seems represent one of the major hardships as a minority to express not only the difficulties of holding an unstable resident status, but also feeling a lack of control over the situation to attain stable resident status, and to maintain their familial duties, due to visa restrictions.

Transnationality

Transnationality is Faist's term that refers to the degree of connectivity between home and host countries, as mentioned in the previous chapter.[16] Faist explains this term:

> The term denotes a spectrum of cross-border ties in various spheres of social life—familial, socio-cultural, economic and political—ranging from travel, through sending financial remittances, to exchanging ideas. . . . In short, transnational ties can be understood

---

16. Faist et al., *Transnational Migration*, 15.

Interpretive Task

as occupying a continuum from low to high—that is, from very few and short-lived ties to those that are multiple and dense and continuous over time. . . . Transnationality is characterized by transactions of varying degrees of intensity and at various stages of the life course; it is not restricted to geographical mobility.[17]

In other words, migrants not only experience assimilation into host countries but also retain ties to their home countries. The degree of this transnationality can vary depending on an individual's own given context, and it is not limited to geographical mobility. Based on Faist's framework of transnationality, the surveys and interviews asked about the transnationality of Korean-speaking young adults. The results indicate that they have strong ties to Korea even while they are experiencing assimilation into American culture. Furthermore, it would seem that this high level of transnationality is not limited to geographical mobility and age at arrival.

Figure 3.4. Arriving Age

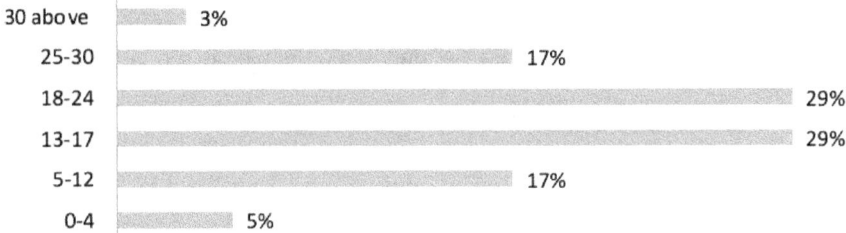

It was surprising that Korean-Speaking young adult departments have a significant number of individuals who arrived in America at an early age. 5 percent of those interviewed were either born in the US or arrived before the age of four, while 17 percent arrived between the ages of five and twelve. Traditionally, people who were born here are considered to be "second generation" and people who came to America during their early teens (usually before twelve) were considered to be "1.5 generation,"[18] as-

17. Faist et al., *Transnational migration*, 16.

18. The Korean 1.5 generation has been generally used for people who born in Korea and came to America before the age of twelve. Danico defined the Korean 1.5 generation as those "who are bicultural and bilingual and who immigrated to the United States during their formative years. They are socialized in both Korean and American cultures and concialized in both Korean and American cultures and consequently express both sets of cultural values and beliefs." Danico, *The 1.5 Generation*, 2.

suming that they were more assimilated into American culture (especially with using English as their primary language) than immigrant generation who came to America at a later age. In traditional studies, people who are born or came in their early childhood are considered mainly as English-speaking people who would be involved in English ministry in their immigrant churches. However, this survey shows that nearly one quarter of the members of the Korean-speaking departments arrived before the age of twelve, and that thus there might be a different way to categorize these young people than the traditional way of categorizing them as belonging to either the 1.5 or second generation.

The survey indicates that Korean-speaking young adults hold strong ties to Korea and Korean culture. According to Pew Research in 2012, Asian Americans have close family ties in their country of origin, and Korean Americans are third on the list of having close family in country of origin with 63 percent, after Indians (69 percent) and Vietnamese (65 percent).[19] In the same light, the survey asked if they have close family in Korea. Out of 404 Korean-speaking young adult respondents, 267 people (79 percent) reported that they had close family members in Korea. This result was even higher than the general Korean American population in Pew Research in 2012.

Figure 3.5. Close Family Members in Korea

Figure 3.6. Answer of "Have You visited Korea After Coming to America?"

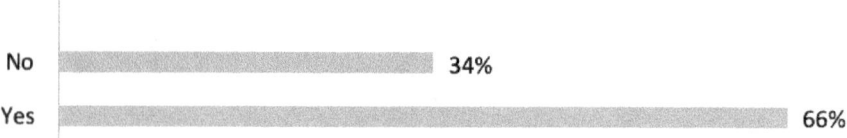

19. See "The Rise of Asian Americans."

Interpretive Task

Figure 3.7. Number of Times to Visit Korea among people who have visited Korea after coming to America

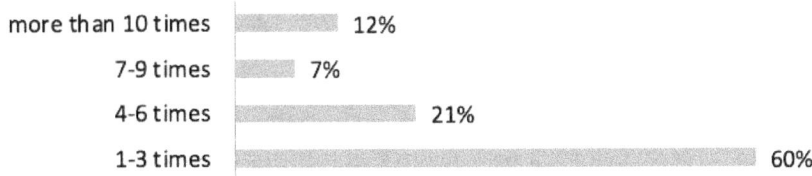

The survey showed that those Korean-speaking young adults often visit Korea after moving to America, if they are able. In the surveys, out of 404 people, 66 percent of the respondents said they had visited Korea after moved in America. Among those who had visited Korea, 81 percent said that they had visited Korea 1–6 times, and 12 percent of the respondents had visited Korea more than ten times. Among those who had not visited Korea, many cited their unstable visa status as a primary reason.

Among the twenty-seven in-depth interviewees, 96 percent explicitly reported that they or their family members had sent or received remittances to or from Korea, and 30 percent said they sent or received money regularly. One hundred percent of in-depth interviewees reported that they regularly use Korean social networking services and media, and all of them reported that they have contacted people in Korea through the Internet, telephone, and/or online messages. Furthermore, 81 percent said that they contacted people in Korea regularly (at least once a week) via the Internet.

Figure 3.8. Close Family Members in America

Although these Korean-speaking young adults have kept strong ties to Korea, this does not mean that their assimilation to America is less pronounced. The result of the survey and interviews show that they were also exposed and assimilated to American culture as well. Out of 404

surveys, 66 percent of Korean-speaking young adults reported that they have close family in America. Out of thirty-seven in-depth interviews with Korean-speaking young adults, all of them reported that they were bilingual, although their level of proficiency in each language varied. All of them were exposed to American culture via education or work settings. Interviewees had all received primary and secondary education, and many had also gone to college. Those from the in-depth interviews who arrived at older ages were still engaged in graduate schools or private education to seek further degrees (or to keep their student status in order to maintain their visa status). Some of them also work in English-speaking work environments. Although some work in Korean-speaking work settings, they still have another place where they are exposed to American culture, such as school or other part-time jobs.

One interesting finding on the topic of assimilating to the culture of the hosting country and maintaining homeland ties is that persons experience different levels of transnationality depending on their backgrounds and contexts. One of the young adult interviewees, who came to America at the age of 9 stated,

> My English is not so fluent. Although I came here when I was 9, I always use Korean more than English. My family speaks Korean. My close friends all speak Korean. In elementary school, there was a bilingual program and I got to use Korean a lot. Even in middle and high school, I always had teachers who were bilingual. I can speak and study in English, but Korean is more comfortable for me.

Another interviewee who also immigrated to the US early in life and matriculated through the American education system said,

> My parents intentionally put me in a middle school where there were no Korean students so that I could learn to speak English well. However, all of the people, like family and friends who have a relationship with me outside of the school, spoke Korean. Although I did not have anyone who spoke Korean in my middle school, that was not a problem. I was bit lonely, but I could meet up with my friends after school. I can speak English to study and work, but I prefer use Korean for my personal life.

These interviews demonstrate the possibility that people who come to America before the age of twelve may still have a hard time speaking and/or developing relationships in English. In other words, the traditional

Interpretive Task

definition of the 1.5 generation of bilingual and bicultural based on their arrival age[20] should be reconsidered or expanded.

While some of the people interviewed had arrived in their new host country at a young age, and would thus be considered part of the 1.5 generation, they expressed that their Korean cultural side is stronger than their American side. Conversely, there are some people who arrived at a later age, whom we would consider to be part of the first generation, that demonstrate significant assimilation to American culture. One of the interviewees, who came to America at the age of twenty-nine and has stayed America for five years, reported,

> I thought I had never been influenced by and assimilated to American culture because my primary social circle is with Korean people here. But I went to Korea last year and I felt that I am not truly Korean anymore. My friends in Korea said I am Americanized. In ways of thinking, talking, and acting, people can tell I am different than Korean people. I don't think I can live in Korea again.

Another interviewee who stayed in America for only two years, beginning at the age of twenty-seven, states,

> Although my English is not perfect, I am comfortable talking to my American friends. I regularly hang out with my American co-workers and friends from school to go to the café or pub, or play sports together. I know some Koreans who hang out with only Koreans. I do not think that is matter of language skills. It is more about how open you are and how willing you are to learn and understand.

Although further study is needed, these interviews demonstrate that even when a person has a late arrival age, people are still able to experience assimilation in significant ways; thus, arrival age might not be the only factor for assimilation. These findings indicate that traditional migrant studies,[21] which are solely categorized by arrival age, should be reconsidered.

The result of surveys and interviews convey that assimilation and cultural maintenance are not mutually exclusive. This study shows that while Korean-speaking young adults experience assimilation into their new surroundings of American culture, they hold strong ties to Korean culture via various channels. In other words, it seems clear that Korean-speaking

---

20. Rumbaut, "Ages," 1160–205; Danico, *The 1.5 Generation*.
21. Cf. Danico, *The 1.5 Generation*; Rumbaut, "Ages," 1160–205.

Ignored

young adults have high degrees of transnationality with various transnational transactions including travel, financial, media, and interpersonal contact to their home country, in addition to education, work, and other communities in their hosting country.

Loneliness and Church as a Survival Place

One of the overwhelming feelings expressed throughout the in-depth interviews was loneliness. It seems that this loneliness is somewhat similar to that of the experiences of American emerging adults. Clark states that contemporary young people are left to discern how to handle their struggles by trying to figure out how to survive by themselves.[22] While agreeing that there is a bright side of emerging adulthood, Christian Smith states that there are dark sides as well. He argues that young people in this stage are more unstable, struggle to figure out their lives, and often find the freedom and exploration associated with emerging adulthood to cause wounds and hurt.[23] In addition, he also mentioned that in this unstable stage, emerging adults experience a kind of social isolation by being surrounded by peers with only limited advice or guidance from adults.[24]

As this study demonstrates, Korean-speaking young adults expressed their loneliness, struggles to survive in this unstable life stage, and lack of advice and resources during the in-depth interviews. Every single Korean-speaking young adult interviewee indicated his or her loneliness in one way or another. A couple of people directly claimed, "Every Korean-speaking young adult is lonely." However, the loneliness that Korean-speaking young adults experience is not merely the same as American emerging adults. Their loneliness is unique and arguably deeper as a result of their ethnic minority status in America. Even though Korean-speaking young adults can speak English (indeed, some of them are perfectly fluent in English), they still experience rejection, feel marginalized, and have a hard time building authentic relationships in American settings like school and work.

In light of these struggles and loneliness, it seems that Korean-speaking young adults are seeking communities in which they can fit. Often, their church communities seem to be the only places where they can belong. Korean-speaking young adult departments offer a unique social sphere where Korean-speaking young adults can forge meaningful

---

22. Clark, *Hurt*, 34.
23. Smith, *Lost in Transition*, 15.
24. Smith, *Lost in Transition*, 234.

relationships. Most of them, including those who are fluent in English, stated that most of their friends are church friends, and that they do not have any friends outside of their Korean-speaking young adult groups. It seems that Korean-speaking young adult groups are the only community in which these young adults can be understood and where there are welcoming people who share their transitional life stage, marginalization as Koreans, and transnational identity.

Surprisingly, 100 percent of the respondents commented that the reason Korean-speaking young people come to church, in addition to reasons of faith, is because they are lonely.

One of the young adults interviewed stated, "People come to church because they are lonely. For Korean-speaking young adults, there is no place to meet decent people. If you don't go to church, basically you are alone. Relationships in school and the workplace are really superficial and don't last long."

Another young adult reported,

> It is true that there are a lot of people who just come to find their partner in the church. When there is a rumor that a certain church has good-looking girls or boys in their young adult department, many people go and become members of that church to meet people. It is also true that many people come to church to hang out with people. Even in my small group, there are couples that just sit there and do not fully participate in the Bible study. They just sit and endure the small group Bible study so that they can go hang out after the small group. And some people even go to drink after church, noting that as the one of the reasons they come to church!

These statements reveal that Korean-speaking young adults carry significant loneliness as emerging adults and ethnic minorities, and that church has been a type of survival place where they can fit in with others of their age, ethnicity, and transnationality.

What Are the Current Practices of the Korean Immigrant Church?

An Important Gateway for Spiritual Formation

Korean immigrant churches have been an important religious place for Korean-speaking young people. This field research, including surveys and in-depth interviews, shows that Korean-Speaking young adult ministries are an important resource for spiritual formation. This is a crucial finding,

Ignored

considering the growing number of religious "nones" and decreasing number of Christians, especially of young people in both America and Korea.[25]

Figure 3.9. Answers of "Did you go to church in Korea?"

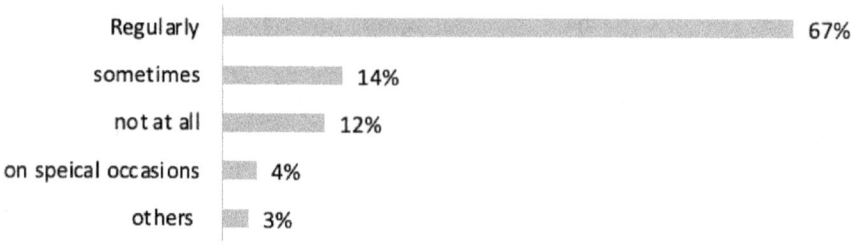

Among the 404 survey respondents, 67 percent of the people regularly attended church before they came to America. Interestingly, 12 percent of those surveyed reported never attending church in Korea but currently attend a Korean immigrant church. Also, the 18 percent of people had not regularly attended church in Korea (14 percent of "sometimes" and 4 percent of "on special occasions only") participated not only in the service but also in small groups at their present churches. In other words, about one third of respondents were more engaged in church in America than they had been in Korea. Considering growing number of religious nones, especially in younger generations, it is important that 30 percent of people who did not have regular church affiliation (12 percent of people who never went to church, 14 percent of people who went to church only sometimes, and 4 percent of special occasion-goers) now engaged more with church. Although it is consistent with the findings of immigrant Korean participation in the ethnic church in the previous studies,[26] the pastors who were interviewed reported that there were more "real" newcomers, those who had never attended church prior to joining the Korean-young adult department. According to these pastors, most new members in the young adult ministry were transplants from other churches who had changed their membership for various reasons.

25. Lipka, "Millennials"; Gallup Korea, "한국인의 종교 [The Religion of Koreans]."
26. Hurh and Kim, "Religious Participation," 19–34; Min and Jang, "Asian Immigrants," 261; Min, *Preserving Ethnicity*; Min and Kim, "Intergenerational Transmission," 263–82; Kim and Kim, "The Ethnic Role," 71–94; Hurh and Kim, "Religious Participation," 19–34.

One of the pastors currently serving in both a Korean-speaking young adult department and adult congregation said

> Comparatively speaking, there are more real newcomers in Korean-speaking young adult departments. In adult departments, we do have a good number of newcomers every year, but there are not many real newcomers who have never gone to church before. Most newcomers in adult congregations are from different churches. However, we meet real newcomers who have never gone to church before in Korean-speaking young adult departments. Whether they come to believe or to get some different help from church, it is a good thing.

Given this significant proportion of new church attendees, it seems the Korean immigrant church serves as a gateway to Christian faith for many.

In addition to its role as a gateway, the churches also serve as hubs for ongoing spiritual formation for Korean-speaking young adults. There were significant numbers of people who experienced spiritual growth in Korean immigrant churches. More than half of the young adults interviewed mentioned that they experienced some spiritual growth and spiritual formation through the Korean-speaking young adult departments, and 37 percent of those interviewed responded that they had experienced crucial and dramatic spiritual growth. One young adult interviewee said,

> I am still struggling with my future and visa status, but I think the more important thing is that I met God and have grown up a lot spiritually. Although my parents in Korea worry that I am still having a hard time getting a job after spending a lot of money and time here, they also think that it was worth it for me to stay here because I have grown near to God. Through my church, I have become a different person, and I am thankful for that.

Transnational Space

Korean immigrant churches and Korean-speaking young adult departments provide transnational spaces, which make it possible to settle in America while keeping ties to Korea. Korean immigrant churches provide different kinds of social services for their members to adjust in the United States. Also, they provide different transactions and activities to maintain and often reinforce members' ties to Korea, such as using Korean language, serving Korean food, practicing Korean cultural behaviors and traditional holidays, and hosting guest speakers from Korea.

Ignored

As many researchers have shown,[27] Korean immigrant churches provide different services for Korean immigrants. With this research, it is clear that the provision of services also corresponds with Korean-speaking young adults as well. Most of the respondents in the in-depth interviews reported that Korean immigrant churches have provided help for their settlement in America. For those who did not have any family or friends in America, churches and their members provide crucial recourse and information to settle. One young adult interviewee said,

> There is a saying: if you go to America, go to a Korean immigrant church. Regardless of your religious background, people go to church to get help to settle and survive. When I came first, I had no one here. But my church people helped me a lot. Finding an apartment, providing rides when I didn't have a car, getting a driver's license, moving to another place . . . there are so many things that I received help to do.

Korean immigrant churches and Korean-speaking young adult departments provide some crucial services and resources to help members get settled.

One of the lay leaders interviewed said,

> People in Korean-speaking young adult departments need these kinds of help. So when a new person comes, the community tries to help them to settle in various ways. I have a pick-up truck from my work, and my car is their favorite. I have helped with people's moving and offered airport rides so many times.

These interviews show that Korean immigrant churches provide various forms of assistance for new immigrants to aid in settlement. This seems to occur informally and by personal outreach within the Korean-speaking young adult department.

Church leaders are also aware of this need. One of the pastors mentioned,

> Because they are not familiar with American culture, our departments have regular programs for outings. We go shopping together to the grocery market or stores like IKEA, since there are people who do not have a car. We go sightseeing together to well-known tourist places or beaches. We go to famous restaurants together. We help people to explore American culture.

27. Min, "Korean Immigrant Churches," 1381–90.

Korean immigrant churches not only provide help for immigrants' adjustment to America, but also provide services for people to maintain their Korean culture. They use Korean language. They usually eat Korean food on Sundays at church. Most Korean immigrant churches celebrate traditional Korean holidays with special activities and food. They treat people according to Korean culture in the immigrant church. In other words, churches provide a place where Korean people can come and maintain their social networks, and often reinforce their Korean culture.

In addition to each individual church's transnational practices, there are institutional transnational ties in the Korean immigrant church. There are branch churches, which have headquarter churches in Korea. In this case, branch churches in America receive financial support and human resources from the headquarter church in Korea. There are also some churches that have relationships with churches in Korea as sister churches. Although the level of transnational ties is different depending on an individual church's relationship with churches in Korea, most Korean immigrant churches have links to Korean churches.

This institutional ties to Korea impact Korean immigrant churches widely. Many Korean immigrant churches use Bible study curricula and ministry programs from Korea, and often they invite guest speakers from Korea. All of the pastors interviewed reported that they use resources from Korea for their ministries, and about 70 percent of them said that their main teaching materials are directly from Korea. Oftentimes, they use monthly devotional magazines for their quiet time practices. These magazines are not only imported from Korea, but the contents include stories of updated Korean news and issues for consideration of how to respond as Christians.

In these transnational links to both America and Korea, Korean-speaking young adults share a similar transnationality, which matters when choosing a spiritual community. Although young adults in Korean-speaking young adult departments are exposed to and assimilated into American culture at different levels, they share common attitudes towards American culture. In the in-depth interviews, there are people who were born in the US and are more comfortable with English, while others just arrived and struggle with their English. With varying levels of assimilation into American culture, most of the Korean-speaking young adult interviewees expressed that more freedom and better personal boundaries is a positive aspect of American culture, as compared to Korean culture, while individualism was considered as a negative aspect of American culture. They also have different levels of ties to Korea. Some people have visited Korea every year and have access to Korean media every day, while other people have seldom visited Korea and only watch Korean TV programs a few times each month. Yet, most of these young adults described Korean culture as hierarchical, competitive, forcing uniformity, and at the same time communal.

Given the level of identification with both Korean and American cultures, the transnationality of Korean-speaking young adults seems to lead them to choose to invest in Korean-speaking young adult groups in Korean immigrant churches. It may be the only option for those who have difficulty with English to choose the Korean-speaking community, but there are many who have enough English proficiency that they could choose English-speaking communities. Based on the interviews, the main reason these young adults chose Korean-speaking communities is the communal-oriented factor of Korean culture. Those who were more comfortable with the Korean language and culture stated that they wanted to know and worship God in their first language, which could touch their heart and emotions. Although there are options as English Ministry for people who use English as their first language or speak English fluently, there are some people who still choose Korean-Speaking Ministry. In the interviews people who were stronger in English than in Korean said they were drawn to the Korean-speaking ministry because they wanted more communal relationships. People who were more comfortable with English or who had experienced the English ministry mentioned that the English-speaking ministry was more individualistic, and that they preferred a more communal-oriented community. One of the pastors interviewed said

> We have a growing number of English-speaking young people in our department. I actually asked them the reason as to why they come to Korean-speaking young adult department instead of the English Ministry. They said that in the English Ministry they did not feel enough care. In the English Ministry, if they come, they come; if they don't, they don't. However, in the Korean-speaking young adult group, they feel much more welcomed. If they don't come, their small group leaders and other members will text, call, or ask why they did not come, encouraging them to come. I think they like being treated that way.

A young adult interviewee who was born in the United States stated,

> English Ministry people are more selfish and individualistic, but Korean-speaking young adult people are warmer. I feel like they are a real community, like a family. They really care about each other. In English Ministry, you meet people only on Sunday. Even if you don't come, no one actually cares. But in the Korean-speaking young adult department, we contact each other and meet during weekdays. We are connected and care for each other. If something happens to you, they will care, ask, and pray together.

With different backgrounds of assimilation, young adults who come to Korean-speaking young adult ministries share similar degrees of transnationality. It is certain that Korean immigrant churches, especially Korean-speaking young adult ministries, provide a transnational space, and that members of Korean-speaking young adult ministries share somewhat similar degrees of transnationality.

FRAGMENTED STRUCTURE

Through surveys and interviews, it is evident that Korean immigrant churches are structurally fragmented. Generally speaking, departments are disconnected within Korean immigrant churches. The Korean immigrant church ministry system runs by department, and there are not many opportunities to connect to different departments. In this overall fragmented structure in Korean immigrant churches, Korean-speaking young adult departments seem to be more segregated from the activities of churches than other departments in Korean immigrant churches. Respondents mentioned that the education departments and English Ministry departments were given greater attention because their members are children of the Korean-speaking adult members. However, because most members of the Korean-speaking young adult ministries do not have family members within their church system, they are the most disconnected and segregated departments, even though Korean-speaking young people use the same language as the adult congregations. One pastor from a church, which has 1,300 members stated,

> Do you know how many Korean-speaking young adults have their parents in the church? It is less than 3 percent. We do have adult members who care about the next generation, but their attention is more focused on their children's education and the English Ministry department. . . . [T]here is no way to inform them of the Korean-speaking young adult department's vision and events,

Ignored

and because the adults do not know about Korean-speaking young adults, there is not enough support for them."

A significant majority of the pastors interviewed (85 percent) reported that their Korean-speaking young adult departments did not have relationships with the other departments. Even more (93 percent) of the young adult interviewees reported that they did not have significant relationships with the adults in the church. Among these, more than half (56 percent) stated that they do not know any adults in the church at all. Although there are some church-wide events, such as special services or church-wide picnics, these seem to be insufficient for building relationships. One of the lay leaders described this segregation as a sad reality:

> I think there are many things we can learn from adults in the church. It is not easy to live with faith and we need to learn how to live from adults. Churches seem to consider us as people who fill the room. They do not have any interest in us. We are so disconnected, it's as if we go to different churches. Sometimes I feel we have a different faith than the adult congregation. . . . We don't have teachers. Look at us. Immature people teach immature people. I don't think this is O.K.

One young adult said,

> I saw many friends had a hard time going to the adult department after they got married because there is no connection; "it feels like going to a new church," they said. People stay within the Korean-speaking young adult groups even after their marriage. However, eventually they need to move on, and many people have left during this transition. I am getting married within a couple months and this has been an issue for us as a couple. We are open to going to different church.

These interviews indicate the way in which the fragmented structure in Korean immigrant churches frustrate those in Korean-speaking young adult departments. Although there are a couple of pastors who stated that their Korean-speaking young adult departments were able to build good relationships between adults and their young adults, it was the result of pastors' individual efforts and investments, not from any structural support.

Hierarchy in the Church

Cultural hierarchy is one of the significant features in Korean culture, and Korean immigrant churches have also been shaped by that narrative. The structure of Korean immigrant churches is hierarchical not only for individuals as a result of their title, gender, age, and social status, but also for departments based on their age group and link to adults. Often, this hierarchy causes struggles for pastors and members of Korean-speaking young adult departments.

Among different hierarchical factors, one of the most frequent struggles for pastors was the status of Korean-speaking young adult pastors. Throughout the pastors' in-depth interviews, their responses show that many pastors who lead Korean-speaking young adult groups struggle in this hierarchical structure in the church. Among the pastoral staff, it seems that they have a lower status than the pastors who serve adults. Most of pastors that I interviewed who serve in Korean-speaking young adult departments worked part-time, although they mentioned they work more than part-time hours. Only 40 percent of the pastor interviewees were full-time pastors, but all of them had additional roles beyond their Korean-speaking young adult ministries, usually in the service of the adult ministry. The full-time pastors who led larger (200+ members) Korean-speaking young adult departments were still involved in some kind of administrative work or adult ministry, while most full-time adult ministry pastors reportedly served only adult ministries in the same churches. The majority (70 percent) of the pastors mentioned feeling somewhat burned out due to overwork. 23 percent of the pastors reported not having enough time to serve Korean-speaking young adults because of ministry requests from other departments. They expressed their struggles, especially that churches and members do not understand or value the importance of Korean-speaking young adult ministries by expecting them to hold roles in addition to their pastorship of the Korean-speaking young adult ministries.

Pastors also raised issues regarding struggles communicating with their senior pastors or elders. Over half (54 percent) of the pastors mentioned that because their senior pastors or elders do not understand or have any interest in Korean-speaking young adults, the pastors felt that they did not have enough support for their ministries. Only a smaller portion (23 percent) of the pastors reported feeling that they had sufficient support from their churches and that their senior pastors adequately valued

Ignored

Korean-speaking young adults departments. One pastor said, "The senior pastor does not care about Korean-speaking young adults. No interests at all. There is not enough financial support. He does not understand why Korean-speaking young adult departments need money."

Another pastor said,

> They are young adults who need to explore and learn, but we are not allowed to try new things. We want to try to worship God in a desert or on a mountain, but our senior pastor and elders do not like that idea. There are some rules to keep, and Sunday service being at the church is one of them. These rules are not negotiable.

Another pastor said,

> As part time pastors, you do not have a choice. I was youth pastor a couple of years ago and the senior pastor put me in charge of the Korean-speaking college group. I did my best to serve these college students, but now he wants me to go to young adult group. It has been only a couple of years in college ministry. We merely set up a system. We need more time to stabilize the ministry but within a couple of weeks, I am going to go to young adult group. I tried to ask the senior pastor if I could stay but he wanted me to obey. It is common in Korean immigrant churches. When your senior pastor puts you in different ministry, you need to go; otherwise, you are challenging his leadership.

Beyond the hierarchy expressed in titles such as pastor, elder, and deacon, there is another hierarchy that impacts Korean-speaking emerging adults: a hierarchy based on department. Although members in Korean young adult departments are no longer minors, they are treated as less than adults. None of the forty interviewees (either pastors or young adults) said that they were involved decision-making processes in the church. They are not invited to make any decisions, not only for church-wide or adult departments, but also their own Korean-speaking young adult departments.

One pastor said,

> Members of the elder committee or any other decision-making parties for Korean-speaking young adult departments do not have any understanding about Korean-speaking young adults and the department. That's why their meeting is just empty talk, and their decisions are not relevant for the Korean-speaking young adult ministry.

One of young adults said,

Interpretive Task

> I have been involved in this church and Korean-speaking young adult department more than ten years now. And we have had eight pastors during those ten years. The interesting thing is that we are always informed that we will have a new pastor one or two weeks ahead of time. You know, when a senior pastor changes, they form search committee, we vote, and listen to sermons of some of the finalists. Therefore, how come when we have a new pastor for the Korean-speaking young adult department, we are just informed, "You will have a new pastor next week?" Is it because our offering is smaller than the adult congregation? In our Korean-speaking young adult department, we have enough people who have a professional job and tithe, so what is the problem?"

Korean-speaking young adult groups often feel treated as less important than the adult ministry. When adult ministries need help or manpower, Korean-speaking young adults are encouraged or forced to volunteer, regardless of their own ministry schedule:

> We do have our own plan and schedule for ministry and events. When adults have a big event, they ask us to come to work or sit in. Sometimes we know in advance, but other times we are called without notice. It is not really respectful of our ministry. If we don't come, we are immature spiritually or just bad young people to the elders.

Unstable System for Korean-Speaking Young Adult Departments

Korean-speaking young adult departments are systemically unstable both in terms of leadership and membership. Many Korean immigrant churches experience serious internal conflicts and a significant number of them undergo bitter church splits through strife, which can involve police activities and lawsuits.[28] Korean immigrant churches' internal conflicts are so common that people say it is part of the Korean immigrant church culture.

70 percent of the pastor interviewees reported that their churches have had internal conflicts, while 62 percent of them stated that they went through some type of pastoral leadership change due to those conflicts. One pastor interviewed stated,

> Church conflict is one of common cultural features of Korean immigrant churches. Many Korean immigrant churches went

---

28. Kim, *A Faith of Our Own*, 21.

> through church splits and there are many churches caught in lawsuits. Some churches are working through multiple lawsuits . . . due to internal conflicts. It is such a shame that so many immigrant churches are mired in internal strife, and it is hard to find a church that has no conflicts.

Internal conflicts and splits themselves make churches insecure environments, and these conflicts cause leadership changes that may add another layer of instability. Pastors reported that pastoral leadership frequently changes in Korean immigrant churches, and this brings many changes to the entire church. Because of the hierarchical structure of Korean immigrant church, every leadership change is likely associated with significant structural and cultural changes to the church, contributing to additional instability.

On top of the instability caused by church-wide conflicts and leadership changes, Korean-speaking young adult groups are one of most unstable departments based on their own leadership and membership changes, according to the in-depth interviews. There are frequent turnovers of pastoral leadership in Korean-speaking young adult departments. Although further research is needed to explain this frequent turnover in a comprehensive way, pastors who lead Korean-speaking young adult departments simply do not stay long. This frequent turnover of pastoral leadership causes different kinds of issues. It brings systemic instability, often leading to conflict between Korean-speaking young adult pastors and members. A pastor stated,

> There is no long-term plan for the Korean-speaking young adult ministry. There is no long-term model, at least in Korean immigrant churches. There is not enough respect for Korean-speaking young adult ministries, and structurally Korean-speaking young adult pastors don't get to stay long enough produce a long-term ministry model. Why? They are either promoted to adult pastors or they are fired by the senior pastors. Most of the time, pastors consider the Korean-speaking young adult position as a stepping-stone for becoming a senior pastor.

One of lay leaders interviewed reported,

> We have had six pastors in the last ten years. I am sure there are different reasons for those changes, but it is extremely painful to go through pastoral leadership changes. Whenever a new pastor comes, we have to stop what we were doing and need to start new

Interpretive Task

things according to the new pastor's vision and style. Sometimes, we have had a new pastor who comes directly from Korea. One did not have any idea of what Korean-speaking young adults were going through. Lay leadership tried to explain why we needed to keep our system, but he did not accept our suggestions. It caused serious conflict between the new pastor and lay leaders. In the end, many members left the church.

Pastors are not the only positions with a high turnover rate. The members in Korean-speaking young adult departments also frequently change. Although their departures are due to various reasons, such as relocation due to school and work, some issue with a previous church, or a relational breakup, memberships of Korean-speaking young adult departments are not stable.

Figure 3.10. Duration of Attendance in the Current Church

The duration of attendance at each person's current church varied in the survey. Through the 404-person survey, 25 percent of the respondents reported that they had attended their current church more than six years, 19 percent had attended three to six years, 26 percent had attended one to three years, and 30 percent had attended their current church for less than a year. Thus, more than half of the members of Korean-speaking young adult ministries have been at their current church for less than three years. Whether these changes are due to recent immigration or church conflicts, the result is that Korean-speaking young adult departments frequently have new members.

A pastor who was serving in a Korean-speaking young adult ministry in a mega church mentioned,

> Every year, we have a huge number of new members. Some of them are new immigrants, and others are from another Korean immigrant church with various reasons for leaving. However, only a small number of them stay. Every year, 70 percent of the people within the entire young adult department are new. There is a lot

Ignored

of in-and-out and quick turnover in the Korean-speaking young adult department. It's not a phenomenon that only occurs in my church. It is a common issue among Korean immigrant churches.

According to the interviews, Korean-speaking young adult departments have a high influx of new members, and simultaneous member losses every year. Their reasons for leaving the church vary, including relocation due to jobs and schools, and issues with a previous church. One of the salient findings related to this issue was that Korean-speaking young people move around to different Korean immigrant churches if they have options; this is a well-known phenomenon among Korean-speaking young Christians. A lay leader interviewee stated,

> People move around. If this church has some internal conflict, we jokingly ask which church would be most beneficent church, which would have people from the church. My church was one of the best churches for Korean-speaking young people for a couple years, but recently our lead pastor was replaced, and many people left. Recently, one of my friends who is lay leader of another Korean immigrant church texted me to say thank-you for sending many people to her church. We are used to this kind of thing happening. I did not get hurt because I know that sooner or later they will go to different church or come back.

Knowledge-Based and One-Way Teaching Focused Spiritual Programming

Although different churches have different spiritual practices, one of the common themes of spiritual growth and formation in Korean-speaking young adult ministries is training-oriented. The interviewees, including pastors and members in Korean-speaking young adult departments, mentioned the training-oriented programs when they talked about spiritual formation and growth. There are 40 percent of pastors interviewees who said that their 'discipleship' program is one of the strengths in their ministry. Among pastors who did not used the term "discipleship," 32 percent mentioned leadership training as one of their important programs. Although pastors did not provide a clear definition of the programs, both discipleship and leadership training programs included Bible study, prayer (usually early morning prayer), and Bible memorization. These practices seemed more focused on knowledge-based spiritual program (and having members complete a certain amount of work) than on holistic spiritual growth. Some pastors mentioned that one of important goals for these programs is growing leaders to serve.

One of the pastors interviewed said,

> Our church has well-established discipleship training. Every leader has completed this discipleship program. This includes Bible reading, memorization, early prayer meeting, Bible study, and daily quiet time. It is not easy, but this strong program helps our church to have stable leadership. For young adults, this is a great challenge. Many people complain or give up, but once they complete the program, they become leaders and grow up so much spiritually.

Alongside of these reports, 56 percent of the young adults reported they have experienced some type of training programs. Indeed, most of the lay leader interviewees became leaders through these spiritual programs.

Although this type of training-oriented and knowledge-based spiritual practice is somewhat helpful for spiritual growth, it seems that the main purpose of these practices is to maintain or reinforce their church system with trained leaders. This training-oriented program is often focused on cognitive knowledge, and it does not impact their daily life. A pastor stated,

> Church members are trained to serve the church. All the discipleship programs lead them to eventually commit themselves to ministry in the church, but it is not linked to their daily life. I think the faith we are teaching is for ministry, not for our life. So, if we serve in event-oriented ministry programs like summer short-term mission trips, people are satisfied, thinking that they did their duty.

Another pastor stated, "There are not many places to think of the Kingdom of God in our ministry and the teaching of our church. We are so busy to keep our ministry going that it doesn't move beyond our church."

These interviews demonstrate that discipleship programs are focused on the church's internal operation more than the individual's spiritual formation. It seems that this knowledge-based spiritual programing perpetuates a non-holistic strategy by focusing on the operations of the church system. Furthermore, this spiritual program seems insufficient for impacting people's holistic spiritual formation beyond church activities.

Ignored

CONCLUSION: INTERPRETATIONS

These findings are drawn from 404 surveys of young adults in Korean-speaking young adult departments and forty in-depth interviews with pastors and young adults in Korean-speaking young adult departments. This study presents some important data for analysis regarding young adults and the current practices of young adult ministries in Korean-speaking young adult departments of Korean immigrant churches.

First, Korean-speaking young adults are carrying doubly painful struggles, not only as emerging adults in-between life stages, but also as ethnic minorities in America. Korean-speaking young people are going through emerging adulthood, as the research and literature demonstrate. They are going through an unstable life stage between adolescence and adulthood. They are not children who are dependent and free from responsibilities, but they are not fully independent to take on full responsibility. They are still growing to figure out how to live with trials and mistakes. They explore life in many different ways: exploring different majors and classes in college, trying different jobs, and moving around to explore different locations. They also try building relationships with different people, including dating relationships. Scholars point out that contemporary young people greatly struggle with the lack of support during this uncertain life stage, given the negative attitudes towards young people shown by adults. Modern young people are left to find a way to grow by themselves. This is true for Korean-speaking emerging adults as well. According to the interviews, their experiences in school and work demonstrate that they seem to be dealing with uncertainty in this in-between stage alone.

With this instability and uncertainty of in-between life stages, Korean-speaking young adults seem to carry burdens and stress as ethnic minorities, stranded between Korean and American cultures. This minority struggle adds even further instability and uncertainty for Korean-speaking young adults. Although most of them clearly claim to be Korean, using Korean language more often than not in America, they are still exploring themselves and exposed to American culture and systems by living in the US Recognizing their assimilation to American culture, which makes them somewhat different from people in Korea, they are trying to figure out their identity. On top of this cultural tension, they struggle with instability as minorities in America concerning their visa and racial status. Many people hold temporary visas and significant numbers of people struggle with an unstable visa status. This struggle also becomes a shared burden among

Interpretive Task

the larger Korean-speaking young adult department, including for those who have permanent residency or naturalized citizenship. Temporary visa status comes with many limits, and this often restricts these young people from visiting their families in Korea, even in crucial times such as a special family gathering or a family member's illness or death. People who have permanent residency or citizenship also struggle as secondary people who are not welcome in mainstream culture in American society, and this also creates tension and anxiety.

Second, Korean-speaking young adults carry great loneliness and often feel frustrated in a fragmented Korean immigrant church system, which creates another layer of loneliness. Loneliness was one of the strongest expressed feelings across the surveys and interviews. Korean-speaking young adults carry loneliness not only as emerging adults but also as ethnic minorities. Studies state that emerging adulthood is a lonely stage in this contemporary culture.[29] Young people have been abandoned and isolated systemically in an adult-oriented world,[30] and are surrounded mostly by peers who similarly lack experience, insight, wisdom, perspective, and balance.[31] This seems not so different for Korean-speaking young people. Korean-speaking young people also feel lonely and carry additional marginalization as ethnic minorities. Korean-speaking young adults expressed loneliness in the interviews. They reported that they feel lonely because many of them live far away from their families and friends. Even those who immigrated with their family still struggle with the loneliness of limited relationships—they need more than their immediate family for meaningful relationships.

It appears that the loneliness Korean-speaking young adults carry draw them to Korean immigrant churches, but they seem to continue to experience loneliness even within their own ethic church enclaves. In the in-depth interviews, 100 percent of young adult respondents reported loneliness as a primary reason for their church involvement; in fact, it seems to be a more crucial reason for church affiliation than spiritual reasons. By joining Korean immigrant churches, Korean-speaking young adults expect to be accepted and belong while they are marginalized and rejected in American society. However, what they are experiencing is another segregation. Over 90 percent of young adult interviewees reported

---

29. Hersch, *A Tribe Apart*, 30; O'Keefe, "Growing Up Alone," 82; Clark, *Hurt*, 34–35.
30. Clark, *Hurt*, 34.
31. Smith, *Lost in Transition*, 234.

Ignored

that they don't have any significant relationship with adults in the church, and about 85 percent of pastor interviewees states that they do not have any connections with the adult departments. More than a half of the young adult respondents reported that they do not know any adults in the church. This shows that Korean-speaking young adults still feel lonely and seriously segregated in their own ethnic church where they hope to find acceptance and belonging.

Third, Korean-speaking young adults share a similar transnationality, and these ties matter to them when choosing communities in which to practice their spirituality. Research indicates that Korean-speaking young adults have strong ties to Korea, while they are exposed to and assimilate into American culture as well. Although the level of assimilation varies depending on an individual's background and context, they have better English skills than previous immigrant generations, and are engaged in American culture through their education and work settings. At the same time, Korean-speaking young adults have strong ties to Korea with many types of transnational transactions, such as visiting Korea, accessing Korean media, utilizing Korean language and culture in daily life, etc. This transnational feature was found to be a crucial factor in choosing community. As we have shown, people in Korean-speaking young adult groups have different backgrounds in terms of their arriving age in the US Although there are many people who speak English fluently and have other options of communities to choose from, such as English Ministry young adult groups, some intentionally select Korean-speaking communities over English-speaking ministries. This demonstrates that whether one is born or has just arrived in America, sharing Korean culture and maintaining ties to Korea are some of the most important factors in choosing their community. In other words, the transnationality of Korean-speaking young adult groups provides a crucial survival space where these young people can belong.

In addition to choosing their community, cultural maintenance in this transnational context is also important, as it matters for their spirituality. Korean-speaking young people choose Korean-speaking young adult groups as their community not only to belong, but also to grow spiritually. Although there are different options for their spiritual formation and growth, Korean-speaking young adults particularly choose Korean immigrant churches to hear Korean-language sermons and teaching, and to engage in Koreanized spiritual practices such as Early Morning Prayer, Tong

Sung prayer, and discipleship training based on curricula from Korea. This shows that culture indeed matters to spirituality.

Fourth, while Korean culture plays a crucial role for Korean-speaking young adults' spiritual formation, there seems to be some dysfunctional cultural forces which lead them to be marginalized and ignored in the church. Although they find some good perspectives and practices in Korean culture, such as a communal-orientation and respect of elders, there are also problematic aspects. Among those cultural illnesses, Confucian hierarchical practices were mentioned the most in the interviews. It seems clear that Korean immigrant churches carry a hierarchical culture in their system and practices. By age and title such as pastor, elder, and deacon, there is an order and a rank in the church. Based on this hierarchy, older or higher-titled persons, such as senior pastors and elders, are treated as more important people. Similarly, adult departments are treated as more important than Korean-speaking young adult departments.

In this hierarchical culture, there were two different cultural illnesses that were expressed in interviews. The first is fragmentation. Korean-speaking young adults were segregated and disconnected from church, especially from older adults. This segregation is so deep that sometimes Korean-speaking young adults feel they are in a different church from the adults. They assume that they are treated as less important, neither connected to nor cared for by adults in the church.

The second is Korean commodification. In this hierarchical culture and system, it is easy to dehumanize people and treat them as commodities. Korean-speaking young people often reported being called to serve adults and their ministries. When there are ministries or events that require additional manpower or attendance, adults assume and often demand that Korean-speaking young adults should do this work. In this hierarchical culture, young people are expected to obey those demands; otherwise they are considered immature or rude to their elders. In other words, even without meaningful relationships, they are obligated to serve the church and adults. These dysfunctional cultural forces seem to lead Korean-speaking young adults to be marginalized and ignored in the church.

Fifth, there are not enough places where Korean-speaking young adults can be heard and cared for. In the surveys and interviews, the participants of this study were able to articulate their struggles and identify issues within their churches and ministries. However, it seemed that there had been few other occasions and spaces for them to do so. Although

Ignored

Korean immigrant churches' current systems are fragmented by department, and all departments are somewhat disconnected, Korean-speaking young adults departments are relatively more segregated compared to other departments. Most of the other departments, including the English Ministry[32] and education departments, have family connections to the adult congregation, but most of Korean-speaking young adults (97 percent) do not have any family members within the church system. This results in less attention and resources being devoted to Korean-speaking young adults from the adult congregation. They feel marginalized and powerless, given their situation. Throughout the interviews, they were able to name their struggles and problems somewhat clearly. Both pastors and young adults stated that they have spoken up to church leadership but that the situation had not changed. Although they were mature enough to reflect and think, and were expected and able to contribute to the church financially and in other ways, they experienced frustration in expressing their struggles and finding solutions.

Furthermore, there is no place or opportunity for Korean-speaking young adults to discuss their difficulties and work on solutions. In a hierarchical system, there is great shame and fear around discussing problems. This shame and fear not only affects the Korean-speaking young adults but also the authorities as well. In this shame and honor culture, discussing negative issues directly is generally uncomfortable and impolite. In this context, authorities are the ones who are have both the power and the responsibility to identify the problems and make changes. Thus, for lower-status people to initiate a discussion of problems and issues is to disrupt the roles and duties of the entire system, bringing shame to all parties. Thus, in such a system, it seems that disconnect between Korean-speaking young adults and authorities deepen.

Through these frustrations, Korean-speaking young adults seem to be craving to be heard and cared for. Throughout the interviews, they expressed their strong desire to belong and connect. They described how important their church is and how much they hope to be cared for. Furthermore, as a researcher I was surprised by how articulate and honest they could be about their life and church experiences to a stranger, especially about such negative aspects of their life as their struggles and pains. In an

32. The English Ministry's relationship with adult congregation varies depending on a church's situation. Some English Ministry departments are independent from Korean-speaking while some are not. But most members of English Ministry departments are children of Korean-speaking adult congregations.

Interpretive Task

honor-shame culture, such as the shared culture of the participants, people typically are not open about their emotions or pain. However, most of the interviews went longer than intended because the interviewees shared so many stories. Sometimes interviewees opened up about their deep wounds with tears. It seems that they were longing for someone to listen to and care about their stories. With the field research, it is clear that Korean-speaking young people were so desperate for their voice to be heard and to matter, but there do not seem to be enough places to share.

4

Normative Task

Migration Theology and Korean Immigrant Churches

DEFINING THE NORMATIVE TASK

IN THE PRECEDING DESCRIPTIVE and interpretive tasks, this study has elucidated the current practices of Korean-speaking young adults in Korean immigrant churches by means of literature reviews, field research (including surveys and in-depth interviews), and data analysis. This study seeks to offer a faithful next step for serving Korean-speaking young adults in Korean immigrant churches. In order to discern such a step, it is important to have a theological foundation derived from thoughtful reflection on Scripture, church history, and theological tradition. Osmer calls this the normative task, which is defined as "using theological concepts to interpret particular episodes, situations, or contexts, constructing ethical norms to guide our responses, and learning from good practice."[1] Asking the question, "what ought to be going on?" is the concern of the normative task, which leads to critical reflection on the current practices based on a biblical and theological framework and provides a foundation to build up new practices.

Osmer offers three interpretive approaches toward the normative task—theological interpretation, ethical reflection, and good practice. Theological reflection is using theological concepts to interpret particular episodes, situations, and contexts, informed by a theory of divine and human action. Ethical reflection is using ethical principles, rules, or guidelines to guide action toward moral ends. Finally, good practice is deriving norms

---

1. Osmer, *Practical Theology*, 4.

from good practice, by exploring models of such practice in the present and past or by engaging reflexively in transforming practices in the present.[2] Osmer states that these three approaches are not mutually exclusive, but rather they are often combined to execute this normative task.[3]

Normative Task in This Study

The normative task in this study seeks to answer what ought to be going on for Korean-speaking young adults in Korean immigrant churches. In order to reflect upon and answer this question, this chapter seeks to discern a holistic ecclesiology for Korean-speaking young adults, as the entire study's focus is on Korean-speaking young adults in Korean immigrant church and their practices. In an attempt to move into the final step (the pragmatic task), this chapter provides a theological foundation for faithful practice for Korean-speaking young adults and Korean immigrant churches.

Although we need to start from the current state of Korean immigrant church ecclesiology in order to seek a holistic ecclesiology for Korean-speaking young adults in Korean immigrant churches, this particular area has only emerged in recent decades among the works of a few theologians. Thus, given a limited context, this study begins by reflecting on the broader discipline of migration theologies, and includes Korean immigrant theologies in order to review and reflect on available ecclesiological works. With critical reflection on current migration and Korean immigrant theologies, this chapter finally demonstrates an ecclesiology for Korean-speaking young adults that accounts for their given context of emerging adulthood, migration, and transnationality.

MIGRATION THEOLOGY

It is only recently that social science has recognized the religious perspective as an important factor when looking at international migration, despite its significant history. Likewise, Christianity—including both Catholic and Protestant churches—has not been attentive to the issue of international migration. Although migration has been a crucial feature throughout Christian history, the church has often been silent on the matter (or even worse, taken an anti-immigrant stance). It was not until the 1960s that substantive theological reflection on human mobility began to

---

2. Osmer, *Practical Theology*, 161.
3. Osmer, *Practical Theology*, 160.

emerge.⁴ In 1961 the World Council of Churches organized a congress in Switzerland on migration and attempted to lay the foundation for a theological perspective on migration, although it mainly involved a biblical reflection on human mobility.⁵ It was not until the end of 1970s when the theology of migration appeared in the United States as part of a new attempt at contextual theology, especially among Hispanic theologians.⁶ Finally in the first years of the twenty-first century, migration theology has been illuminated and considered seriously in wider theological fields with multiple conferences, symposia, and research projects.

Although Christian responses to migration vary depending on their context and doctrine, I will address the main themes of recent theological reflection on migration. First, migration theology claims that the very nature of God is migratory. That is, a theology of migration begins with God's migratory act. Catholic theologian Peter Phan argued that creation could be interpreted as God's migratory act from the absolute Spirit to finite matter. He continues, "In creative act, God experiences from the first time the precarious, marginalized, threatened, and endangered condition of the migrant."⁷ God's migratory action in the incarnation of Jesus of Nazareth is another common theme in migration theology. After the fall, God took a risk and migrated to earth himself in order to give new life to his people.⁸ Furthermore, Amos Yong has added an emphasis on the Holy Spirit's migratory work with a Pentecostal theology of migration. According to Yong, Pentecostalism is a missionary religion, and it links to migratory acts, illustrating the early church's missionary activities in the books of Luke and Acts.⁹ In the totality of God's Trinitarian nature (Father, Son, and Spirit), Peter Phan states that "migration means movement, and that the Christian God is a 'mover' par excellence."¹⁰

Second, given that the very nature of God is migratory, migration theology argues that a true Christian response to the God who migrated first is to go on pilgrimage toward God. As demonstrated in migratory

---

4. For brief history of the theology of migration, see Campese, "The Irruption of Migrants," 3–32.

5. Campese, "The Irruption of Migrants," 7.

6. See Deck, "Illegal Immigration," 39–53; Lopez, "Theology of Migration," 68–71.

7. Phan, "Stranger," 99.

8. Phan, "Stranger," 100; Diaz, "Migrants," 238–39.

9. Yong, "The Im/migrant," 134–44.

10. Phan, "Stranger," 98.

movements of God's people in the Bible, migration theology claims that migration is one of Scripture's core themes, including the journey of Abraham, the long history of exile, and the early Christian migrant community in the New Testament. With such ample history in the Bible, Orthodox theologian Kondothra George states that Christian existence was thus considered a pilgrimage.[11] Based on this history, migration theology finds and rediscovers "the fundamental value of the richness, tenacity, and beauty of the faith of the migrants, a faith conveyed through popular expressions (such as devotions) that allowed these people to survive as human beings and believers in difficult and dangerous situations."[12] Migration theologians believe that this journey is a faithful response to God, as migrants participate and complete his mission, confirming their status as a metaphor of the true Christian in contemporary times.[13]

Third, migration theology urges hospitality and considers the church a refuge. Kondothra George states that hospitality was one of the vital Christian virtues, especially in the Bible's history of pilgrimage. He reminds how Abraham received into his tent three strangers and provided hospitality. He also argues that the apostolic tradition in the New Testament maintained hospitality as a core virtue. With this tradition, George insists that the church needs to be sensitive and to provide hospitality especially to the poor, the marginalized, and the vulnerable in its pilgrimages.[14] Nancy Bedford admits that Protestantism has not always done well to respond to migration issues and even sometimes has made the worst choices by being anti-immigration, choices that have been linked to white supremacist ideas. She claims that Protestants are now recognizing the matter of migration by providing a safe space for migrants.[15]

Peter Chan goes a bit further by saying that migration is not just a historical phenomenon, but also a permanent feature of the church. Given his research about the reality on migration, he insists that churches should demonstrate appropriate ethical behavior toward migrants. It is true that Catholic churches have a more developed theology than other churches

---

11. Kondothra, "Theology of Migration," 66–67.
12. Campese, "The Irruption of Migrants," 23.
13. Groody, "Undocumented Immigrant," 314–16.
14. Kondothra, "Theology of Migration," 72–74.
15. Bedford, "Migration," 114.

Ignored

concerning migration, and thus often engage with the issues related to providing resources to migrants.[16]

Forth, theology of migration considers migration as a missional journey and migrants as missionaries. This approach derives more from Protestant churches than Catholic ones, and is often expressed as an approach of Southern migrants (Africans and Latinos) in the context of the United States. Pointing out the bankruptcy of the Christendom ideal and the marks of the end of Western missionary dominance, Jehu Hanciles claims that the migration movement has historically been a prime factor in global religious expansion.[17] He demonstrates how major waves of immigration in American history have consistently revitalized American religious life and also have had a missionary impact on American society, through the formation of new congregations.[18] In this light, immigrants have not only transformed America into the most culturally diverse nation on the planet, but have also been rapidly changing the face of American Christianity. Thus, Hanciles states that every Christian migrant is a potential missionary.[19] In the same vein, Juan Martinez also addresses Latino Protestants' contribution to religious life in the United States today with a different concept of mission: doing mission from below. Like the church of the first century, it is the powerless engaging in mission to the powerful, which is totally opposite from the traditional Western practice of mission.[20]

Fifth, theology of migration includes a sense of ecclesial solidarity beyond nation-states. Dealing with the transnational identities of home and hosting countries, migration theology demonstrates that the primary identity of Christian migrants is being a Christian beyond borders. Catholic scholars like Michael Budde and William Cavanaugh claim that Christians living in ecclesial solidarity need to find ways to participate in the common good of God's life together as pilgrims.[21] In fact, Cavanaugh goes so far as to claim that the United States has never sought its natural purpose, which is to seek the common good; by contrast, the church should actively seek

---

16. Phan, "Stranger," 106. For more on legal and social science perspectives on serving immigrants, see Kerwin and Gerschutz, *And You Welcomed Me*.

17. Hanciles, "Migration and Mission," 146.

18. Hanciles, *Beyond Christendom*, 378.

19. Hanciles, "Transformations," 20.

20. Martinez, *Los Protestantes*, 176.

21. See Budde, *Baptism*; Cavanauch, *Migration*.

solidarity.²² This ecclesial solidarity in Catholic churches often ends up being demonstrated through social justice, seeking visible and tangible ways to express a Christian's conviction and vocation to bring the good news to the world's poor and oppressed of all sorts.

Critical Reflection on Current Migration Theology and Ecclesiology

Based on these five common themes in migration theology, theologians and churches have sought to develop ecclesiology within the migration context. Although it is still emerging, and there is a serious ecclesiological lack of attention to migration, there are three common migration ecclesiology concepts in current studies. According to Susanna Snyder, "Migration calls us to rediscover conceptions of the church as a pilgrim community (called to transgress boundaries), a kingdom community (called to challenge injustice), and an inclusive community (called to be neighbors to the 'other')" based on World Council of Church statement from its 2012 conference on migration and ecclesiology.²³ These three concepts of church on migration in general correspond to current migration theology discussions. A pilgrimage ecclesiological community is based on the nature of a migratory God and his people, and the journey of a true Christian to the Kingdom of God. The kingdom community concept is based on ecclesial solidarity beyond nation-states and seeking the common good. Finally, an inclusive perspective of the church is related to hospitality and welcoming strangers in current migration theology.

Although there have been great efforts and insights to provide a foundation for contemporary migration theology and ecclesiology, migration is still considered "their" story rather than our own in contemporary ecclesiology, which has created limitations. First, migration has been seriously ignored in church studies based on this notion of migration as someone else's story. Gioacchino Campese stated, "even the most recent studies in ecclesiology and reflections on the states of church in Italy and the United Stated by well-known theologians are basically silent about immigration," although migration is an issue of crucial importance in both countries.²⁴ Migration is not some one else's story anymore. It is a global movement, which we witness everywhere, including in our neighborhoods. Generally

---

22. Cavanauch, *Migration*, 45.
23. Snyder, "Introduction," 7.
24. Campese, "Somebody Is Missing," 79.

Ignored

speaking, however, there is a serious lack of research and studies on migration theology and ecclesiology, regarding contemporary global human mobility. In other words, theology and church studies haven't enough paid attention to context and real life. Campese points out that although there are significant numbers of migrants in the United States, migration has not yet received the attention it deserves.[25]

Second, the us-and-them attitude toward migration sees migrants as passive recipients at best. When migrants are viewed as others, and not one of us, they become people whom we must support, instead of people with whom we have the opportunity to live together. With this assumption, contemporary responses to migration in church studies are merely ethically focused on underprivileged migrants, notably refugees, people seeking asylum, trafficking survivors, and the undocumented.[26] Susanna argues that these responses treat migrants as if they were outside the church and recipients of Christian welfare rather than migrants being part of the church, pointing out that ecclesiological reflections that go beyond the moral duty of the church on migration have been noticeably absent.[27] Although migrants are part of the church, with whom churches should live and walk together, the tendencies of existing migration theology and ecclesiology have not responded that way.

Third, when migrants are considered to be an appendage of the church, it is hard to build up a holistic ecclesiology for discerning God's work in the world. Campese critiques current ecclesiology as often too nationalistic, Eurocentric, or Western-Centric, pointing out that contemporary ecclesiology often does not take into consideration the fact that God could be speaking to the churches though the "foreign" and "strange" voices of the immigrants.[28] While there have been great efforts to help migrants in various ways, current ecclesiology has not taken steps to consider migrants as an important parts of churches, capable to build up communities and discern God's call for the contemporary church. In this light, migration theology from other ethnic theologians is merely their story, not our story that the church should pay attention to.

---

25. Campese notes that "at least one in five people in the United States today is a first- or second-generation resident." Campese, "The Irruption of Migrants," 11.
26. Snyder, "Introduction," 4.
27. Snyder, "Introduction," 5.
28. Snyder, "Introduction," 79–81.

KOREAN IMMIGRANT THEOLOGY

Korean Immigrants and Their Church

Korean immigration in the United States began with the Korean immigrant church. When the first immigrants settled as migration workers in Hawaii on sugarcane farms in 1903, they began to establish churches.[29] Since then, Korean immigrant churches have been a crucial place for Korean immigrants. Given this history, among other Asian immigrant groups, Korean immigrants have one of the highest rates of affiliation with church. Pew Research shows that about 70 to 80 percent of Korean immigrants were affiliated with Korean immigrant churches by research in 1990,[30] and over 80 percent of Korean immigrants attended church at least once per week in 2012.[31] Scholars point out that Korean Protestant immigrants' overwhelming church affiliation relates to more than just religious reasons.[32]

Although religious functions constitute one of the most important reasons why Korean immigrants come to the church, studies have shown that there are other significant functions which Korean immigrant churches have provided. One of the leading Korean American scholars, Pyong Gap Min, identified four major social functions for the Korean immigrant church based on his field research with Korean immigrants.[33] First, the Korean immigrant church provides a comfortable place for social interaction and fellowship. For Korean immigrants who feel a sense of alienation in a foreign environment, association with co-ethnic members is crucial for coping with this alienation, and the Korean immigrant church has provided an ideal place for association among Korean immigrants. Second, the Korean immigrant church helps immigrants to maintain their cultural traditions. Korean immigrant church helps to preserve Korean culture in several ways. By using and observing Korean language and customs, providing Korean language programs for children, and celebrating traditional Korean holidays, Korean immigrants maintain their cultural tradition through their church. Third, the Korean immigrant church provides different resources and social services. The church offers services to immigrants for their successful adjustment to life in a new context, including

---

29. See "A Chronicle of the Last 100 Years."
30. Hurh and Kim, "Korean Immigrants," 19–34.
31. Min and Kim, "Intergenerational Transmission," 267.
32. Min and Jang, "The Diversity," 269.
33. Min, "Korean Immigrant Churches," 1381–90.

information and counseling on employment, business, housing health care, social security, children's education and so forth. Forth, Korean immigrant churches provide social status and social position for Korean immigrants. Most Korean immigrants experience downward mobility in terms of their socio-economic context due to language barriers and other disadvantages. This brings about difficulty and dissatisfaction for many Korean immigrants. In this context, the Korean immigrant church provides meaningful status, including leadership, staff, and volunteer positions. Chandler Im adds one more social function for the Korean immigrant church: the Korean immigrant church's political and ethical contribution to Korea. Im reports that the Korean immigrant church contributed to the Korean independence movement during the Japanese forced occupation period.[34] The solidarity of Korean immigrant churches on issues in Korea remains a powerful force today; recently, Korean immigrant churches prepared a petition on the sinking of Sewol ferry in 2014.[35]

Themes on Korean Immigrant Theology

Korean immigrant/American theology hasn't been developed fully yet and is still emerging. With limited studies, Korean immigrant/American theology has generally been understood as a contextual theology. One of the leading Asian American theologians, Jonathan Y. Tan, states, "Whatever their confessional leanings may be, broadly speaking Asian American theologies are best understood as *contextual* theologies that seek to juxtapose the life experiences of Asian Americans with the gospel's soteriological, prophetic, ethical, and transformative power."[36] Peter Phan describes Asian American theology as a hybrid theology. He says, "Paradoxically, while neither fully Asian nor fully American, an Asian American theology is both Asian and American, embodying the resources, methodologies, and characteristics of both theologies, and in this sense, will be richer than either theology by itself. An Asian American theology is by nature an *intercultural* theology, forged in the cauldron of the encounter between vastly different cultures"[37] In the same light, Korean immigrant theology has emerged as a hybrid, intercultural, and contextual theology.

---

34. Im, "The Korean diaspora," 136.
35. Amennet, "세월호 사고 관련 성명서 [Petition for Sewol Ferry]."
36. Tan, *Asian American Theologies*, 78.
37. Phan, *Asian Face*, Xiv.

From the perspective of contextual theology, there are four main themes among the limited studies in Korean immigrant/American theology. First, Korean immigrant theology starts from the context of marginality. Approaching "marginality" in its own way is one of the major differences between Latino and Asian American theologies. Campese states that because of complex historical and geographical context, "Latino theologians consider 'migrant analogy' unable to signify the peculiar condition of the Latinos, while Asian American theologians do not seem to have any problem using the same image to identify themselves."[38] Unlike many Latino immigrant theologians, Korean immigrant theologians often accept and start their theology from marginal context.[39] Chun Hoi Heo, who teaches Korean Theology at Knox College, University of Toronto, emphasizes marginality as the unique context of Korean immigrant theology. He argues, "A theology of Korean immigrants needs to be neither traditional Korean theology nor Korean Minjung theology,[40] nor mainstream North American theology, but a unique theological contract arising out of immigrant experiences of marginality."[41] In the same light, one of the first Korean immigrant theologians, Jung Young Lee, affirms his theology as a theology of marginality, and theology of marginality is also a theology of emigration.[42] Sang Hyun Lee also starts his theological reflection on Korean immigrants and their church with "the Wilderness of Marginality."[43]

Korean immigrant theology recognizes and reflects upon this context of marginality with immigrants' minority experience. This marginality is illustrated as wilderness, in-between-ness, non-acceptance,[44] alienation, and existential nothingness.[45] Sang Hyun Lee, a pioneer Asian American theologian, sees the context of Korean immigrants as marginality with "Forced Liminality." This forced liminal place resulted from

---

38. See Campese, "The Irruption of Migrants," 16–18.

39. However, there are some Latino scholars who accept marginality as the starting point of their theology. See De La Torre, *Christian Ethics from the Margins*.

40. *Minjung* theology emerged in the context of the Christian experiences in the Korean political situation and the struggles for social justice in the 1970s. See Commission on Theological Concerns, *Minjung Theology*.

41. Heo, *Multicultural Christology*, 51.

42. Lee, *Marginality*, 74.

43. Lee, "Pilgrims," 41.

44. Lee, "Pilgrims," 41.

45. Lee, *Marginality*, 75.

marginalization is a frustrated and oppressed place where people are caught without belonging or freedom.[46]

Second, this reality of marginality brings an important motif to move forward. Korean immigrant theology does not stop recognizing the pain and wounds of being marginal only. Rather, it pushes beyond. Although being in-between and in the forced liminal place as a minority brings many wounds and difficulties, Korean immigrant theology considers that this painful reality can actually bring different perspectives on life. The pain and wounds associated with being immigrants in the margins can provide an opportunity to reflect on how powerful God is. Using the traditional Korean concept of *Jeong*, which is a radical from of love that encompasses compassion, affection, solidarity, rationality, vulnerability, and forgiveness,[47] Wonhee Anne Joh claims that a Christology of *jeong*—the love of Jesus—is can powerfully bring wholeness and healing from the abjection and pain of immigrant experiences.[48]

This marginal reality also can bring about a creative perspective on marginality with an understanding of God's marginality. Jung Young Lee insists that a new marginality is a creative core, which can impact others, as Jesus experienced marginality with his incarnation and earthly life, and yet overcame marginality to bring about a new margin—creative core—of God's reign over the world.[49] Sang Huyn Lee also claims that conversion to Christ yields a new liminality which makes it possible for Korean immigrants to be open to others and build community and solidarity with them, with joy and happiness in God, while forgetting nothing.[50]

Third, with new perspectives on marginality, Korean immigrant theology leads to a new identity for Korean immigrants as pilgrims who are on the journey according to God's calling. In the context of migration, people experience marginalization, unsettledness, and a lack of acceptance that causes frustration, hurt, and anxiety. Migrants are not only unsettled in the hosting land but also in their homeland. Migrants might turn to their origins, but the origins are forever changing while they themselves have also changed.[51] In this ongoing unsettled context of in-between-ness, migrants

---

46. Lee, *Liminal Place*, 5.
47. Joh, *Heart of the Cross*, xiii.
48. Joh, *Heart of the Cross*, 106.
49. Lee, *Marginality*, 99.
50. Lee, *Liminal Place*, 147–60.
51. Joh, *Heart of the Cross*, 9.

face ontological questions of "who am I" and "why am I here?" For this specific ontological question, Korean Immigrant theology seeks to provide an answer, claiming that immigrants are pilgrims who are on a journey to follow God's call. Sang Hyun Lee claims that the biblical notion of pilgrimage may be the key concept, most appropriate for discerning the theological meaning of our marginal existence.[52] He continues that Christian pilgrimage emerges as a compelling image for Asian immigrants facing the inevitable uprootedness that results from emigration.[53] Arguing that Korean American Christians should be pilgrims who are on a journey toward God's promised-goal, he insists that the Korean immigrant church should reinterpret Asian American existence with the help of an understanding of Christian existence as pilgrimage.[54]

Jung Young Lee also sees migrants as people on a journey because of God's call. He parallels Korean immigrants with journeys in the Bible including Abraham and Sarah, Moses, Amos, and the disciples of Jesus in the New Testament. With these journeys in the Bible, Lee claims that God's call for his people is to leave and take a journey as the marginalized to transform the margins into a creative core.[55] This perspective answers the existential and ontological question of migrants: they are pilgrims fulfilling God's calling.

Fourth, Korean immigrant theology seeks justice and reconciliation for harmonious life in the context of migrants. Korean immigrant theology, like other migrant theologies, urges harmonious coexistence in a multicultural context as a new way of life, in contrast to the oppressive reality of social discrimination against migrants. Demonstrating reconciliation as living together with God and neighbors, brothers and sisters in Christ, proclaiming that the dividing walls among us are broken down, Chun Hoi Heo claims that Korean immigrant theology should focus more on living in harmony through reconciliation rather than liberation, a more common perspective among Latino and African migrants.[56] In the same vein, Hee An Choi insists on seeking 'a postcolonial self,' which is defined as 'I and with others', claiming peaceful coexistence among other individuals and the Korean ethnic community, and between the Korean ethnic community and other ethnic

---

52. Lee, "Pilgrims," 43.
53. Lee, "Pilgrimage," 81.
54. Lee, "Pilgrims," 44.
55. Lee, *Marginality*, 111–19.
56. Heo, *Multicultural Christology*, 189.

communities.⁵⁷ She argues that by practicing radical hospitality, Korean immigrant churches should take the role of forming the immigrants' identity from the "marginalized self" to the "post-colonial self."⁵⁸

In pursuit of harmony, Korean immigrant theology advocates reconciliation based on justice and believes Korean immigrants have the potential to practice reconciliation. Jung Young Lee claims that one of the core missions of church is the reconciliation of all by the liberation of others from social injustice and the elimination of deeply rooted dominant ideologies; such reconciliation is impossible without justice.⁵⁹ Seeking justice and reconciliation, he insists that as Jesus accepted and loved others unconditionally on the cross, migrants should seek the harmonious coexistence of all people in a genuinely pluralistic society.⁶⁰ Seeking justice and reconciliation, Andrew Sung Park argues that the oppressed can only recognize other people's wounds due to their experience, and thus Korean immigrants who have been suffered can help others who are suffering, seeking justice.⁶¹ Furthermore, Park claims that Korean immigrants, as victims, should initiate the reconciliation process, since the oppressors rarely come to repentance by themselves, as their own wrongs prevent them from seeing reality.⁶² In the same respect, Sang Hyun Lee also states that through forced liminal experiences, Korean immigrants should seek justice not only within the Korean community, but also with other ethnic minorities, such as the Latino community, by treating and paying them fairly in their business settings. In addition to this solidarity with other ethnic minority communities, Lee argues that the Korean immigrant community should seek reconciliation with all those who are marginalized, resisting power-centered ideologies.⁶³

Critical Reflection on Current Korean Immigrant Theology

While these main points of Korean immigrant theology have provided a useful lens to Korean immigrants and their churches, there are also limits and challenges. One of the biggest challenges for Korean immigrant theology is a lack of research. As mentioned previously, Christianity and its

57. Choi, *A Postcolonial Self*, 135.
58. Choi, *A Postcolonial Self*, 127.
59. Lee, *Marginality*, 140.
60. Lee, *Marginality*, 73.
61. Park, *The Wounded Heart*, 132.
62. Park, *The Wounded Heart*, 172.
63. Lee, *Liminal Space*, 180.

communities play a crucial part on Korean immigrants' lives as a result of high church affiliation and the more than twelve thousand Korean immigrant churches in the United States. However, there has been a lack of research on the Korean immigrant church. In sociological academia, Pyong Min Gap states that the topic of Asian immigrants' religious experiences has not received the level of scholarly attention it deserves, even though there is an understanding that religious experiences and religious institutions play an essential role in Asian immigrant studies.[64] It is no different in the theological academy, as there are only a few publications that give serious attention to Korean immigrants in scholarly theology.

Another issue with current Korean immigrant theology is its lack of recognition within the contemporary context. Most Korean immigrant theologies have been published more than ten years ago: *Asian-American Theology: Called to Be Pilgrims* by Sang Hyun Lee (1993); *The Wounded Heart of God: The Asian Concept of Han and the Christian Doctrine of Sin* by Andrew Sung Park (1993); *Marginality: The Key to Multicultural Theory* by Jung Young Lee (1995); and *Multicultural Christology: A Korean Immigrant Perspective* by Chun Hoi Heo (2003). Although there some more recent research has been conducted, such as *A Postcolonial Self: Korean Immigrant Theology and Church* by Hee An Choi (2015), it has been criticized for focusing only on a traditional perspective and lacks up-to-date experiences and narratives of Koreans and Korean churches.[65] In this respect, most Korean immigrant theologies deal with only traditional concepts, such as Han and Jeong, with theologians' own autobiographical immigrant experiences in the past.

However, the global migrants' contexts are different from the past, especially considering the development of new technologies. Korean immigrants and their context have also changed significantly. One of the crucial differences in contemporary Korean immigrants is their transnationality. Previous Korean immigrant generations had limited access to Korea at the same time as they struggled with English. However, there are growing numbers of new Korean migrants in America who are fluent in English, while simultaneously fluent Korean and actively practicing Korean cultural in America.[66] Furthermore, contemporary migrants have instant contact with Korea through more accessible transportation

---

64. Min, "Asian America," 5.
65. Chung, "A Review," 224.
66. Min, "The Immigration of Koreans," 31.

and the Internet, including email and online messengers. Their strong ties and instant connection have brought about a different reality of immigrant life, and even their religious life in immigrant churches. Additionally, migration has become more of a global phenomenon, and there is a growing number of non-immigrant visitors from Korea in the United States, as was described in the previous chapter. This has led to a demographic change in Korean immigrant church, from legal permanent residents and naturalized citizens to nonimmigrant short-term residents.[67] However, the contemporary context of Korean immigrants has not been given enough attention, and most Korean immigrant theologies are disconnected from the changing reality of Korean immigrants and their churches.

Lastly, the existing Korean immigrant theology and ecclesiology is still in keeping with an us-and-them notion of the church. Korean immigrant theologies have long been considered to be a version of contextual theology, which marks their ideas as exclusively Korean. Although there are growing numbers of Korean/Asian people in the United States, and they now belong to American society and churches, Korean immigrant theology is not receiving sufficient attention from other people outside of the Korean or Asian American church communities. Limited recognition and connection to theology outside of the Korean immigrant context and community has been offered.

At the same time, Korean immigrant theologies are also limited in their audiences to Korean immigrants or Asian immigrants at best. This implies that Korean immigrant theology is also based on an us-and-them mindset, which separates Korean immigrants from the rest of the church in the world. Although some scholars reference the importance of reconciling with other ethnic groups, this is rarely anything other than an ethical or moral step in ecclesiology. Contemporary migration patterns have brought about many changes beyond national and state borders, and in this context God has been working beyond nation and state. In light of this, Korean immigrant theology should not merely be restricted to Korean immigrants, but should carefully discern how Korean immigrant churches respond to God's calling beyond the boundaries of Korean immigrant churches in the world.

---

67. Im and Oh, "Korean Diaspora," 316.

SEEKING AN ECCLESIOLOGY FOR KOREAN IMMIGRANTS AND THEIR YOUNG PEOPLE IN THE TRANSNATIONAL CONTEXT

In order to discern a faithful next step for the Korean immigrant church and Korean-speaking young adults, we need a theological framework that can be the foundation for the next step. For its theological framework, this study carefully reviewed current discussions of migrant theology and Korean immigrant theology. Although these discussions provide a helpful perspective on ecclesiology, Korean-speaking young adults also need an in-depth theological framework based on their context as emerging adults who experience transnationality. In this section, I attempt to provide an ecclesiology for Korean immigrants and their young people who speak Korean based on theological reflection on the contemporary Korean immigrant context. With a theological framework of ecclesiology, I will argue that the Korean immigrant church should be a community where people find their identity and dignity, where people experience belonging and formation, and where people participate and contribute to God's mission.

Community Where People Find Their Identity and Dignity beyond State and Nation

Church should be a community where people find their identity and dignity beyond the confines and allegiances of state and nation. Identity is an important issue for everyone. However, it is even more important for Korean-speaking young adults, who are both emerging adults and migrants. Identity explorations are one of the most important features during emerging adulthood. Although identity formation starts from adolescence, it intensifies in emerging adulthood as people explore themselves in areas of love, work, and other circumstances.[68] As young people question who they are, they often face confusion and frustration. During this time, young people need care and guidance from mature people. Considering that contemporary society is adult-oriented and that young people are disconnected from adults, emerging adults desperately need other mature, concerned adults in their community who genuinely care about and for them as they form their identities.[69] Korean-speaking young adults are also going through emerging adulthood while coping with an adult-oriented society. Furthermore, this

---

68. Arnett, *Emerging Adulthood*, 10.
69. Smith, *Lost in Transition*, 7.

Ignored

research indicates that they experience isolation even in their churches.[70] In this regard, Korean immigrants should be aware of how crucial the identity task is for Korean-speaking young adults, and how important the Korean immigrant church's role in this process really is.

Identity is a significant matter for migrants as well. In the context of migration, people experience social changes within the new culture. Most often, these changes bring negative experiences for marginalized, disregarded people settling in a new country. These migration experiences often challenge people's identities, not only in their cultural identity, but also their dignity in terms of their worth and value. Scholars point out that identity is an important issue even in the language of migration. Common terms like *refugee, migrant, forced migrant, immigrants, undocumented, internally displaced person,* and *alien* are such limited labels which carry political, legal, and social consequences, but do not define human identity.[71] Roger Zetter states, "Far from clarifying an identity, the label conveys, instead, an extremely complex set of values, and judgments which are more than just definitional."[72] While facing marginalization and being categorized by political and legal terms, migrants experience shame and rejection related to their presence in new society. It is the context in which Korean immigrants and Korean-speaking young people live. This is the reason ecclesiology should start from a foundational quest for identity in the context of the Korean immigrant church.

Imago Dei

In terms of identity, the concept of *Imago Dei* offers a critical perspective. Beyond state and nation, beyond ethnicity and culture, and beyond gender and age, human beings are created in the image and likeness of God (Gen 1:26–27; 5:1–3; 9:6; 1 Cor 11:7; Jas 3:9). This is a fundamental truth of human identity. Although this is primarily a Judeo-Christian contribution to a theology of migration, Groody points out that it is often ignored in public discourse.[73] However, defining migrants first and foremost in terms of *imago Dei* brings a totally different perspective than that which defines them with the label of political and legal status.[74] *Imago Dei* brings three

---

70. See chapter 2.
71. Groody, "Migration and Refugees," 642–43.
72. Zetter, "Labeling Refugees," 40.
73. Groody, "Crossing the Divine," 645.
74. Groody, "Crossing the Divine," 645.

important perspectives on an ecclesiology of migration theology, especially for Korean immigrants and their young people.

First, *imago Dei* reminds the church that it should be a community that learns who God is. *Imago Dei* demonstrates that human beings are created in the image and likeness of God (Gen 1:26–27). This means in order to understand human nature and identity, we must first understand the Creator of humanity. Groody argues, "*Imago Dei* names the personal and relational nature of human existence and the mystery that human life cannot be understood apart from the mystery of God."[75] This puts the church's priority on God, not people and their agenda. Whether a church is in the United States or Korea, and whether a church has more migrants or fewer, the church is first and foremost a community for learning about and experiencing the God who created humanity in his image.

Second, *imago Dei* demonstrates human value and worth in terms of identity. The unchangeable identity for Christians is "the result of God's decision to uniquely create us. God has chosen to create each one of us out of his sovereign will."[76] This is ultimate identity, where every young person should locate the origin of his or her identity formation. Furthermore, in the context of migration, which can involve being labeled with dehumanizing terms based on political, legal, and social status, *imago Dei* challenges us with the intrinsic value of human beings. This approach "helps those on the move discover an inner identity that fosters their own agency rather than an imposed external identity that increases their vulnerability and subjugation."[77]

Third, *imago Dei* shows human capacity as subjects exercising agency before God. Because human beings are created in God's image and likeness, they have capacity as subjects and agents who are able to reflect, discern, and respond.[78] Bearing precious and great value, *imago Dei* also conveys human beings' capacity based on God's image. This is an important piece in identity especially in the context of migration where migrants are often considered weak and worthless objects. While dehumanized approaches on migration doubt migrants' capacity and ability due to their language barriers, cultural clumsiness, or poor financial background, *imago Dei* strongly countervails against this with the firm foundation of humanity's ability and

---

75. Groody, "Crossing the Divine," 645.
76. Clark and Clark, *Disconnected*, 55.
77. Groody, "Crossing the Divine," 644.
78. Groome, *Sharing Faith*, 8.

Ignored

capacity based on God's image and likeness, regardless of their social, ethnic, cultural, and financial background.

Community Where People Experience Belonging and Formation Together

Church should also be a community where people can be accepted as who they are and learn from each other. One of the most important roles for church is to provide spiritual formation. This spiritual formation cannot happen merely by passing along information and knowledge at a cognitive level. It requires more. In this spiritual formation process, belonging and mutual learning are crucial elements. Belonging is fundamental to a proper understanding of the church. Graham Ward defines *ekklesia* as not just an assembly of citizens, solders, or believers in Christ, but also a corporation of those who have been called out, *ekkaleo*, to function collectively where belonging is exercised.[79] Belonging is also crucial for emerging adults. In the process of individuation (as becoming a unique individual), young people quest for belonging.[80] Finally, belonging is an important issue for migrants. As they migrate to another country, they grieve the loss of relationships in their home country, and their sense of belonging is weakened. Furthermore, as someone who is a marginalized minority, it is not easy to find where to belong in a new land.

Another element is mutual learning. Human beings are created to be in relationship. People cannot live and grow by themselves but only in and through relationships. Thomas Groome states that "authentic being of people always realized in relationship with others and authentic subjectivity can be achieved by caring for and receiving care from other people." He continues that this authentic subjectivity in relationship enables leaning and spiritual formation.[81] However, contemporary young people seem not to have enough of an opportunity to experience community and belonging. Chap Clark points out the younger generation's loss of a sense of meaningful relationship, along with their loneliness and segregation, labeling this a systemic abandonment by institutions and adults.[82] Christian Smith also argues that contemporary emerging adults are rejected, without sufficient

79. Ward, "Belonging to the Church," 1.
80. Clark and Clark, *Disconnected*, 58.
81. Groome, *Sharing Faith*, 9.
82. Clark, *Hurt*, 39–56.

attention and care, facing problems that they are told are entirely their own, unrelated to the adults around them.[83]

For Korean-speaking young adults, this segregation is always doubled (as emerging adults and migrants). As the results of the field research have shown, Korean-speaking young adults carry a great deal of loneliness. They deal with rejection and systemic abandonment in American society as emerging adults and migrants. Additionally, they experience a great deal of segregation from Korean immigrant churches as well. Thus, an ecclesiology that seeks and provides a community of belonging and growing is crucial.

Adoptive Ministry

On the topic of a church being a community with belonging and growing by mutual learning, Chap Clark introduces a helpful concept of adoptive ministry in his recent work of *Adoptive Youth Ministry: Integrating Emerging Generations into the Family of Faith*. Adoptive youth ministry is an approach to understanding the church as a community of God's adoptive children, and ministry as an organic movement of God's family rather than in terms of its institutional functions.[84] In the adoptive ministry approach, there are three important elements that are helpful as we seek an ecclesiology for Korean immigrants and their young people. First, adoptive ministry illuminates the fundamental calling of a church as a connected and intimate community of God's household. Chap Clark argues that church is not just a gathering of people, but people who are invited and called together as God's children.[85] Thus, the church is to attempt to build a community among those who gather together as God's people; such a community draws people into the family-like intimacy to which we have been invited in Christ.[86] This relational connectedness and intimacy of belonging is not limited to the local church community. Because God is the one who created and reigns over the world, God's adoption leads his children to be a local and global family.[87] This approach to church is crucial for Korean-speaking young people for two reasons. First, it demonstrates to young people the ultimate answer for the quest of belonging. As mentioned earlier, belonging is an important quest for young people asking, "where do I fit?" In this context, the

---

83. Smith, *Lost in Transition*, 11.
84. See Clark, *Adoptive Youth Ministry*.
85. Clark, *Adoptive Youth Ministry*, 2.
86. Clark, *Adoptive Youth Ministry*, 11.
87. Clark, *Adoptive Youth Ministry*, 8.

understanding of the church as God's household with adopted children, which draws them into local and global family of God, demonstrates a deep belonging that speaks to their ultimate identity as children of God. Second, it confirms and reinforces the sense of belonging for Korean-speaking young adults as migrants who have experienced a loss of crucial relationships and belonging in their home country. This connectedness to God's household not only provides for migrants a new sense of intimacy and belonging in the local church, but it also reminds them that God's household remains steadfast beyond any state or nation.

Second, adoptive ministry leads to mutual relationship, defining Christians as co-siblings and adopted children of God. In adoptive ministry, the church is not a hierarchical, top-down system, but rather a mutual and equal relationship in community. Because all Christians, regardless of their age, gender, and ethnicity, are adopted children of God, they are equal. Clark writes about this functional equality, which points to the fact that young people are co-siblings with all others in the community, even as they need to be nurtured and led into maturity.[88] In this light, Clark claims that the contemporary church "should dismantle the institutional baggage of power and hierarchy by recognizing that we are all in this together, young and old alike, because we are God's family."[89] Although this is an important perspective in general for any church dealing with a younger generation that is often segregated and abandoned in an adult-oriented system, it is even more crucial in a Korean church community where Confucianized hierarchy is actively practiced.

Third, adoptive ministry demonstrates living in community, which leads to growth and spiritual formation through organically living as a family, and not merely with institutional functions. Understanding the church as a living organism of family, adoptive ministry seeks a different journey than institutional functions. Adoptive ministry commits to the messy, unpredictable life of a living entity by being willing to experiment together as community.[90] It is not that a few of the older generation teach and ensure order, but rather that everyone in the community experiments with their unknown life together. Throughout various movements and seasons, the church as a living organism learns, grows, and deepens in spiritual formation. It is not like simply passing information, but must

88. Clark, *Adoptive Youth Ministry*, 16.
89. Clark, *Adoptive Youth Ministry*, 16.
90. Clark, *Adoptive Youth Ministry*, 16.

include living and learning together. As Dean argues, "Faith is a way of life, not only a body of information to master."[91] Everist states, "In church community, people experience all kinds of teaching activities, both verbal and nonverbal, that include cognitive, affective, and other life activities, as describing church as a learning community."[92] In other words, the church is a living community where people experiment and learn together as living out together. Considering Korean-speaking young adults that have been treated as young and immature, and thus been led and ordered around by adults in a Confucianized setting, adoptive ministry provides a theological framework to create an environment where young people can mutually learn and live together with adults as community.

Community Where People Participate and Contribute to God's Ongoing Redemptive Work

The church should be a community seeking to participate in God's work. It is not a just gathering of people; it is an assembly of God's people who are called according to his purpose (Rom 8:28) in his name (John 14:13).[93] This understanding of calling is not only essential in ecclesiology generally, but in particular for migrants' and emerging adults' context by providing an ontological framework. For young people, the question of why we live and what life is about is an important one as they mature in life. In this respect, it is important to understand God's call, which is the purpose of life. As they learn their ultimate identity as God's beloved children, understanding the call from God provides young people with an ontological reason for life. This call is crucial for migrants as well: considered as strangers, aliens, marginalized, and minorities who are weak and helpless, migrants have been treated as inferior in American society. In this context, it is easy to consider migrants as passive recipients of service in the church's mission. However, this is not God's intention for church and its community. It is a misunderstanding of a Western, colonial, and unilateral perspective of mission as giving to the migrants whatever they need.[94] God's intention for his people is to participate in God's mission as community. The entire community of the including migrants, should

---

91. Dean, *Almost Christian*, 117.
92. Everist, *The Church*, 22.
93. Clark, *Adoptive Youth Ministry*, 1.
94. Campese, "Theologies of Migration," 180.

seek to participate in God's redemptive work. God has called people to be part of this great work. This provides the church's purpose and recognizes migrants as God's agents, not inferior recipients.

Missional Church

With an understanding of the church as a community participating in God's mission, a missional church approach also brings a helpful perspective. The missional church model is based on *Missio Dei*: that God has sent his Son, his Spirit, and his people to be part of God's mission as being a sent one.[95] In recent years, missional church approaches have provided helpful ecclesiological reflection and missiological practices, demonstrating that it is God (not the church) who initiates, works through, and completes the mission, of which the church is called to be a part. Thus, being a missional church is more about creating an environment where all church members are ready to be engaged in God's initiatives by learning, reflecting, and discerning together.[96] These missional church approaches provide a helpful theological framework for an ecclesiology for Korean-speaking young adults in four ways.

First, the missional church recognizes people as agents of God who are capable of contributing to God's mission. Instead of an ecclesiocentric understanding of mission, which has been the practice of Western mission, the missional church requires a profoundly theocentric reconceptualization of Christian mission. Mission is not merely an activity of the Church but the result of God's initiatives, rooted in God's purposes to restore and heal creation.[97] In this approach, the missional church considers the church (and its people) as being a sent one who plays a crucial role in God's mission. Because people are created in God's image (*Imago Dei*), they are valuable and able to be agency of God in his mission (*Missio Dei*). This understanding recognizes God's people, including Korean-speaking young people, with their ultimate identity and valuable life calling. In terms of emerging adulthood, this provides an ontological foundation as Korean-speaking young adults seek the meaning of life. Furthermore, in terms of the migration context, a missional church approach not only recognizes migrants' identity as agents of God (rather than marginalized, inferior strangers), but also recognizes their capacity and call from God. While migrants are

---

95. For *Missio Dei*, see Bosch, *Transforming Mission*; Guder, *Missional Church*, 237.
96. Branson, "Perspectives," 38.
97. Guder, *Missional Church*, 4.

Normative Task

considered weak, helpless, and passive recipients, the missional church approach argues that they are valuable and capable of participating and contributing to God's mission in the world.

Second, the missional church requires the community to discern God's will together. The missional church emphasizes that the mission is initiated by and belongs to God.[98] God is at the center.[99] In this context, the church is the instrument of God's mission, participating in his work.[100] Responding to God's invitation, the global church participates in God's mission and each local church is to be part of the work. In this context, it is an important task for each local church to discern what is their part within the entire kingdom work. Alan Roxburgh argues that church should focus on God as the chief actor and should shape people to discern and join with what God is already doing ahead of us.[101] While discerning to participate in God's work, one important task is listening. This listening is not only to God and neighbors but also to each other in the church community.[102] The missional church urges participating in God's mission as an entire community, not merely few leaders with passive followers. Kevin Haah states that since the church is a community of God's people, the direction of the church must be discerned communally.[103] This means that regardless of age, gender, nation, and ethnicity, each member in the church is a full agent of God and needs to be carefully heard in order to discern God's mission. This theological framework reminds us that each person in the church is an important player to discern God's work as community. Although each member has a different background, history, and maturity level, it is important to create an environment to listen to all of them, believing that God is working through everyone in the community.

This understanding is related to one crucial task for young people, namely autonomy. Starting from adolescence, young people develop their autonomy, asking, "Do I and my choices matter?"[104] From adolescence onward, young people are shifting from having an external locus of control to

---

98. Guder, *Missional Church*, 4.
99. Roxburgh, *Joining God*, 42.
100. Guder, *Missional Church*, 4.
101. Roxburgh, *Joining God*, 50.
102. Roxburgh, *Joining God*, 60.
103. Haah, "Diversity," 104.
104. Clark and Clark, *Disconnected*, 56.

Ignored

having an internal locus of control as they develop their autonomy.[105] In the missional church context, all people (including the youth) experience both listening and being heard as the community discerns God's work. As they are heard and taken seriously, which might even impact the community decision, young people recognize the significance of their voice and thoughts. In other words, they develop their autonomy as they experience the reality that both they and their voice matter. Furthermore, this approach also restores the weakened autonomy and significance of migrants who have been mistreated as marginalized strangers. Not only does it recognize the voice of migrants as valuable, but it also provides an important opportunity to listen and discern God's work, which has been ignored.

Third, the missional church takes the given context seriously. On the premise that God is the one who initiates and owns the mission, missional churches believe that God is already working and continuing the work ahead of the church.[106] In order to participate in God's work, missional churches pay serious attention to a particular context to discern what God might be up to in the given context. Context—a specific place, people, history, culture, and story—matters because God initiated and continues work there. Similarly, being attentive to both the local and global contexts, the missional church approach enables Korean immigrant churches and Korean-speaking young adults to reflect upon and appreciate their migrant context within the global migration phenomenon. This brings attentive hearts for each one of its members in Korean immigrant churches and their immigrant stories, treating them as an important part of God's work. As serious attention to a context of Korean immigrants and their young people who speak Korean is given, the missional church provides opportunities to reflect upon and appreciate a community's given context as migrants and young adults. Furthermore, reflecting upon their given context, missional churches recognize and illuminate Korean-speaking young adults who have been marginalized and ignored as an important channel for engaging God's work.

---

105. "Locus, meaning 'center of activity,' can refer to the source of someone's ability to make decisions as they move through life. It is usually described as being somewhere on a continuum between external and internal locus of control. During childhood, for instance, the locus of control is primarily external, meaning that the parents are responsible for that child. As adults, the more developed our sense of personal power and ability and our willingness to take responsibility for our choice, the stronger our internal locus of control." Clark and Clark, *Disconnected*, 57.

106. Roxburgh, *Joining God*, 114.

Normative Task

Fourth, the missional church fosters a new imagination beyond local church settings. The missional church approach encourages going beyond the boundaries of the church based on the theological assumption of God's reign and work over the world. Based on the ministry of Jesus and his disciples in Luke and Acts, Roxburgh finds theological foundation of Holy Spirit's work in boundary breaking beyond the Jews. He argues, "The reason for this boundary-breaking work of the Spirit is that God is about something in the world that is far bigger than the confines of an ethnotribal religion, even if that ethnotribal religion is the Judaism of the Scriptures."[107] With this theological framework of boundary breaking, the missional church urges a new imagination of church and is ministry beyond church boundary. This implies important perspectives for seeking ecclesiology for Korean-speaking young adults at multiple levels.

First, this boundary breaking brings about a new imagination concerning the marginalized as migrants and young people. Typically, they have been treated as passive recipients by the church. However, as Jesus used Gentiles and ordinary people to bring different insight and reflection to the Jews, the young, marginalized migrants can be far more than inferior recipients; instead, they can bring insights that impacts the community discerning and participating in God's work. Second, boundary breaking with a different understanding of the marginalized breaks apart typical ethnic boundaries. As the New Testament demonstrates, the Holy Spirit working beyond Jewish boundaries and bringing people into God's community regardless of their ethnic background, a missional church-oriented theological framework encourages churches beyond state and national boundaries.

Traditionally, migration studies and theology have been considered other's stories, not ours. Latino theology and migration is only about Latinos/as, just as African or Asian theology and migration is only for African or Asian. However, this missional church understanding of boundary breaking implies that the church can and should break those boundaries to discern and participate in God's work because God is working beyond the ethnic boundaries. Recent theologians critique Euro-centric and colonial perspectives of mission, which consider migrants as inferior recipients, and argue that migrants are actually impacting a bigger map of Christianity as active agents, especially in the American migration context. Jehu Hanciles points out that migrants have consistently revitalized American religious life

---

107. Roxburgh, *Joining God*, 112.

Ignored

and impacted on American Christianity in the case of African migrations.[108] Juan Martinez also addresses how Latino Protestants contribute to Christianity in America. He states that like the first-century church, powerless migrants actually impact the powerful Americans and their Christianity, which is totally opposite from the traditional Western mission.[109] Thus, the missional church approach of breaking-boundaries can bring about a new imagination for God's work beyond ethnic boundaries in the same way that migrants impact American Christianity.

With this boundary breaking, Korean-speaking young adults can have a new imagination about their role in the Korean immigrant church and furthermore in the United States, against all current assumptions that they are merely inferior recipients as a younger generation and migrants. Furthermore, this new imagination could also bring about a new era for the Korean immigrant church beyond the us-and-them perspective, such that we are able to discern and participate in God's work holistically.

Sociologist Helen Rose Ebaugh, a leading scholar on transnationality in religion, points out that migration studies in religious contexts had focused how religions and their communities impact migrants' adaptation in immigrant country, before they moved to focus on the connection between the hosting and home countries with their religion. She continues that the field of migration and religious studies recently began to move into "how religious beliefs, practices, norms, and institutions operate as immigrants migrate from their home communities to new areas of settlement around the world."[110] She argues that as migration becomes easier and more people are mobile, many of them have relationships in two or more countries simultaneously. Thus, migrants' political, social, economic, cultural, and religious activities across borders reverberate not only between their home and host societies, but everywhere in the world where migrants settle and people maintain ties with one another.[111]

This understanding of transnational links and their influences beyond both home and hosting country can bring about a new imagination for Korean churches. There are more than seven million Korean migrants in about two hundred different countries throughout the world.[112] There are over

---

108. Hanciles, *Beyond Christendom*, 379.
109. Martinez, *Los Protestantes*, 176.
110. Ebaugh, "Transnationality," 111.
111. Ebaugh, "Transnationality," 112.
112. Ministry of Foreign Affairs, "재외동포 현황 [Korean Diasporas]."

five thousand Korean immigrant churches in over 120 different countries throughout the world.¹¹³ Given the context of Korean immigrant churches all over the world, theological reflection on the missional church and breaking boundaries may bring about a whole new imagination for joining God's work, not only for Korean migrants in local churches, but also for churches in the United States. Furthermore, it can illuminate the influence on the home country, Korea and around the world where Korean migrants are based on spontaneous transnational links. Therefore, this missional church approach can help Korean immigrant churches to see God and their role beyond gender and age, beyond state and nation, and beyond us-and-them.

---

113. Shu, "4,233 교회 됐다 [4,323 Korean Churches]."

5

Pragmatic Task

Changes for Korean Immigrant Churches

DEFINING THE PRAGMATIC TASK

Utilizing the practical theology method, this study has explained the current practices of Korean-speaking young adults in Korean immigrant churches (descriptive task), offered analysis on the current practices (interpretative task) and provided a biblical and theological framework of ecclesiology for Korean-speaking young adults (normative task). Based on the research of the previous chapters, this chapter presents a way forward to faithfully serve Korean-speaking young adults.

Osmer uses the term "pragmatic task" to highlight the work of discerning the next step. He defines the pragmatic task as "determining strategies of action that will influence situations in ways that are desirable and entering into a reflective conversation with the 'talk back' emerging when they are enacted."[1] The pragmatic task is not merely concerned with creating a new practice based on a new idea, but also includes a process of discerning a new practice in response to the previous tasks of the practical theology method. In this respect, the pragmatic task leads to changes based on an assessment provided by the descriptive and interpretive tasks and the insight brought on by the normative task.

In the pragmatic task, Osmer focuses on leading change via three forms of leadership, namely task competence, transactional leadership, and transforming leadership. Task competence is "the ability to excel in performing

1. Osmer, *Practical Theology*, 4.

the tasks of a leadership role in an organization."[2] Transactional leadership is "the ability to influence others through a process of trade-offs."[3] Finally transforming leadership is to "lead an organization through a process of 'deep change' in its identity, mission, culture, and operating procedures."[4] In light of these three leadership forms by which people lead change in churches, Osmer claims that the goal of change can be explained as servant leadership, defined as "leadership that influences the congregation to change in ways that more fully embody the servanthood of Christ."[5]

Pragmatic Task in this Study

The pragmatic task in this study is twofold. First, this chapter proposes four different changes that Korean immigrant churches need to make in order to serve Korean-speaking young adults faithfully. These changes, which are shaped as a result of the research, first demonstrate the current praxis with descriptive and interpretive explanations of the current reality for Korean-speaking young adults and associated ministries. Then, we will move to suggested changes based on the normative reflections (theological and ecclesiological framework) for Korean-speaking young adults, which finally lead to the faithful next step of the pragmatic task.

The four changes deal with fostering intergenerational connections, seeking spiritual formation through an adoptive family of siblings, forming a missional church leadership culture, and being a globally connected community in a transnational context. These four suggested changes are not the "right" changes or the "only" changes appropriate for the Korean immigrant context. Rather, the suggested changes reflect prominent themes that emerged from this research and could be helpful within a contemporary Korean immigrant church setting. I am fully aware that the suggested changes are not exhaustive, and that any adjustments will depend on each church's context. Thus, these four changes represent a starting point for conversation.

Secondly, this chapter explores how to process these changes in local church settings. Since every church has different stories and a unique history, it is impossible to find one right model and one way to implement change for every context. Thus, this chapter focuses instead on a process

2. Osmer, *Practical Theology*, 176.
3. Osmer, *Practical Theology*, 176.
4. Osmer, *Practical Theology*, 177.
5. Osmer, *Practical Theology*, 192.

of leading change in different contexts rather than presenting the answer or a quick fix strategy. For processing such changes, Alan Roxburgh's *The Missional Change Model* is a helpful tool for effecting cultural changes in church settings. The missional change model offers ways that local churches could practice the suggested four changes in different contexts. With the missional change model, this chapter recommends Appreciative Inquiry as a starting point.

THEOLOGICAL IMPLICATIONS OF CHANGES FOR KOREAN IMMIGRANT CHURCHES

From Fragmented Structure

What Is Happening?

In this research, one of the significant findings on the current practices for Korean-speaking young adults is the reality of being disconnected. Literature reviews reveal that emerging adults are in general disconnected from adult society. Arnett points out that interpretations of emerging adulthood are mostly negative because young people take longer to reach full adulthood today than it did in the past.[6] Christian Smith pushes even further, stating that contemporary emerging adults are viewed as problems.[7] In these contexts, Chap Clark claims that young people have been abandoned in external systems, including school and other social structures, as well as in the internal system of their homes.[8] As a result, loneliness is a central experience in this systemic abandonment, and the consequence of this abandonment and loneliness for young people is that they create their own world to survive.[9] Christian Smith also points out that emerging adults are surrounded mostly by their peers, which is sociologically an odd way to help young people to learn how to be responsible, capable, mature adults.[10] Korean young adults' context is not very different from that of American young adults in general. Just like young people in America, young people in Korea do not receive enough attention from the greater society either.[11]

---

6. Arnett, "Emerging Adulthood," 70.
7. Smith, *Lost in Transition*, 10.
8. Clark, *Hurt*, 28–35.
9. Clark, *Hurt*, 51–54.
10. Smith, *Lost in Transition*, 34.
11. Kim, "성인모색기 [Emerging Adulthood]," 331; Lee, "소통의 위기 [Crisis of Communication]," 279.

Pragmatic Task

With this lack of attention, and feeling disconnected from adult society, young people in Korea are often considered to be failures, as they are compared to those from previous generations who experienced stunning economic achievements in very different circumstances.[12]

Korean-speaking young adults in Korean immigrant churches are in the same situation. The field research, including surveys and in-depth interviews, reveal a great deal of loneliness that Korean-speaking young adults carry. In the in-depth interviews, 100 percent of the young adults reported loneliness as a primary reason for their church involvement. Facing such loneliness, these young people hold their church as their survival space with the expectation of being accepted and finding belonging. However, they still experience a disconnection in their churches. The result of the research indicates that Korean-speaking young adults are surrounded by their peers in the church as well. The majority of pastor interviewees (85 percent) reported that their Korean-speaking young adult departments do not have relationships with other departments. Additionally, a significant number of Korean-speaking young adult interviewees (93 percent) reported that they do not have any significant relationship with adults in their church. Among them, more than half of Korean-speaking young adult respondents (56 percent) stated that they do not know any adults except their pastoral staff in their churches. This segregation is so deep that one of the Korean-speaking young adult interviewees, a lay leader, lamented, "We are so disconnected, it is as if we are in different churches."

Change to Intergenerationally Connected Community

Human beings are created to be in relationship, as they are created in the image of the triune God who exists eternally in relationship. People are designed to be connected and to belong. This is true for all humans, young and old. Throughout the Bible, including both Testaments, there is strong evidence that people were connected intergenerationally as community. During the exile, when God set his people of Israel in order, no generation was excluded.[13] Holly Allen and Christine Ross demonstrate that when Israel gathered for important events, all generations were present (Deut 29:10–12; 31:12–13; Josh 8:34–35; 2 Chr 20:13).[14] Generations are also required to be connected so as to pass on God's word to their younger

---

12. Lee, "소통의 위기 [Crisis of Communication]," 271.
13. Kirk, *Heirs Together*, 17.
14. Allen and Ross, *Intergenerational Christian*, 78.

Ignored

generations in the Old Testament (Deut 6:6–9). In the same respect, the New Testament also shows that in the early church all generations met together in homes (Acts 2:46–47; 4:32–25; 16:31–34). Diana Garland also states that a Hebrew household ranged between fifty and one hundred people, including young and old, and "for most people, work and home, family and work colleagues, religious expression, and the ebb and flow of daily life were intertwined in the same world of existence—household."[15] In these ancient times, people were intergenerationally connected in their daily life.

Practicing an intergenerationally connected community is not only God's intention, which we have seen to be substantiated in Scripture, but living in such a community also brings important benefits for community members. Allen and Ross demonstrate four possible benefits of intergenerational community: belonging, support for troubled families, character growth, and unique benefits by age and stage.[16] One of important perspective from Allen and Ross is that these benefits are not only for the young or weak, but for every member. They particularly explore the benefits that people in each life stage can offer and receive. This implies that all people from different life stages need to be connected intergenerationally as a community.

Although an intergenerationally connected community is important for all ages of people, it is crucially important for young people. Intergenerational community provides resources for young people to meet their essential need to belong. It also provides mature mentors to help young people grow exponentially more than they would by being surrounded only by their peers. Furthermore, intergenerationally connected communities can bring opportunities for young people to serve beyond their age group. Social science research has already indicated positive impacts on young people that stem from intergenerational religious community involvement.[17] Such benefits include lowering high-risk behaviors like drinking, drug use, smoking, deviant behaviors and sexual related problems,[18] better mental health with less anxiety and depression,[19] personal well-being fostered by

---

15. Garland, *Family Ministry*, 26.

16. Allen and Ross, *Intergenerational Christian*, 47–63.

17. For a literature review on potential benefits and risks of religiousness and spirituality for emerging adults Magyar-Russell et al., "Potential Benefits," 39–55.

18. Yonker et al., "The Relationship," 299–314.

19. Smith and Snell, *Souls in Transition*.

a sense of purpose in life, directives about what is right and wrong, greater perception of boundaries in social relationships,[20] distinctive sets of coping strategies for dealing with life stressors,[21] and the provision of belonging in a safe, communal space where young people can establish their worldview and gain access to peers, mentors, and elders.[22] Thus, a religious community is a unique intergenerational environment where emerging adults can be in the presence of a wide range of individuals who can offer perspectives from different life stages.[23]

According to the research in this study, most Korean immigrants do not have a space to connect intergenerationally. Respondents reported that a few annual events are the only times when they might meet the entire church community. However, this low frequency is insufficient for two reasons. First, it simply does not provide enough opportunities. Meeting only a couple of times per year with those outside of one's generational peer group does not provide space to connect intergenerationally. Korean immigrant churches should find ways to create more space to allow people from different generations to meet more often. Such opportunities could include events, activities, service, small groups, or something else of the sort. Since there is a lack of opportunities to meet each other, anything can be a starting point to share stories and live in community together. Second, annual events are not enough because people do not experience relationship building. According to in-depth interviews, the role of Korean-speaking young adults in annual events was mainly volunteering. Often, Korean-speaking young adult interviewees expressed frustration that they were forced to work for adults without receiving care and attention from them. In this respect, Korean immigrant churches should take initiative to build up community where people can connect and shape authentic, intergenerational relationships.

---

20. Smith, *Lost in Transition*; Smith and Snell, *Souls in Transition*.
21. Mahoney et al., "Religious Coping," 341–54.
22. Good et al., "Just Another Club?," 1153–71.
23. Magyar-Russell et al., "Potential Benefits," 42.

Ignored

From Knowledge-Based and One-Way Teaching of Discipleship Programing

What Is Happening?

The result of this study indicates that spiritual practices in the Korean immigrant church are heavily focused on knowledge-based and lecture-style discipleship programs. Discipleship programs have shaped the Korean church throughout a significant portion of its history. Korean discipleship was widely introduced in the 1960s by the Navigators; the Sarang Church discipleship movement also made an important impact on the Korean church in the 1980s.[24] Recently, a study of Korean discipleship movements provides an overview its history and evaluates the current practices of discipleship. The research has been done by four different experts—a theologian, a religious sociologist, and two practitioners—and includes literature reviews and field research.[25] The authors suggest that Korean discipleship has been used as a strategy for church growth, and as such, Korean discipleship programs have been raising lay leaders to grow or sustain church systems without actually caring for their lives of outside of the church or providing a theological foundation. Furthermore, the research reviews that current discipleship programs lack holistic spiritual formation because they are based primarily on a Bible study curriculum facilitated in a classroom-type environment.

This research on Korean-speaking young adults also indicates that Korean immigrant churches are similar to their global counterparts. Throughout the in-depth interviews with Korean-speaking young adults and their pastors, it was evident that most of Korean immigrant churches maintain some type of training or discipleship program, and that those are mainly focused on information-based, lecture-style teaching using Bible study curricula from Korea. Spiritual practices in Korean immigrant churches are also primarily a knowledge-based, teaching-style of discipleship programing. According to the interviews, many are under the impression that this type of discipleship programing is for the purpose of training people to serve. One of pastor interviewee mentioned that their program is to "lead people to eventually commit themselves to ministry in the church, but is not connected to their daily life." It indicates that the main purpose of these programs is to

---

24. Song, "Introduction," 9.
25. Jung et al., 제자훈련 [*Discipleship*].

maintain or reinforce the church system rather than foster an environment of holistic formation for the members of the community.

Change to Spiritual Formation through an Adoptive Family of Siblings

Faith is not something that is achieved by getting information; as Dean summarizes, "It is a way of life, not only a body of information to master."[26] In this particular way of life, we are invited to grow more like Jesus, which is called spiritual formation: "Spiritual formation is a life long process of becoming, of being formed and developed in the likeness of Christ."[27] This is the formation and growth that we need to experience. It is much deeper than knowledge-based teaching. It requires both intimate community and institutional organization.

We are called and accepted as God's children. Throughout the Bible, in both Testaments, God's people are depicted as a familial community. Scripture uses the family metaphor to demonstrate that God's people are called to be in a community where people share family-like intimacy.[28] In this adoptive family, everyone is equal as adopted siblings, and young people are nurtured and led into maturity.[29] This community is not top-down, in which one or a few leaders order or teach the entire community, but it is a community where each person needs the entire community to learn and grow. Because we are living out a new life in Christ with faith, seeking to become like Jesus, we need community to learn from one another, experiment, and grow together.

In this respect, the Korean immigrant church should reflect and evaluate the current knowledge-based discipleship program, and seek to create space for spiritual formation. The church is not a functional institution that seeks to maintain or reinforce a system and produce a profit, but rather it is a living organism like family. The Korean immigrant church should broaden its perspective of spiritual formation beyond training leaders to keep up their own ministries, and should find creative ways to grow beyond knowledge-based discipleship programing. This type of formation could include different types of learning styles, both verbal and nonverbal, including cognitive and affective dimensions, and related

26. Dean, *Almost Christian*, 117.
27. Naidoo, "Spiritual Formation," 187.
28. Clark, *Adoptive Youth Ministry*, 2.
29. Clark, *Adoptive Youth Ministry*, 16.

Ignored

to other life activities.[30] As a different way of growing, the Korean immigrant church should recognize that each one of their members in the community, including younger people, could offer important lessons and perspectives for spiritual formation. Everyone is equal as adopted siblings in God's family, precious and important as children of God. As each community seeks to engage in spiritual formation, Korean immigrant churches should seek a model for holistic growth, which invests not only in cognitive development from information found in Scripture, but also in holistic Christ-like spiritual life transformation.

From Hierarchical Leadership

WHAT IS HAPPENING?

The research indicates that Korean-speaking young adults are not only disconnected from church, but also treated as second-class members whose voices do not carry weight in their churches. As seen previously, contemporary young people in general are living in an adult-oriented society, and this is no different in church settings as well. Anabel Proffitt, Associate Professor of Educational Ministries at Lancaster Theological Seminary, points out that contemporary churches are only interested in "how to keep the young people in the church" to sustain and prove their vitality.[31] She pushes further, noting that young people are viewed as a commodity in this setting.[32] Whether churches treat young people as a commodity intentionally or not, the implication is that young people in church settings are considered not to be full members of the community, but rather as second class—a marginal part, which is peripheral to the adult congregation.

Korean literature also demonstrates similar ideas, as scholars claim there has been a lack of research about young people in the contemporary Korean church context.[33] In the face of this lacuna, many Western books that are more focused on numerical church growth, with so-called youth ministry experts providing *the* model to apply, have been translated and have influenced Korean churches. This has made an impact on the Korean church because it has offered the perspective that Korean young people are

---

30. Everist, *The Church*, 22.
31. Proffitt, "Countering Commodification," 3–4.
32. Proffitt, "Countering Commodification," 3–4.
33. Park, "기독교신앙교육, [Christian Faith Education]," 4; So, "성인 발현기 [Emerging Adulthood]," 21.

supposed to grow numerically in order to increase the attendance of the entire church, with little attention paid to their spiritual growth.

In the field research conducted, including surveys and in-depth interviews, this reality—young people being treated as second class—appeared even more significantly. Although there were over four hundred people interviewed or surveyed, including pastors and young adults in fifteen different cities from six major denominations of Korean immigrant churches, not one person interviewed was involved in the decision-making processes in their churches. In every single case, the people that make decisions for their churches were either elders or committees comprised of only adult leaders. In other words, Korean-speaking young adults were and are excluded from making decisions for their churches. This reality is the same even when churches make decisions about Korean-speaking young adult departments. One of the pastor interviewees reported, "People on the decision-making committees are all elder adult leaders that do not have any understanding of Korean-speaking young adults; and that is the why reason their decisions are not relevant for Korean-speaking young adult ministries." The result indicates that Korean-speaking young adults often feel treated as less important than their adult counterparts. Korean-speaking young adults are often asked and even required to serve and work when the churches need manpower for church-wide activities and events, but they were not invited to contribute any influence on the decisions being made.

Changes to Missional Church Leadership

It has been demonstrated that the leadership style of the Korean immigrant church is hierarchical and embodies a top-down approach. Although this traditional leadership approach might have worked in the past, the research indicates that it also causes troubling issues. Throughout the field research, it has been shown that the traditional hierarchical leadership style and structure makes people feel less important, abandoned, frustrated, and even abused, as seen in chapter 3. In this respect, one of prominent and crucial changes Korean immigrant churches should effect is a change in leadership style. During interviews, Korean-speaking young adults expressed their desire to see a different leadership style.

As seen in the normative task in this study, Korean immigrant churches need to provide intimacy and belonging, caring and communication in authentic relationships, and to promote the value of each member of the community. Given this understanding, the missional church approach provides a helpful framework as a different style of leadership. As mentioned in the previous chapter, missional churches approach and recognize people as fully valued agents of God, learn and grow from one another as community, and discern and participate in God's work together in the journey of life in a changing world. In the leadership style embodied by a missional church, the roles of leaders are different. Leaders are less likely to go about ordering, planning, and providing answers anymore. Branson states, "Leadership is about shaping an environment in which the people of God participate in the action-reflection cycle as they gain new capacities to discern what God is doing among and around them."[34]

For Korean immigrant churches to make adjustments in leadership style would first require leaders to revisit the leadership style currently in place. Although a top-down, centralized leadership style has been used in many cultural settings, the Korean church's leadership style has a unique history. Many scholars point out that the Korean church and its leadership have been shaped by Confucianized Reformed theology. Confucianism is one of the prominent narratives in Korean culture, and still has deep roots in daily life for people in Korea.[35] Studies show that Confucianism is not necessarily a type of religion in contemporary Korea, but more of a lifestyle; and this type of lifestyle is heavily rooted in Korean Christianity as well.[36] Furthermore, Korean Christianity has been greatly impacted by fundamental reformed theologians and missionaries. These two narratives—Confucianism and Reformed theology—have been interwoven and have led the leaders of the Korean church in a particular direction. Thus, it would be necessary for Korean church leaders to revisit and reflect on how the current authoritative, Confucianized leadership style has been constructed before adapting it in an innovative direction.

This requires not only theological reflection, but cultural reflection as well. In revisiting and analyzing the current hierarchical leadership style, the Korean immigrant church should listen more carefully to how different factors have shaped the current leadership model and how the current leadership model has affected the community. With this reflection, Korean immigrant churches may understand how to process change as missional

---

34. Branson and Martinez, *Leadership*, 55.

35. See Śleziak, "The Role of Confucianism"; Park and Chesla, "Revisiting Confucianism"; Jung, 문화적 문법 *[Cultural Grammar]*, 194–347; Baker, "The Transformation," 425–55.

36. Lee, "Revisiting the Confucian Norms"; Park, "Korean Protestant Christianity," 59–64.

leaders, reflecting on the current context of authoritarian leadership and the normative framework of biblical leadership.

From Traditional "Immigrant" Church

What Is Happening?

The classic role of religion in immigrant society is to provide cultural continuity of the homeland and the psychological benefits of religious faith following the trauma of immigration.[37] This research shows that the Korean immigrant church has operated out of the same perspective. One representative scholar in the field of Korean immigrants, Pyong Gap Min, demonstrates the major functions that the Korean immigrant church provides in fostering fellowship, maintaining Korean cultural traditions, facilitating social services for Korean immigrants, and offering social status and positions for Korean adult immigrants.[38] Considering the Korean immigrant church as an ethnic enclave, V. H. Kwon also shows that Korean immigrant churches provide space and services for their members to maintain their ethnic identities and heritage, providing social support and relational benefits.[39]

However, the demographic of the Korean immigrant church is changing. While it has been assumed that Korean immigrant churches would transition to English-speaking second- or third-generation churches, such as other European and Japanese immigrant churches, this research indicates that Korean immigrant churches are not experiencing the transition to English-speaking services; rather, English-speaking Korean Americans are leaving their parents' churches.[40] Im and Oh argue that the Korean immigrant church is facing a membership shift from legal permanent residents and naturalized citizens to nonimmigrant short-term residents and temporary visa holders; their data shows increasing numbers of English-speaking young adults leaving Korean immigrant churches, and increasing numbers of nonimmigrant Koreans visiting the United States.[41] In other words, Korean immigrant churches are no longer

---

37. Hirchman, "The Role of Religion," 1206.
38. Min, "Korean Immigrant Churches," 1370.
39. Kwon, "Houston Korean Ethnic Church," 111–18.
40. Kim, *Faith of Our* Own; Min and Kim, "Intergenerational Transmission"; Im and Oh, "Korean Diaspora."
41. Im and Oh, "Korean Diaspora," 316.

Ignored

a traditional "immigrant" church for people who immigrated and do not expect to move back to their home country.

This study discovered demographic changes as well. Out of the 404 surveys of Korean-speaking young adults, only about half of the respondents (53 percent) were legal permanent residents and naturalized citizens, with the other half (47 percent) reporting that they hold nonimmigrant visas. Throughout the in-depth interviews, about half of interviewees stated that they desire or plan to go back to Korea (22 percent) or are open to going back to Korea (26 percent). Korean-speaking young adult interviewees also reported that they had strong, active, and instant connections to Korea via Internet, phone, mass media, and even accessible transportation. This shows that the demographics and the context of the Korean immigrant church are changing, and that a different perspective and a new set of ministry practices are required.

Change to Transnational Church with Korean Language

A fundamental understanding of the Korean immigrant church is based on the classical assimilation theory of immigrants, which portrayed assimilation as a uni-directional process.[42] This theory claimed acculturation and assimilation to the hosting country was an automatic process, expecting immigrants to be fully assimilated after not more than a couple of generations. However, this theory has since been widely critiqued, particularly in light of recent immigrant patterns. Studies have shown that assimilation happens in a multi-directional process with varying degrees on a continuum.[43] Furthermore, with a changing reality of migration patterns, scholars working in migrant studies have recently adapted a transnational perspective on immigrants' lives, considering not only how migrants assimilate into their hosting countries and maintain their homeland ties, but also how their transnational ties impact their local and global societies.[44]

Although the reality of the immigrant context has changed, as studies demonstrate, Korean immigrant churches still base much of their understanding on a traditional, outdated framework of migration. Korean

---

42. See Gordon, *Assimilation*; Warner and Srole, *American Ethnic Groups*.

43. See Alba and Nee, *Remaking the American Mainstream*; Zhou, "Segmented Assimilation"; Center for Migration Studies, "Immigrant Adaptation"; Portes and Rumbaut, *Immigrant America*.

44. See Ebaugh, "Transnationality"; Faist et al., *Transnational Migration*; Levitt and Jaworsky, "Transnational Migration Studies," 129–56.

immigrant churches still mainly focus on cultural continuity and the psychological benefits of providing services such as Korean-language school programs, celebrating Korean holidays, and social and relational resources. Furthermore, based on the framework of classical assimilation theory, many still think that Korean immigrant churches will eventually transition to English-speaking churches, claiming that the future of the Korean immigrant church depends on the so-called second generation, which is comprised of English-speaking younger people.[45]

However, the demographics of the Korean immigrant church are changing. There are an increasing number of non-immigrant visitors, and these new migrants from Korea tend to have a higher education background and better English skills than the previous immigrant generation.[46] With technological developments, contemporary migrants have easier access to visiting Korea, as well as instant connections to Korea via the Internet, phone, and mess media. In this new reality, the Korean immigrant church should not and cannot remain committed to a traditional "immigrant" church model any longer.

Korean immigrant churches should recognize these changes and learn how they play a role in the dynamics in each local church setting. Furthermore, Korean immigrant churches should seek beyond their traditional assimilation framework to be transnational churches with Korean language ministries. In other words, Korean immigrant churches should seek transformation from being an isolated ethnic enclave to a vibrant transnational community. The Korean-speaking church in the United States needs to focus not merely on cultural continuity and its transition to the second generation, but even more on the new reality of the transnational ties of their members and how these ties could impact their local churches, the Korean church in Korea, and the Korean diaspora churches around the world.

PROCESSING THE CHANGES

So far, this study has presented careful observations of the current practices of the Korean immigrant church, interpretations of those practices among

---

45. Seminars, events and forums for the next generation of Korean immigrant churches are still only on English-speaking young people (the so-called second and 1.5 generations). The main concern of theses events are how to keep English-speaking young generation in Korean immigrant churches. See Kim, "한인교회 미래 [The Future of Korean Immigrant Church]"; Lim, "20년후 한인교회 [After 20 Years, the Korean Immigrant Church]."

46. Min, "The Immigration of Koreans," 31.

Ignored

Korean-speaking young adults, and a theological framework for ecclesiology for the Korean immigrant church and its young people. The study has also suggested four prominent changes that the Korean immigrant church should take based on data gathered during the research process. However, having some ideas of the changes that should be effected does not in itself bring about any real changes in the community. Roxburgh states that because our habits are so strong, merely having a good idea, even a brilliant one, does not mean it will be accepted or change the way people think, work, or act.[47] In other words, knowing what to change is not the end of the task, but rather the very beginning of the real changes.

Although this study has suggested four prominent changes Korean immigrant churches need to consider, it would not lead to real change unless each community works together to process theses changes in their context. The task of making changes should look different depending on context because each context includes different people, places, and stories. For example, the new practices appropriate for an intergenerational, connected community would vary depending on each church's unique context. Some churches might seek to find a way to be connected with all generations in a small group, while other churches find a way to be connected through their Sunday services. It is because each context is different that each community needs to discern how God is working within a particular context.

From this perspective, this study suggests a way to lead the process of change instead suggesting any particular, normative model to apply.

The Missional Change Model

In terms of leading the process of change within a particular context, Alan Roxburgh's "The Missional Change Model" offers a helpful way to do this in a local church setting.[48] The Missional Change Model is not a quick fix strategy that is clean and linear; rather, it provides a way to lead the process of change by moving back and forth among the steps without knowing in advance how long each step will take. The process is focused on how a local church community can actually experience and commit to cultural change.

---

47. Roxburgh and Boren, *Missional Church*, 138.
48. Roxburgh and Boren, *Missional Church*, 133–46.

Figure 5.1 Missional Change Model

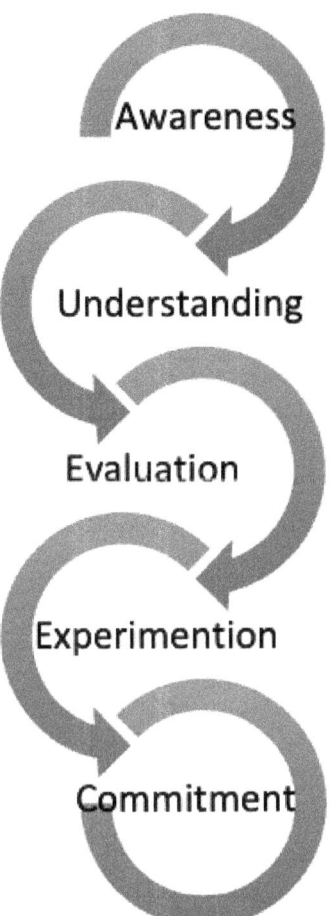

The first stage of the Missional Change Model is awareness. Awareness is a stage where people become aware of what is happening and find a way to express that in their own language. This step is more about creating a space where people believe that they are being listened to and in which they are able to give voice to their experience.[49] This careful listening and attention can help a church to move beyond mere preoccupation with tasks toward recognition of what is happening. This work requires leaders to function differently than they may be used to doing (namely,

---

49. Roxburgh and Boren, *Missional Church*, 148.

Ignored

less ordering, planning, and teaching). Roxburgh and Boren clarify the role of leaders in this stage:

> The role of the leader is to cultivate these safe spaces and assist people in finding (but not provide) the means whereby they can name what is happening. People need time and opportunity to work through their feelings to the place of a new awareness, and they need the space to discover language for what is happening in their rapidly changing world. When others provide language in nearly packaged sound bites, sermons, or programs, they deny people the opportunity to discover together the place where they find themselves.[50]

There are different ways to cultivate awareness. Roxburgh and Boren suggest a couple of tools for awareness, including pastoral care, Appreciative Inquiry, workshops, and listening teams.[51] However, those are not the only right ways to engage the process. Each church can find different and creative ways to progress through this step. Particularly in the Korean church context, a preparation step might be required before leaders are ready to begin the step of gaining awareness to reflect on the traditional leadership style and structure in the Korean church, and to develop listening skills and the tact to ask good questions.

Furthermore, even if leaders are able to progress beyond this step with a different style of leadership, because of the congregation, it could take significantly longer than expected. People are only familiar with following a few leaders' orders in most Korean immigrant churches, and often plan without reflecting and expressing their voices. Thus, even if congregations receive opportunities to be heard, it might take some time for people to find their voices and express them in the Korean immigrant church context.

As awareness grows, the community can seek deeper understanding. Roxburgh and Boren differentiate the understanding stage from the awareness stage in this way:

> In the awareness stage we invite each other to find the language that makes sense of our internal experiences and feelings of being in the clearing. The understanding stage begins as people tentatively find this language and are therefore able to talk to one another about their experiences. In one sense, then, awareness is a more personal, internal process of finding that *aha* place where

---

50. Roxburgh and Boren, *Missional Church*, 138.
51. Roxburgh and Boren, *Missional Church*, 150–54.

I am able to give words to my experiences, while understanding is when I begin to test this awareness in *dialogue* with each other.[52]

One important leadership role in this stage is deepening people's understanding of their awareness by creating time and space for conversation. Although there may be some attempts to jump to solutions as people become aware of what is happening, leaders have to slow down and invite people to go deeper with the issues, exploring the meaning of what they are learning through their interactive engagement with one another.[53]

The understanding stage can be processed in different ways; Roxburgh and Boren suggest conducting a listening report, online surveys soliciting feedback, and feedback seminars.[54] This stage, like other stages, requires some creativity within the Korean context. Korean immigrant churches can use regular ministry settings like weekly small groups and informal fellowship dinners and gatherings to process what has been learned in this stage. Because this stage is more about giving people the space to explore what they are learning with one another, leaders should intentionally provide opportunities for people to listen and talk. In this particular case, Koreans might need some directed practices to engage in conversations beyond their social status. Due to the cultural forces of the traditional Korean way of conducting conversations (in which older males of higher status speak more while others are encouraged to listen), developing conversations with mutual participation might present a challenge.

Once the community has gained awareness and deepened their understanding of what is happening, they can move on to the evaluation stage. During the evaluation stage, people are invited to talk about the implications of their conversations in the awareness and understanding steps for the current life of the church.[55] This stage involves asking how the newfound awareness and understanding speaks into the current practices of church.[56] Although speaking and evaluating the current practices might be critical, because people have hopefully experienced safety and trust throughout the previous stages, the evaluation stage is less critical and negative, and includes deeper engagement.[57] Roxburgh and Boren empha-

---

52. Roxburgh and Boren, *Missional Church*, 157.
53. Roxburgh and Boren, *Missional Church*, 143.
54. Roxburgh and Boren, *Missional Church*, 158–61.
55. Roxburgh and Boren, *Missional Church*, 143.
56. Roxburgh and Boren, *Missional Church*, 163.
57. Roxburgh and Boren, *Missional Church*, 144.

size the need not to rush, but rather to spend sufficient time in this stage by recommending a four-month process of dialogue groups in which a feedback report is processed together.[58] They warn that there are two possible temptations during this stage, both of which move the process too fast. One temptation is to put the work in the hands of experts and professionals (i.e., reverends, pastors, and people with doctorates and master's degrees), and the other is to attempt to find a guru who promises people that the person has discovered *the* way (ancient or new), and is now ready to guide the people.[59] However, because this is work for people as a community, not for a few, churches should resist both of these temptations.

Those temptations are important considerations in the Korean context as well because traditional ways of finding new practices dictate that planning and coordinating such changes have been the role of experts and leaders. Thus, it would be easy to fall back into the old pattern without noticing if a community does not intentionally reflect upon and resist this temptation. One helpful theological point in relationship to working with people is that "the spirit of God is among the people of God, not in the experts and the ordained, but right in the midst of all the ordinary men and women of the local church."[60] As leaders find different roles to cultivate an environment for people to listen, they might need to learn how to handle some unexpected emotions like anxiety grief as they let go of old ways of being. Resisting the temptation to go back to the old ways, and accepting the uncertainty of not knowing how God would lead, takes a lot of physical, mental, emotional and spiritual energy on the part of leaders. Therefore, it would be helpful not only for the people but for the leaders to create a safe place to share their stories.

Once people are aware of, understand, and have evaluated their current practices, they are ready to move forward. The experimentation stage helps people start making changes. Experimentation does not pursue total change, but allows new concepts to be tried without requiring complete commitment; a community experiences a course of action that they tentatively adopt without knowing exactly what the results will be.[61] Roxburgh and Boren state that the reason for experiments is to give people permission to fail, given that the North American church is a risk-averse culture. They demonstrate that

---

58. Roxburgh and Boren, *Missional Church*, 164.
59. Roxburgh and Boren, *Missional Church*, 164–65.
60. Roxburgh and Boren, *Missional Church*, 165.
61. Roxburgh and Boren, *Missional Church*, 181.

Pragmatic Task

because the North American church carries a theological undergirding of perfectionism based on evangelical and restoration expressions (under the guise of sanctification), professionals (clergy) are about only the ones who have control and knowledge over the mysteries of what God is doing. The result of this is that leaders on church boards are expected to have abilities to manage the existing paradigms of church life, and such boards often risk getting shut down due to the weight of anxiety.[62]

Much of Roxburgh and Boren's interpretations on the North American church in regard to its risk and experiment-averse culture are also true in Korean church as well, since the Korean church has been influenced and shaped by North American churches and theologians in many ways. However, one must always go even deeper with traditional cultural narratives such as Confucianism. One cultural narrative that causes even more aversion to risk within Korean culture is the cultural norm of seeking harmony that comes from Confucian metaphysics. Because Korean culture is still heavily based on the collectivistic traditional mentality of the Confucian ideal of harmony,[63] any changes that would take risk and possibly disrupt harmony and bring shame to the community would not be accepted. In this particular context, it might take longer to experiment and risk failure, because to experiment is to give people permission to fail. Some Korean immigrant churches would not have a difficult time experimenting, while other churches would cease moving on to the next step because of fear of failing and bringing shame on the community.

Finally, based on the people's opportunity to learn from the experiments, communities are ready to make commitments to experiment. At this commitment stage, people experience real change and transformation, and choose not to go back to old habits.[64] Emphasizing that this journey from awareness to commitment takes time, Roxburgh and Boren mention that it will take a local church five to six years to make this transition.[65] It may take longer in the Korean context with some unique cultural narratives such as hierarchical leadership, ideal harmony, and shame. This is a journey that takes a long time and a strong commitment. Some may say that such a journey is only possible in American churches, and thus impossible in Korean church culture. However, every journey begins with a faithful first

---

62. Roxburgh and Boren, *Missional Church*, 183–84.
63. Śleziak, "The Role of Confucianism," 46.
64. Roxburgh and Boren, *Missional Church*, 185.
65. Roxburgh and Boren, *Missional Church*, 193.

step before moving forward. Thus, I would like to suggest a practical tool for the first step that Korean immigrant churches can take.

Developing Listening Proficiency

The transition for a Korean immigrant church seeking to create a different environment—from a fragmented, one-directional method of teaching and a traditional, hierarchical, and one-way assimilation-based church to an intergenerationally connected, adoptive family of siblings with missional church leadership and transnational church ties—takes time and commitment. This may sound impossible within the Korean context; however, this transition could begin from one small step. I would like to suggest that this small yet powerful first step is none other than listening.

Throughout these transitions, listening is a core task. Listening is crucial because as a church we are invited to participate in God's initiatives. Without listening to God, it is impossible to join God's work. Without listening to God, all of a community's best intentions for work and ministry are just good deeds disconnected from God's kingdom. Because God is the one initiates and continues the redemptive work and role of the church, we are not called to create a new work, but rather to join his work by listening and seeking God's kingdom. Secondly, listening is important within the community because God is working through each and every one of the community members. Discerning God's next faithful step for the community requires listening to the stories of the community. Because each member of a community, regardless of age, gender, and ethnicity, is a crucial part of what God is doing in the world,[66] listening to each other in community is important. Lastly, listening is crucial because it brings healing and helps build up authentic relationships within the community. Studies have shown that listening is a powerful way to heal in the disciplines of clinical phycology, education, pastoral counseling, etc.[67] Especially in the context of migrants, listening can bring recognition, empathy, and healing to the painful wounds of marginalized life.

Although listening is crucial for a church to be a faithful community of God, it requires practice to develop proficiency. In particular, in the Korean context where Confucianized hierarchy has been deeply rooted in daily practice, it may take more effort and practice than in other cultural settings. Although there are different ways to develop a community's

66. Roxburgh, *Joining God*, 58.
67. See Akhtar, *Listening*; Waks, *Listening*; Underwood, *Empathy and Confrontation*.

listening capacity, I would like to suggest Appreciative Inquiry as a practical and useful tool, especially in the Korean context.

Appreciative Inquiry

Appreciative Inquiry (AI) is a theory and practice developed first by David Cooperrider and Suresh Srivastva at Case Western Reserve University in 1987.[68] While the problem-solving approach considers an organization as a problem to solve, AI searches for the best in people, their organization, and the world to bring about positive and innovative changes.[69] Watkins, Mohr and Kelly define AI in this way:

> Appreciative Inquiry is, essentially, a collaborative and highly participative, system wide approach to seeking, identifying and enhancing the "life-giving forces" that are present when a system is performing optimally in human, economic and organizational terms. It is a journey during which profound knowledge of a human system at its moments of wonder is unconcerned and used to co-construct the best and highest future of that system.[70]

With this positive and innovative approach, AI has been widely used in different organizational settings, including business and education, as well as in church settings. Mark Lau Branson, in his book *Memories, Hopes, and Conversation: Appreciative Inquiry, Missional Engagement and Congregational Change*, demonstrates how AI can be used well in a church setting. His first edition (2004) included First Presbyterian Church, Altadena (California) as a case study; in his second edition (2016), he displayed forth 5 different church narratives on how AI can impact and bring change in a ministry setting. Branson states that, for churches, AI "provides a process to bring our own narratives into conversation with the biblical and historical narratives of our faith. AI can guide and nourish (reconstruct) the organization along the lines of its best stories as discerned alongside God's initiatives."[71]

Although AI is powerful tool in many ways, it can particularly contribute to the cause of Korean-speaking young adults within the Korean immigrant church community in at least three ways. First, AI helps create

---

68. See Cooperrider and Srivastva, "Appreciative Inquiry," 129–69.
69. Cooperrider et al., *Appreciative Inquiry*, 5.
70. Watkins et al., *Appreciative Inquiry*, 22.
71. Branson, *Memories*, 21.

Ignored

a mutual space for conversation regardless of age, gender and ethnicity. As has been noted, Confucianized hierarchy is one of the deeply practiced features in the Korean immigrant church. In this kind of setting, it is easy for a few of the leaders, elders, and higher-status people to speak, teach, and order others in conversation while the young and people with less power are encouraged and often forced just to listen. However, AI provides positive questions to develop opportunities for everyone in the conversation to speak and listen. Because AI is not about finding the right or wrong answer, but is more interested in personal stories, emotions, and hopes, anyone can participate in the conversation of sharing and listening to each other, and everyone in the group is given an opportunity to speak.

Second, AI relieves shame, which people might experience in conversations about community, by focusing on maintaining a positive perspective and framing narratives positively. Although there are many arguments on the topic of shame, generally speaking, shame is the primary ethos for Asian culture, while guilt is that for Western culture.[72] In a shame-based culture, it is important to keep harmony, and the lack thereof often causes shame. When people bring up something that disrupts the harmony and peace in a community, they are often met with shame. Conversations and evaluation of an organization tend to be negative, as the conversations often trend toward discussing deficits; this can create a high level of tension. Harmony and peace are often compromised in such interactions, particularly in the context of intergenerational conversations. However, AI can foster a positive and non-threatening way of conversing about the community by focusing on positive narratives in the community.

Third, AI facilitates a next faithful step for participating in God's ongoing work in a creative way by embracing the idea of mystery. One basic assumption of the AI method is that an organization is a mystery that should be embraced as a human center of infinite imagination, capacity, and potential. The problem-solving approach, on the other hand, considers an organization to be a problem with the working assumption that there is one way to fix it.[73] Because church communities are called to trust God in the uncertainty of life together, and to discern the mysteries of God's ongoing work through and within the community, it is important to find a way to discern how a church can join in God's work

---

72. This does not mean that a shame-based culture does not also have a guilt mechanism. Creighton, "Revisiting Shame and Guilt Cultures," 285.

73. Cooperrider et al., *Appreciative Inquiry*, 15.

Pragmatic Task

with a creative imagination. Particularly in Korean culture, in which the problem-solving approach and top-down leadership are deeply embedded, AI can bring different and helpful perspective to help a community embrace mystery with creative imagination.

Appreciative Inquiry can be used in every step of leading change in a church setting. Branson's *Memories, Hopes, and Conversations: Appreciative Inquiry, Missional Engagement, and Congregational Change* has five church narratives, which demonstrate how each church used AI in their context. Furthermore, he offers a detailed guideline and schedule for implementing the AI process. That being said, it should be acknowledged that the AI process might still make some churches and leaders feel anxiety at the start. Thus, I would like to present some initial AI questions, which could provide a starting point.[74]

1. Reflecting on your entire experience at our church, remember a time when you felt the most engaged, alive, and motivated. Who was involved? What did you do? How did it feel? What happened?

2. What are the most important contributions the church has made to your life? Tell me when this happened who made a difference? How did it affect you?

3. What are the essential, central characteristics or ways of life that make our church unique?

4. Make three wishes for the future our church. Describe what the church would look like these whishes come true.

With these simple questions, any leader, whether a senior pastor or an associate pastor of one small department, can start a conversation in any setting with pastors, staff, lay leaders, and those of a younger generation over a meal or coffee time, a small group or a regular meeting. Most practices are not well explained with words only, but they become much clearer when they are practiced in action. Although these AI questions look almost too simple to bring about any changes, it may bring unexpected, constructive ways to change once implemented. Branson claims, "AI is not something that is done once or every few years as part of strategic planning—it is a way of continually forming an interpretive community that can thereby perceive, think, converse, and create with the most life-giving

---

74. Branson, *Memories*, 76.

Ignored

resources."[75] The Korean immigrant church, which is in need of cultural change, needs to recognize that such cultural change cannot be done overnight, but requires a long-term process in community. It might look impossible at the outset, and it may move slowly even if with great effort. Changes that come with a missional church change model and through AI could be more understandable and feasible when embarking on the journey together. Although there are bound to be some trials and errors, taking one small step at a time by simply trying out the aforementioned AI questions could yield great hope for moving forward.

---

75. Branson, *Memories*, 24.

Conclusion

SUMMARY OF THE STUDY

THIS STUDY ADDRESSES A major concern: Korean immigrant churches that focus on English-speaking young adults as they look forward to the future, while overlooking significant groups of Korean-speaking young people. Given that this particular population of Korean-speaking young people in Korean immigrant churches has not been studied in depth, this study sought to bring to light this hidden population in order that Korean immigrant churches might better understand and serve the Korean-speaking young people in their communities. From the overarching research question "How should Korean immigrant churches as communities understand and serve Korean-speaking young people?" Four sub-research questions emerged: (1) Who are the Korean-speaking young adults in the Korean immigrant church? (2) What are the current practices of Korean immigrant churches in regard to Korean-speaking young adults? (3) What is an ecclesiology that the Korean immigrant church should seek that accounts for Korean-speaking young adults as part of the community? (4) How should the Korean immigrant church as a community, including Korean-speaking young adults, move forward to discern a next faithful practice to participate in God's ongoing redemptive work?

Ignored

Who Are the Korean-Speaking Young Adults in the Korean Immigrant Church?

This study reveals a marginalized and ignored population of young people in Korean immigrant churches: Korean-speaking young adults. Although most study, research, and ministry attention has been focused on English-speaking young people, most Korean immigrant churches have a Korean-speaking young adult ministry.

The findings of this study indicate that Korean-speaking young adults share many perspectives in common with North American emerging adults. Both are experiencing a prolonged transition to adulthood. While there is bright side for emerging adults who are exploring life in various ways with fewer commitments, Korean-speaking young adults experience a dark side to this period as well. Instability, loneliness, and abandonment are also common experiences during this particular transition. In addition to the general struggles of emerging adulthood, Korean-speaking young adults also face challenges as ethnic minorities including marginality, unstable visa status issues, and cultural and language barriers.

This study reveals that Korean-speaking young adults are lonely. Loneliness was one of the strongest and most frequently expressed emotions throughout the surveys. Korean-young people deal with loneliness as they transition into adulthood like other emerging adults, and also as they transition as migrants. All of the interviewees, both young adults and pastors, mentioned that Korean-speaking young people are lonely, and that loneliness is a major reason why they come to church. However, due to the fragmented and hierarchical structure of Korean immigrant churches, this study reveals that Korean-speaking young adults face loneliness in their churches as well; in fact, churches can compound their experience of loneliness.

Korean-speaking young adults are transnational. Unlike previous immigrant generations, contemporary Korean-speaking young adults have better English skills and a more in-depth understanding of American culture. Yet they also demonstrate strong ties to Korea through different types of transactions, which include making visits to Korea, accessing Korean media instantly and consistently, and utilizing Korean language and culture in daily life. The fact that Korean-speaking young adults simultaneously experience assimilation into American culture and maintain Korean culture makes them different. In this Korean-speaking young adult group, there are not only people who arrived in America recently, but also people who were born in America or arrived at an early age. In other words, this group of young people is not categorized by their arrival age or language skill; rather, they share similar levels of transnationality.

What Are the Current Practices of Korean Immigrant Churches in Regard to Korean-Speaking Young Adults?

This study indicates that the Korean immigrant church plays crucial role for the spirituality of Korean-speaking young adults. Korean immigrant churches have been an important gateway for spiritual growth. There is a comparably high rate of newcomers who have never previously been to church in Korean-speaking young adult departments, compared to all the other departments in the Korean immigrant churches. Considering that there are increasing numbers of religious nones, especially among young people, this suggests that Korean immigrant churches provide a crucial religious space for young people. Furthermore, the findings indicate that Korean-speaking young people experience spiritual growth in Korean immigrant churches.

While Korean culture plays a crucial role in Korean-speaking young adults' spiritual formation, some dysfunctional cultural forces appear to lead them to be marginalized and ignored in the church. The research indicates that the current practices and systems of the Korean immigrant church have been rooted in the Confucianized hierarchy of traditional Korean culture. Based on that context, the Korean immigrant church conveys an authoritarian leadership style and a fragmented church structure. In this study, Korean-speaking young people expressed their frustrations of feeling marginalized and isolated in their churches.

In the current structures and practices of Korean immigrant churches, there are simply not enough places in which Korean-speaking young adults can be cared for and truly heard. Korean-speaking young adult departments are often isolated, and they do not provide enough opportunities for Korean-speaking young people to interact and build relationships with others in the church. The findings demonstrate that there are only a few times each year when those young adults meet older adults, and that even on those occasions Korean-speaking young people are mainly asked to serve and help with events. Furthermore, within a disconnected and isolated system, Korean-speaking young people struggle to communicate with adult leaders. Both pastors and young adults expressed frustration that they were not heard during church decision-making processes.

Ignored

What Is an Ecclesiology That the Korean Immigrant Church Should Seek That Accounts for Korean-Speaking Young Adults as Part of the Community?

Based on these findings, this study offered an ecclesiology for Korean immigrants and their young people in a transnational context with particular reference to current migration theology. First, Korean immigrant churches should seek to be communities in which people find their identity and dignity beyond the state and nation, based on the *imago Dei*. As emerging adults in an adult-oriented society and hierarchical cultural context, and as Korean immigrants in America, Korean-speaking young adults struggle to understand their identity. They often doubt their dignity, feeling ignored and marginalized. In light of these realities, restoring their ultimate identity and dignity in God is the foremost task for the church.

Second, Korean immigrant churches should create communities where people experience belonging and grow together. Church is not merely a place where people gather. Rather, it is a community where people experience acceptance, belonging, and formation. As young people in a prolonged transition to adulthood, and as those in between cultures, Korean-speaking young adults struggle with loneliness and a desire to belong. Furthermore, Korean immigrant churches should create environments where people can grow together. Instead of a top-down operation, church communities should be places where the people of God gather as adoptive siblings to learn from each other, regardless of age, gender, and social status.

Third, Korean immigrant churches should be communities in which people participate and contribute to God's ongoing redemptive work from a missional church perspective. Church is not a community where only the members matter. Rather, church is a community that God has called to be a partner in his ongoing redemptive work. In this light, Korean immigrant churches should discern and participate in God's mission as a community, and should recognize that Korean-speaking young people play an important role in that mission. Furthermore, considering their transnationality, Korean immigrant churches may able to find creative and unexpected ways to participate in God's work beyond cultural and geographical boundaries.

Conclusion

How Should the Korean Immigrant Church as a Community, Including Korean-Speaking Young Adults, Move forward to Discern a Next Faithful Practice to Participate God's Ongoing Redemptive Work?

This study suggests four changes as possible next steps for Korean immigrants churches regarding their Korean-speaking young adults. These four changes should not be viewed as the only correct possible changes, but rather as suggestions that reflect prominent themes that emerged throughout the research. Because each church has a different and unique context, this study offers these four changes as possible ideas so that each church can find a creative way to move forward.

The first suggested change as a faithful next step is to move from a fragmented church structure to an intergenerationally connected community. The findings of this study indicate that Korean immigrant churches have fragmented structures and that Korean-speaking young adults do not have enough relationships with adults. There are not enough opportunities for members to connect with others outside of their peer group. In this light, Korean immigrant churches should seek ways to create communities where people can connect and build authentic relationships beyond their own generation.

Secondly, Korean immigrant churches should make a shift from knowledge-based, didactic discipleship programs toward holistic spiritual formation as an adoptive family of siblings. This study shows that spiritual practices in Korean immigrant churches are heavily focused on knowledge-based and lecture-style discipleship programs. As such, after finishing the given training program, people easily become church resources (workers for the church). However, spiritual growth is not merely about gaining cognitive knowledge, or even serving in the congregation. It is more about a comprehensive lifestyle transformation to become more like Jesus—this is spiritual formation. Spiritual formation is about a process of becoming, and this is only possible within community. It is not about a few leaders passing down information, but about living and experiencing life together as a community. In this light, each church member is a sibling of God prepared to help others grow.

Thirdly, this study encourages Korean immigrant churches to change their leadership style from hierarchical leadership to missional church leadership. The findings of this study demonstrate that leadership styles of Korean immigrant churches are based on a Confucianized hierarchical Korean culture, which is male-oriented, top-down, and authoritarian. The research indicates that such a leadership style and structure makes people feel less important, abandoned, frustrated, and even abused. From this current leadership framework, Korean immigrant churches should consider a different leadership style that creates an environment where people can reflect upon, share, discern, and participate in God's will as a community.

Lastly, this study demonstrates that Korean immigrant churches need to consider becoming transnational churches that retain Korean language. Korean immigrant churches have been expected to experience a transition to English-speaking, Korean American churches. This was the primary reason why many focused their primary attention on the English-speaking younger generation. However, the research indicates that English-speaking young people are leaving Korean-speaking churches, either to create their own spiritual space or to leave Christianity altogether. In light of this trend, there has not been (and might never be) a transition to English-speaking ministries in Korean immigrant churches. Furthermore, demographic changes have transpired recently in the Korean immigrant church. There are now growing numbers of non-immigrant visa holders, who are different than traditional immigrants. The findings of this study indicate that the demographics and the context of Korean immigrant churches are changing, and this requires a different perspective and new set of ministry practices, in light of their increasingly transnational reality.

With these four suggested changes, this study offers a way forward for leading change based on Roxburgh's missional change approach, rather than providing an exact model to apply to every church. This missional change model demonstrates how each church could process the changes from where they are. Furthermore, as a means to demonstrating the process of leading change in Korean immigrant churches, this study introduced Appreciative Inquiry as a starting point. Appreciative Inquiry encourages and helps communities to take the simple but important next step of listening in the midst of complex and overwhelming situations.

CONTRIBUTIONS

This study of Korean-speaking young adults in Korean immigrant churches makes significant contributions in at least three different areas. First, this study contributes to Korean American immigrant studies by illuminating the hidden population of Korean-speaking young adults and their unique context. Traditionally, Korean immigrant studies have focused only on

English-speaking generations—the so-called 1.5 and second generations—in their research of younger generations, including questions about the relationships between generations, cultural adaptation and conflicts, assimilation, and identity formation. However, there has only been limited research that focuses on the issues related to Korean-speaking emerging generations. This study broadens the general understanding of Korean immigrants by offering insight into Korean-speaking young adults, a population that has yet to be thoroughly researched.

Given this neglected population of Korean-speaking young people and their unique context, this research contributes to Korean American immigrant studies by providing a transnational perspective. Traditionally, Korean immigrant studies have been framed by a classical assimilation perspective, which is based on one particular way of assimilating into the culture of a host country. However, this study demonstrates how Korean-speaking young adults are able to keep their ties to Korea strong, while simultaneously allowing themselves to be exposed to and to assimilate into American culture. With a transnational framework, this study expands and challenges the current understanding of Korean immigrants, which reductively categorizes people by their arriving ages based on classical assimilation theory.

Secondly, this study contributes to Korean immigrant church studies. Korean immigrant church studies have also been mainly framed by classical assimilation theory, which asserts that Korean immigrant churches would transition to English-speaking churches in the near future. In that framework, Korean immigrant church studies have focused primarily on English-speaking generations of young adults, assuming that they would be the future of the Korean immigrant church. However, the transition to English-speaking Korean churches has not occurred, and with increasing numbers of short-term migrants, Korean-speaking ministries are often growing. This study illuminates this changing reality of the Korean immigrant church by providing data that contributes to a better understanding of Korean-speaking young adults and brings a holistic perspective to contemporary immigrants in the immigrant church context.

Furthermore, with surveys and in-depth interviews of more than 400 people from 13 churches, this study provides findings that contribute to our understanding of the current practices of Korean immigrant churches, including reflections on their current structure, leadership styles, and spiritual programs. In addition, based on a broad understanding of Korean immigrants and the current practices of Korean immigrant studies, this

Ignored

study reflects on transnational ties not only at the individual level, but also at the institutional level by addressing the ways in which these ties impact church members' spiritual formation and community selection. The data and findings about Korean-speaking young adults at the levels of individual and institutional transnationality suggest another way of thinking about the future of the Korean immigrant church.

Lastly, this study contributes to Korean migrant and diaspora studies, as well as to Korean immigrant church studies. There are more than seven million Korean immigrants in over 190 countries in the world[1] and there are almost six thousand Korean immigrant churches globally.[2] This study suggests a different way to understand the Korean diaspora and their churches that moves beyond traditional immigrant studies. In particular, this research will help the Korean diaspora and their churches to identify the important but marginalized groups of people like Korean-speaking young adults in order to broaden their understanding. This research also contributes to the study of Korean migrants in a global context by encouraging a new imagination regarding the communities of the Korean diaspora and the churches beyond their local territory. In the contemporary transnational context, the potential impact is significant, as there are more than seven million people in the Korean diaspora, with global networks. As such, this study, which illuminates the transnationality of young Korean migrants, can prompt creative ways of understanding the Korean diaspora and its churches, and of participating in God's ongoing work throughout transnational links in a global context.

SUGGESTIONS FOR FURTHER STUDIES

This research particularly focuses on Korean-speaking young adults in Korean immigrant churches, yet it brings some important insights for further research in broader migration and immigrant church studies. In this light, I would like to suggest at least three different directions that this research could be taken further in the future. First, this study identifies Korean-speaking young adults as a unique population—a hidden population within Korean immigrant studies—and this can be studied further by identifying younger immigrant generations of other ethnic groups who speak their home languages. Traditionally, migrant studies interested in younger generations are mainly concerned with English-speaking young people, or the

1. Ministry of Foreign Affairs, "재외동포 현황 [Korean Diasporas]."
2. Shu, "4,233 교회 됐다 [4,323 Korean Churches]."

so-called second or 1.5 generation. However, this study shows that there are young people who speak the language of their home country, and who actively engage with their home culture. Researching the younger generations of other immigrants who speak the language of their home country language could bring about a broader understanding of migrants.

This study shows that Korean-speaking young adults are not only young people who arrived in America during their early adult years. Korean-speaking young adults actually include people who were born in America as well. Further studies of immigrant young people who speak the language of their home country can challenge the traditional way of categorizing immigrants such as first, second, or 1.5 generation based on their arriving age, and bring a more comprehensive understanding of assimilation. In addition, this nuanced approach toward addressing migrant communities and their younger generations can be further expanded to include questions of transnationality and the retention of home culture while experiencing assimilation, and to analyze the ways in which transnationality and transnational links shape the identity and lifestyle of immigrants.

Second, this study demonstrates not only the current practices but also the changing context of the Korean immigrant church and Korean-speaking young adults, which raises important issues and topics for further reflect and research. Korean immigrant churches, like other immigrant or non-immigrant churches in America, have been concerned with and put great effort toward identifying how to do and be the church in a rapidly changing context. Thus, this study sheds light on changing factors related to immigrant church studies, including issues related to transnationality and changing visa status for Korean-speaking young adults. These findings can be adapted for further research on the Korean immigrant church to study how churches should serve contemporary migrants who are different than previous immigrant generations. Moreover, this type of research can also initiate further studies to look at how the Korean migrant community in America can participate in God's kingdom by making an impact not only on their own ethnic people, but also beyond their ethnic enclave, locally and globally through transnational links.

Lastly, this study presents that the transnationality of Korean-speaking young adults matters to them when choosing a religious community and practicing spirituality. As a result, this study can pave a pathway for further research about how transnationality impacts and shapes spirituality. Although religion and religious communities have played significant roles

Ignored

for migrants, and many scholars have called for further studies, there is still a lack of research on this topic. In this light, there should be more studies on the role of religion and religious communities in the life of migrants. Furthermore, research should be undertaken in the matter of the intersection between the spirituality and the transnationality of migrants. Although there are a few studies on religion and the religious community of migrants, most only focus on social functions that religious communities provide for migrants and describe migrants as passive recipients. However, in the changing context of immigration, there are growing numbers of people who maintain strong ties to their home country while also assimilating fluently into the hosting country. These contemporary migrants' needs may be different than previous immigrant generations, even as their roles are different in their local communities in the hosting country and in their homeland community. In this changing transnational context, further studies are needed on how spirituality shapes and is being shaped by transnationality, how transnational spirituality builds up global networks, and how these links precipitate changes in a global context.

FINAL REMARKS

This study is not merely about migrant issues or transnationality. Neither is it only about the immigrant church. This research is about people who have been ignored and marginalized despite their important role in their community and their enormous potential for the future. As I started this research, I was very excited to reveal a hidden population and their potential to impact local and global communities. However, throughout the study I realized that I too have treated these precious people as objects—a commodity for my research as I dreamt about writing a great dissertation—without knowing and understanding them.

However, as I met many young people and their pastors, I was able to learn about them as precious creatures. For young adults in Korean immigrant churches, there are many good aspects about being in America, and there are also many ways that these young people can impact not only their local communities, but also communities in Korea and globally. At the same time, there is deep sense of pain and sorrow that these young people carry as young adults and ethnic minorities. Although some of their experiences were predictable, others stories would never have been imagined without carefully listening with a willingness to understand.

Conclusion

Over the course of completing this project, I met many young people and their pastors. Some people admittedly had hard time opening up, but others shared painful but rich stories from the depths of their hearts. These unforgettable conversations with each one of the respondents in my research taught me to listen and seek to understand them as human beings, rather than as research subjects. As I began to listen and learn about these important people, their painful stories often brought me to tears. After many difficult and sleepless nights, I have learned how a researcher can treat and respect research subjects as precious and beloved human beings first and foremost, and I am grateful to each of them for the many lessons learned.

As I mentioned already, this study is significant, as it contributes important insights for further research in many ways. Furthermore, these groups of Korean-speaking young adults are crucial for us to engage in order to understand contemporary migrants and their churches. However, the most important thing we must do is to listen and pay attention to the stories others share during the research process as human beings rather than objects. I hope and pray that this research can promote a way to care for and respect the young people that I have come to know and love. May God's will be done through and for those who mourn, and those who listen to their mourning.

Appendix A

Survey Questions with Korean-Speaking Young Adults

A. Basic Info
   1. 나이 Age
   2. 성별 Gender
   3. 이민상태 Immigrant status
      - 한시적 비자 Temporary Visa
      - 영주권 혹은 시민권 Green Card or Citizen
      - 그외 Other _____
   4. 미국에 왔을때 몇살이었나요? How old were you when you arrived in the states? _____
   5. 미국에 지내는 동안 비자를 몇번 바꾸셨나요? How many times have you changed your visa/status during your staying in the state? _____
   6. 학업 상황 Education background (check if graduated)
      - 고졸 High school graduate
      - 커뮤니티 칼리지 졸 Community College graduate
      - 대졸 BA
      - 석사 MA
      - 박사 PhD

Appendix A: Survey Questions with Korean-Speaking Young Adults

7. 직업 (해당되는 모든 사안에 체크해주세요) Current work/school status (check all that apply)

    - 풀타임 직장 Full-time work
    - 파트타임 직장 Part-time work
    - 풀타임 학생 Full-time student
    - 파트타임 학생 Part-time student

8. 미국에 온 목적 (해당되는 모든 사안에 체크해주세요) Purpose of immigration (check all that apply)

    - 교육 Education
    - 직장 Job
    - 가족과 함께 있기 위해서 Be with family
    - 더 나은 삶을 위해서 Find a better life
    - 그 외 Other

9. 일년에 몇번 정도 한국에 방문하시나요? How many times do you visit Korea per year? _____

10. 미국에 온 이후에 한국에 몇번 다녀오셨나요? How many times have you visited Korea, after you came to the States? _____

11. 한국에 가족들 (직계가족)이 있으신가요? 있으시다면 몇명이 있으신가요? Do you have immediate family members in Korea? If yes, how many? _____

12. 미국에 (직계가족)이 있으신가요? 있으시다면 몇명이 있으신가요? Do you have immediate family members in the States? If yes, how many? _____

B. Church Experience

13. 이 교회를 다니신지 얼마나 되셨나요? How long have you been involved in this church? _____years, _____months

14. 미국에 계신동안 몇개의 교회를 다녀보셨나요? How many churches did you attend during your time in the States? _____

15. 미국에 오시기 전에 교회를 다니셨었나요? Were you a churchgoer before you come to the States?

    - 정기적으로 Regular member

Appendix A: Survey Questions with Korean-Speaking Young Adults

- 가끔씩 Occasionally
- 특별한 날에만 Only special occasions
- 한번도 가지 않았었다 Never
- 그외 Other

16. 교회를 선택하실때 가장 중요한 요인 두가지는 무엇인가요? What are the top two important criteria for choosing a church?

    - _____
    - _____

17. 교회에 다니는 이유는 무엇인가요? What are the reasons to come to church?

    - Belonging
    - Social services church provides
    - Strengthen my faith
    - Relationship with other members
    - Worship (music)
    - Other _____

PART II: For the following section, please provide on a 1–5 scale:

1—전혀 아니다. False, 2—아니다 Somewhat False, 3—그냥 그렇다/ 잘 모르겠다. Not Sure, 4—그렇다. Somewhat True, 5—완전 그러하다. True

A. Identity

16. 나는 안정적으로 자리를 잡았고 성인이 될 준비가 되었다. I feel settled and ready to move into adulthood   1   2   3   4   5
17. 나는 내가 누구인지 안다. I know who I am.   1   2   3   4   5
18. 성인이 되었지만, 나는 내가 누구인지 잘 모르겠다. Although I am an adult, I am not sure who I am.   1   2   3   4   5

B. Autonomy

19. 나는 내가 누구인지 알고 내 은사/달란트를 어떻게 사용하여야 하는지 알고 있다. I know myself and know how to use my gifts.   1   2   3   4   5

165

Appendix A: Survey Questions with Korean-Speaking Young Adults

    20. 나는 내가 우리 교회와 세상에 영향을 줄수 있다고 믿는다. I am confident that I have ability to impact my church and the world. 1 2 3 4 5

    21. 나는 내가 무엇을 잘하는지 무엇을 위해 부름 받았는지 잘 모르겠다. I am not sure what I am good at or called to (or for). 1 2 3 4 5

C. Belonging

    22. 어른들이 나를 안다고 생각한다. I feel known by older adults. 1 2 3 4 5

    23. 교회 전체는 나에게 가족같다. Broader church community is like a family to me. 1 2 3 4 5

    24. 내가 속해있는 부서와 리더들을 제외하고는 이 교회에서는 아무도 나를 모른다. Other than my peers and direct ministry leaders, nobody knows me at this church. 1 2 3 4 5

D. How they perceive themselves

    25. 한어권 18세 이상의 청년들을 가장 잘 설명할 수 있는 단어 세 가지를 나열해주세요. Please provide three words that in your opinion best describe how Korean-speaking emerging adults feel about their life?

Appendix B

Informed Consent Form

Fuller Theological Seminary
School of Theology

저는 풀러신학교에서 Chap Clark 교수님 밑에서 박사과정 논문을 쓰는 중이고 저의 논문을 위해 자료를 수집하고 있습니다. 바쁘시겠지만 여러분께서 이 리서치에 참여해주시기를 부탁드립니다. 아래에 리서치에 대한 디테일을 설명드리겠지만 혹시 질문이 있으시면 주저말고 알려주시고 혹은 나중에라도 질문이 있으시면 기쁘게 답해드리도록 하겠습니다.

My name is Jinna Sil Lo Jin, and I am collecting research as part of my doctoral degree at Fuller Theological Seminary under Chap Clark. I would like you to participate in a research project described below. I will explain this document to you in detail. Please feel free to ask questions. If you have more questions later, I will be happy to discuss them with you at any time.

프로젝트 설명:

한어 청년부서가 거의 모든 한인 이민교회에 있지만 실제로 이 한어 청년들에 대한 연구가 거의 이루어 지지 않고 있습니다. 이 연구를 통해 보다 한어 청년들에 대한 정확하고 온전한 이해가 이루어져 사역에 도움이 되고자 합니다.

이 논문에 사용하고자 한어 청년부를 섬기시는 사역자들의 포커스 그룹을 실행하려고 합니다. 바쁘시겠지만 참여해주시기를 부탁드립니다.

Appendix B: Informed Consent Form

이 리서치 중에서 여러분이 참석하시게 될 부분은 온라인 설문조사입니다. 본 연구의 목적은 아래와 같습니다.

1. 한인 이민교회 안에 한어 청년들에 대한 이해
2. 현재 한인 이민교회가 어떻게 한어 청년들을 사역하고 있는지에 대한 이해
3. 어떻게 하면 한인 이민 교회가 한어 청년들을 보다 더 잘 섬길 수 있을 것인지에 대한 고찰

이 연구의 목적은 한인 이민 교회안에 한어 청년들에 대한 보다 깊은 이해에 있으며 특별히 이 설문조사를 통해서는 여러분들의 이민, 가정, 교육, 그리고 교회 배경에 대해 질문하게 될 것입니다..

Description of the Project:

Although almost every Korean immigrant churches has a Korean-speaking young adult ministry, almost no research has been done about this population. With this research, I hope to provide an accurate and holistic understanding of this important group of people so that we can serve them better.

You were invited to participate in this study because you are currently serving in a Korean-speaking emerging adult ministry, and I encourage you to participate in this survey to contributeto this study.

The current study invites you to participate in a survey. The goals of this study are:

1. *To understand who are Korean-speaking emerging adults in Korean immigrant churches.*
2. *To identify the current practices of Korean immigrant church ministry for Korean-speaking emerging adults.*
3. *To understand how Korean immigrant church can serve Korean-speaking emerging adults in a holistic way.*

The purpose of this study is to gain a deeper understanding of Korean emerging adults in Korean immigrant churches. More specifically, the survey will ask questions about your immigration, education, family and church background, etc.

Appendix B: Informed Consent Form

절차:

만일 참여하시기로 결정을 하시게되면 다음과 같은 절차로 이루어집니다; 영어와 한글 이중언어로 된 설문조사지를 받게 되실 것입니다. 이 설문조사는 10-20분 정도 소요될 것이며 조사의 익명을 유지하기 위해 동의서를 조사지와 따로 걷도록 하겠습니다.

Procedures:

If you decide to take part in this study here is what will happen: You will be given bilingual survey questionnaires. This is a simply survey which will take only ten to twenty minutes. In order to keep anonymity, please tear off the consent form. The consent form will be collected separately.

위험 혹은 불편 요소:

본 리서치는 최소위험수치의 연구입니다. 여러분의 비자 상태를 물어보는 질문에 답하시면서 불편감을 느끼실 수도 있습니다. 하지만 모든 질문에 대답은 전적으로 여러분의 자유에 있으며 특정한 질문에 대해 대답하지 않으셔도 됩니다.

Risks or Discomfort:

There is minimal risk with being involved with this research study. You may feel vulnerable when answering questions about your visa status. However, answering questions is completely up to you, and you may skip questions.

이 연구의 혜택:

이 포커스 그룹에 참여하심으로서 얻으시는 직접적인 혜택은 없으나, 연구자가 한어 청년 사역을 더 깊이 이해 할 수 있습니다. 또한 이 리서치의 결과는 논문을 통해 집합적으로 발표되게 될 것입니다.

Benefits of This Study:

Although there will be no direct benefit to you for taking part in this study, the researcher may learn more about the current ministry of Korean-speaking emerging adults. Furthermore, the research will share aggregative results of the survey through the dissertation.

Appendix B: Informed Consent Form

비밀 및 익명보장:

이 리서치에 대한 여러분의 참여는 철저히 비밀이 보장됩니다. 여러분에 대한 어떤 정보도 유출 되지 않을 것입니다. 어떠한 자료도 연구자인 저 외에는 볼 수가 없으며 디지털로 저장된 모든 자료에는 비밀번호가 함께 붙여지게 되어 다른 사람에게 쉽게 노출 되지 않을 것입니다. 손으로 작성된 문서들은 디지털 문서로 곧 변환되며 손으로 작성된 문서는 폐기 될 것입니다. 리서치를 통한 결과를 통해 참석자가 누구인지 드러나지 않게 될 것이며 이름과 장소의 명칭을 변경하여 외부독자로 부터 보호받게 되실 것입니다.

Confidentiality:

Your part in this study is confidential. None of the information will identify you by name. All records will be available only to myself, the researcher, and will be saved and backed up digitally and will be password protected. All handwritten documentation will be transcribed digitally and the hard copies will be disposed of. Only after names and places have been changed will any findings or data be revealed or available to any outside party.

자발적 참여와 참여 취소:

이 리서치의 참여는 자발적으로만 진행됩니다. 여러분에게는 이 리서치를 거절할 권리가 있으십니다. 만일 참여하시기로 결정하셨다가 마음이 바뀌시면, 어떤 시점에서라도 취소하실 수 있습니다. 또한 어떤 질문에도 답하지 않으시고 넘어가실 수 도 있습니다. 무엇을 결정하시던지 개인에게 어떠한 피해가 가지 않습니다.

Voluntary Participation and Withdrawal:

Participation in research is voluntary. You have the right to refuse to be in this study. If you decide to be in the study and change your mind, you have the right to drop out at any time. You may skip questions. Whatever you decide, you will not lose any benefits to which you are otherwise entitled.

질문, 권리 그리고 항의:

만일 이 리서치 프로젝트에 대해 어떠한 질문이 있으시면 Jinna Jin 진 실로 626-584-5596이나 jinnajin@fuller.edu로 연락하실 수 있습니다. 만일 참여자로 이 리서치에 대해 질문이나 걱정이 있으시면 선교연구센터 디렉터 David Scott (626-584-5269, cmr@fuller.edu)으로 연락하시면 됩니다.

Appendix B: Informed Consent Form

Questions, Rights, and Complaints:

If you have any questions about this research project, please call Jinna Jin at 626-584-5596 or email at jinnajin@fuller.edu. If you have any questions or concerns about your rights as a research participant in this study, please direct them to David Scott, CMR Associate Director at the School of Intercultural Studies (626.584.5269, email: cmr@fuller.edu);

동의서:

이 동의서는 여러분이 18세 이상이고 이 동의서를 잘 읽으셨으며 여러분이 가지고 계신 모든 질문이 해결되었음을 동의하는 문서입니다. 또한 여러분께서는 어떤 시점에서라도 참여를 취소하실 수 있으며 그로인해 어떤 피해도 받지 않게 됨을 이해하신다는 것을 동의한다는 문서입니다. 연구자 Jinna Jin, 진실로 에게 답하게 되시는 모든 답은 보안이 유지됩니다. 또한 이 논문이 출판되기 전에 결과를 보실 수 있는 권리가 있습니다.

Consent Statement

This statement certifies the following: that you are 18 years of age or older and you have read the consent and all your questions have been answered. You understand that you may withdraw from the study at any time and that you will not lose any of the benefits that you would otherwise receive by withdrawing early. All of the answers you provide to Jinna Jin will be kept private. You should know that you have the right to see the results prior to their being published.

나는 Jinna Jin 진실로가 진행하는 한어 청년에 대한 연구에 참석함을 동의합니다. 동의서를 찢어가고 조사지에 답을 함으로 이 설문조사에 임하는 것을 동의합니다.

I consent to participating in being involved in a survey for Korean-speaking emerging adults being conducted by Jinna Jin.

_____   _____
Signature of Participant 참석자 서명   Date 날짜

_____   A copy of the informed consent
Typed/Printed Name 참석자 이름   will be given to you. 동의서 복사
                                    본이 여러분께 제공됩니다.

Appendix C

In-depth Interview Questions with Pastors

1. 한어 대학+청년부를 사역하시는 동안 가장 동기부여가되고 흥분되었던 순간이 있으셨다면 언제입니까? During your ministry with Korean speaking emerging adults, when were you most motivated and excited about your ministry?
2. 현재 섬기시는 교회의 어떤 부분이 가장 가치 있고 중요하다고 생각하십니까? What do you value most about your church?
3. 현재 섬기시는 부서에 어떤 부분이 가장 가치 있고 중요하다고 생각하십니까? What do you value most about your department?
4. 사역하시면서 겪으시는 어려들 중에 가장 큰 두가지를 설명해주세요. What are the top two challenges your ministry faces, and how do you deal with them?
5. 현재 섬기시는 청년+대학 부서와 교회 전체와의 관계에 대해서 설명해주세요. Tell me about the relationship of the emerging adults to the rest of the church.

Appendix D

Informed Consent Form

Fuller Theological Seminary
School of Theology

저는 풀러신학교에서 Chap Clark 교수님 밑에서 박사과정 논문을 쓰는 중이고 저의 논문을 위해 자료를 수집하고 있습니다. 바쁘시겠지만 여러분께서 이 리서치에 참여해주시기를 부탁드립니다. 아래에 리서치에 대한 디테일을 설명드리겠지만 혹시 질문이 있으시면 주저말고 알려주시고 혹은 나중에라도 질문이 있으시면 기쁘게 답해드리도록 하겠습니다.

My name is Jinna Sil Lo Jin, and I am collecting research as part of my doctoral degree at Fuller Theological Seminary under Chap Clark. I would like you participate in a research project described below. I will explain this document to you in detail. Please feel free to ask questions. If you have more questions later, I will be happy to discuss them with you at any time.

프로젝트 설명:

한어 청년부서가 거의 모든 한인 이민교회에 있지만 실제로 이 한어 청년들에 대한 연구가 거의 이루어 지지 않고 있습니다. 이 연구를 통해 보다 한어 청년들에 대한 정확하고 온전한 이해가 이루어져 사역에 도움이 되고자 합니다.

이 논문에 사용하고자 한어 청년부를 섬기시는 사역자들과 인터뷰를 실행하려고 합니다. 바쁘시겠지만 참여해주시기를 부탁드립니다.

이 리서치 중에서 여러분이 참석하시게 될 부분은 온라인 설문조사입니다. 본 연구의 목적은 아래와 같습니다.

Appendix D: Informed Consent Form

1. 한인 이민교회 안에 한어 청년들에 대한 이해
2. 현재 한인 이민교회가 어떻게 한어 청년들을 사역하고 있는지에 대한 이해
3. 어떻게 하면 한인 이민 교회가 한어 청년들을 보다 더 잘 섬길 수 있을 것인지에 대한 고찰

이 연구의 목적은 한인 이민 교회안에 한어 청년들에 대한 보다 깊은 이해에 있으며 특별히 이 설문조사를 통해서는 여러분이 섬기시는 교회의 크기, 사역 프로그램, 목적 그리고 어려움 등에 대해 여쭙게 될 것입니다.

Description of the Project:

Although almost every Korean immigrant churches has a Korean-speaking young adult ministry, almost no research has been done about this population. With this research, I hope to provide an accurate and holistic understanding of this important group of people so that we can serve them better.

You were invited to participate in this study because you are currently serving in a Korean-speaking emerging adult ministry, and I encourage you to participate in this interview to contribute to this study.

The current study invites you to participate in an in-depth interview. The goals of this study are:

1. *To understand who are Korean-speaking young adults in Korean immigrant churches.*
2. *To identify the current practices of Korean immigrant church ministry for Korean-speaking young adults.*
3. *To understand how Korean immigrant church can serve Korean-speaking young adults in a holistic way.*

The purpose of this study is to gain a deeper understanding of Korean young adults in Korean immigrant churches. More specifically, the survey will ask questions about your church size, ministry programs, goals and challenges, etc.

Appendix D: Informed Consent Form

절차:

만일 참여하시기로 결정을 하시게되면 다음과 같은 절차로 이루어집니다; 연구자와 한번 90분동안 만나셔서 인터뷰를 하시게 됩니다. 인터뷰 동안에는 제가 질문을 하게 될 것이며 여러분들은 한어 청년 사역자로써 여러분들의 경험을 나누시게 될 것입니다. 구체적으로, 여러분 사역의 가치, 가장 의미 있었던 순간들, 어려움들, 다른 부서와의 관계등에 대해서 나누게 될 것입니다.

Procedures:

If you decide to take part in this study, here is what will happen: You will meet with the researcher for a 90-minute interview. I will ask questions, and we will discuss together your ministry experience, highlights, values, the challenges of your current ministry, and the relationship between your department and other departments in your current church. This session will be recorded so that I will not have to take notes during the discussion. After the session, I will listen to the recording and take notes on what we discussed.

위험 혹은 불편 요소:

본 리서치는 최소위험수치의 연구입니다. 모든 질문에 대답은 전적으로 여러분의 자유에 있으며 특정한 질문에 대해 대답하지 않으셔도 됩니다.

Risks or Discomfort:

There is minimal risk with being involved with this research study. Answering questions is completely up to you, and you may skip questions.

이 연구의 혜택:

이 포커스 그룹에 참여하심으로서 얻으시는 직접적인 혜택은 없으나, 연구자가 한어 청년 사역을 더 깊이 이해 할 수 있습니다. 또한 이 리서치의 결과는 논문을 통해 집합적으로 발표되게 될 것입니다.

Benefits of This Study:

Although there will be no direct benefit to you for taking part in this study, the researcher may learn more about the current ministry of Korean

Appendix D: Informed Consent Form

speaking emerging adults. Furthermore, the researcher will share aggregative results of the survey through the dissertation.

비밀 및 익명보장:

이 리서치에 대한 여러분의 참여는 철저히 비밀이 보장됩니다. 여러분에 대한 어떤 정보도 유출 되지 않을 것입니다. 어떠한 자료도 연구자인 저 외에는 볼 수가 없으며 디지털로 저장된 모든 자료에는 비밀번호가 함께 붙여지게 되어 다른 사람에게 쉽게 노출 되지 않을 것입니다. 손으로 작성된 문서들은 디지털 문서로 곧 변환되며 손으로 작성된 문서는 폐기 될 것입니다. 리서치를 통한 결과를 통해 참석자가 누구인지 드러나지 않게 될 것이며 이름과 장소의 명칭을 변경하여 외부독자로 부터 보호받게 되실 것입니다.

Confidentiality:

Your part in this study is confidential. None of the information will identify you by name. All records will be available only to myself, the researcher, and will be saved and backed up digitally and will be password protected. All handwritten documentation will be transcribed digitally, and the hard copies will be disposed of. Only after names and places have been changed will any findings or data be revealed or available to any outside party.

자발적 참여와 참여 취소:

이 리서치의 참여는 자발적으로만 진행됩니다. 여러분에게는 이 리서치를 거절할 권리가 있으십니다. 만일 참여하시기로 결정하셨다가 마음이 바뀌시면, 어떤 시점에서라도 취소하실 수 있습니다. 또한 어떤 질문에도 답하지 않으시고 넘어가실 수 도 있습니다. 무엇을 결정하시던지 개인에게 어떠한 피해가 가지 않습니다.

Voluntary participation and withdrawal:

Participation in research is voluntary. You have the right to refuse to be in this study. If you decide to be in the study and change your mind, you have the right to drop out at any time. You may skip questions. Whatever you decide, you will not lose any benefits to which you are otherwise entitled.

Appendix D: Informed Consent Form

질문, 권리 그리고 항의:

만일 이 리서치 프로젝트에 대해 어떠한 질문이 있으시면 Jinna Jin 진실로 626-584-5596이나 jinnajin@fuller.edu로 연락하실 수 있습니다. 만일 참여자로 이 리서치에 대해 질문이나 걱정이 있으시면 선교연구센터 디렉터 David Scott (626-584-5269, cmr@fuller.edu)으로 연락하시면 됩니다.

Questions, Rights, and Complaints:

If you have any questions about this research project, please call Jinna Jin at 626-584-5596 or email at jinnajin@fuller.edu. If you have any questions or concerns about your rights as a research participant in this study, please direct them to David Scott, CMR Associate Director at the School of Intercultural Studies (626.584.5269, email: cmr@fuller.edu);

동의서:

이 동의서는 여러분이 18세 이상이고 이 동의서를 잘 읽으셨으며 여러분이 가지고 계신 모든 질문이 해결되었음을 동의하는 문서입니다. 또한 여러분께서는 어떤 시점에서라도 참여를 취소하실 수 있으며 그로인해 어떤 피해도 받지 않게 됨을 이해하신다는 것을 동의한다는 문서입니다. 연구자 Jinna Jin, 진실로 에게 답하게 되시는 모든 답은 보안이 유지됩니다. 또한 이 논문이 출판되기 전에 결과를 보실 수 있는 권리가 있습니다.

Consent Statement

This statement certifies the following: that you are 18 years of age or older and you have read the consent and all your questions have been answered. You understand that you may withdraw from the study at any time, and that you will not lose any of the benefits that you would otherwise receive by withdrawing early. All of the answers you provide to Jinna Jin will be kept private. You should know that you have the right to see the results prior to their being published.

Appendix D: Informed Consent Form

I consent to participating in being involved in an interview about Korean-speaking emerging adults being conducted by Jinna Jin. 나는 Jinna Jin 진실로가 진행하는 한어 청년에 대한 연구에 참석함을 동의합니다.

_____   _____
Signature of Participant 참석자 서명   Date 날짜

_____   A copy of the informed consent
Typed/Printed Name 참석자 이름   will be given to you. 동의서 복사본이 여러분께 제공됩니다.

Appendix E

In-depth Interview Questions with Korean-Speaking Young Adults

Age

Occupation

Gender

Arriving age

   A. Migration experience (if applicable)[1]

   1. Life in Korea

      - 한국을 떠나시기전의 생활에 대해서 설명해주실수 있으세요? (살았던 동네, 가족, 교육, 일, 먼저 이민온 가족등). Can you tell me something about what your life was like before you left Korea? (Area where you lived, family, education, work, history of migration in your family)

   2. Migration experience

      - 미국으로의 이주경험을 설명해주실수 있으세요? 왜 그리고 어떻게 오시게 되셨나요? (이유, 국가 선택의 이유, 가족과의 관계) Can you describe why and how you migrated? (Reasons, choice of country, family networks/came alone)

      - 오셨을때 어떤 비자로 오셨어요? What visa status did you have when entering the U.S.?

   ---

   1. If the interviewee was born in the States, I will ask about the migration experience of his/her parents.

Appendix E: Questions with Korean-speaking Young Adults

- 지금은 어떤 비자를 가지고 계세요? What visa status do you hold at this moment?

3. Settling in the United States

    - 처음에 미국에 왔을때의 경험을 이야기 해주실수 있으세요? Can you tell me about your first experiences of moving to the United States?
    - 어떤 기분이셨어요? How did you feel?
    - 이곳에 가족이 이미 계셨었나요? Did you have family already in the United States?
    - 처음 정착할때 도움이 된 사람들이나 공동체가 있었나요? Were there any particular people and/or community that helped you during the initial period?

4. Education (if any, formally)

    - 이곳에서 공부한 경험을 나누어 주실수 있으세요? (학교 친구들과 교수들과의 관계, 어려움, 공부 프로그램, 도움들, 차별들) Can you share with me about your experiences of studying in school? (Relationship with peers and teachers, challenges, programs, cares, discrimination)

5. Work (if you have a job)

    - 이곳에서 일한 경험에 대해서 나누어 주실 수 있으세요? (시간, 일의 양, 트레이닝, 차별, 일하는 환경) Can you share with me about your work experience? (Hours, workload, training, discrimination, working environment)

B. Ties with Korea

1. Family and friends

    - 한국에 중요한 사람들이 있으세요? Do you have significant others in Korea?
    - 그들과 어떻게 연락하세요? (얼마나 자주 그리고 어떤 방법으로?) How do you keep in touch with them? (How often and in what ways?)

Appendix E: Questions with Korean-speaking Young Adults

- 한국에 혹은 한국으로 부터 돈이나 물건을 받거나 보내신적이 있으세요? Do/did you send any money or goods to/from Korea? (If so, to whom and for what purpose?)

2. Church

    - 한국에서 다녔던 교회와 연결이 있으세요? Do you have any connections from Korean churches you attended?
    - 있으시다면 어떻게 연락하세요? If so, with whom and how do you keep in touch?
    - 그 교회로부터 지속적인 영향을 받고 계세요? Do you have any interactions with your church in Korea?

3. Media

    - 한국 미니어와 얼나나 자주 연결하세요? (이떤 이유로 그리고 어떻게?) How often do you connect to Korean media? (For what and how?)

4. Visiting

    - 한국에 얼마나 자주 방문하세요? 어떤 이유로? How often do you go back to Korea? For what purpose?

5. Returning plan

    - 한국에 돌아가실 계획을 가지고 계신가요? 왜요? Do you expect to go back to Korea? Why?

C. Experiencing American culture

1. Relationship

    - 미국인들과 개인적으로 어떤 관계를 가지고 계세요? What types of personal relationships do you have with Americans?

2. Media

    - 얼마나 자주 미국 미디어와 연결하세요? (어떤 이유로 그리고 어떻게?) How often do you connect to American media? (For what purpose and how?)

Appendix E: Questions with Korean-speaking Young Adults

    3. Cultural assimilation

- 어떤때 그리고 어떤 방법으로 내가 미국문화에 동화되어가고 있다고 생각하세요? When and in what ways do you feel you are assimilating into American culture?

  D. Church experience

    1. Church experience in Korea

- 한국에서도 교회를 다니셨나요? Were you a church member in Korea?
- 얼마나 자주 교회에 다니셨어요? How often did you attend church in Korea?
- 이민교회와 비교했을때 한국교회만이 가지는 점이 있다면 어떤게 있을까요? What are the unique characteristics of churches in Korea, as compared to Korean immigrant churches in the United States?
- 종교적인 이유말고 교회를 다니셨던 이유가 있으셨나요? Did you attend church for any reasons apart from religious reasons?

    2. Previous Church experience in the States

- 미국에서 경험하셨던 교회에 대해서 설명해주세요. Please share your experience of church in the U.S.
- 지금 교회에 정착하기전에 얼마나 많은 교회에 다녀보셨나요? How many churches did you go before you settled in your current church?
- 교회를 옮겨보신적이 있다면 어떤 이유로 그러셨고 또 어떻게 새 교회를 찾으셨나요? If you have changed churches, what were the reasons and how did you find a new church?
- 한국 교회와 비교했을때 어떤 점이 이민교회의 독특한 점일까요? What are the unique characteristics of Korean immigrant churches, as compared to churches in Korea?

Appendix E: Questions with Korean-speaking Young Adults

- 종교적인 이유말고 교회를 다니시는 이유가 있으신가요? Do you attend your church for any reasons apart from religious reasons?

3. Current church experience

    - 출석하시는 교회에 대해 설명해주세요. Please describe the church you are currently attending.
    - 이 교회에 출석하신지는 얼마나 되셨나요? How long have you attended your current church?
    - 이 교회를 선택하신 이유들이 있으신가요? What are the reasons you chose this church?
    - 출석하시는 한어 대학 청년부에 대해 설명해주세요. Please describe the Korean-speaking young adult department you are currently attending.
    - 교회에 출석하는 한어 대학 청년들에 대해 설명해주세요. Please describe the Korean-speaking young adults in your church.
    - 한어 청년들이 이민 교회에 출석하는 이유는 무엇이라고 생각하세요? What do you think are the reasons why Korean-speaking emerging adults attend Korean immigrant churches?
    - 청년부 안에 관계의 다이나믹에 대해서 설명해주세요. Please describe the relational dynamic in your Korean-speaking young adult department.
    - 한어 대학 청년들이 한국에 있는 청년들, 이민교회의 장년들 그리고 영어권 청년들과 비교하여 어떤 부분들이 유사한지요? What are the similarities that Korean-speaking young adults demonstrate, as compared to the Korean-speaking older generation and English-speaking Koreans in your church, as well as to young adults in Korea?
    - 한어 대학 청년들이 한국에 있는 청년들, 이민교회의 장년들 그리고 영어권 청년들과 비교하여 어떤 부분들이 다른지요? What are the differences that Korean-speaking young adults demonstrate, as compared to the Korean-speaking

Appendix E: Questions with Korean-speaking Young Adults

older adults and English-speaking Koreans in your church, as well as to young adults in Korea?

- 다른 부서에 속하신 어른들이나 다른 분들과의 관계에 대해서 대해서 설명해주세요. Please tell me about the relationship between the Korean-speaking young adult department and other departments, such as adult congregation.

- 한어 청년들을 더 잘 섬기기 위해서 한인 이민 교회에 필요한 것은 어떤 것들이 있을까요? What are those things that the Korean immigrant church needs to do to serve Korean-speaking young adults better?

Appendix F

Informed Consent Form

Fuller Theological Seminary
School of Theology

저는 풀러신학교에서 Chap Clark 교수님 밑에서 박사과정 논문을 쓰는 중이고 저의 논문을 위해 자료를 수집하고 있습니다. 바쁘시겠지만 여러분께서 이 리서치에 참여해주시기를 부탁드립니다. 아래에 리서치에 대한 디테일을 설명드리겠지만 혹시 질문이 있으시면 주저말고 알려주시고 혹은 나중에라도 질문이 있으시면 기쁘게 답해드리도록 하겠습니다.

My name is Jinna Sil Lo Jin, and I am collecting research as part of my doctoral degree at Fuller Theological Seminary under faculty advisor Dr. Chap Clark. I would like to invite you to participate in a research project described below. I will explain this document to you in detail. Please feel free to ask questions. If you have more questions later, I will be happy to discuss them with you at any time.

프로젝트 설명:

한어 청년부서가 거의 모든 한인 이민교회에 있지만 실제로 이 한어 청년들에 대한 연구가 거의 이루어 지지 않고 있습니다. 이 연구를 통해 보다 한어 청년들에 대한 정확하고 온전한 이해가 이루어져 사역에 도움이 되고자 합니다.

이 논문에 사용하고자 한어 청년부를 섬기시는 청년들과 인터뷰를 실행하려고 합니다. 바쁘시겠지만 참여해주시기를 부탁드립니다.

Appendix F: Informed Consent Form

이 리서치 중에서 여러분이 참석하시게 될 부분은 심층 인터뷰 입니다. 본 연구의 목적은 아래와 같습니다.

1. 한인 이민교회 안에 한어 청년들에 대한 이해
2. 현재 한인 이민교회가 어떻게 한어 청년들을 사역하고 있는지에 대한 이해
3. 어떻게 하면 한인 이민 교회가 한어 청년들을 보다 더 잘 섬길 수 있을 것인지에 대한 고찰

이 연구의 목적은 한인 이민 교회안에 한어 청년들에 대한 보다 깊은 이해에 있으며 특별히 이 인터뷰를 통해서는 여러분의 이민경험과 이민교회의 경험에 대해 여쭙게 될 것입니다.

Description of the Project:

Although almost every Korean immigrant church has a Korean-speaking young adult ministry, almost no research has been done about this population. With this research, I hope to provide an accurate and holistic understanding of this important group of people so that we can serve them better.

You were invited to participate in this study because you are currently attending a Korean-speaking emerging adult ministry.

The current study invites you to participate in an in-depth interview. The goals of this study are:

1. *To understand who are the Korean-speaking young adults in Korean immigrant churches.*
2. *To identify the current practices of Korean immigrant church ministry for Korean-speaking young adults.*
3. *To understand how Korean immigrant churches can serve Korean-speaking young adults in a holistic way.*

The purpose of this study is to gain a deeper understanding of Korean young adults in Korean immigrant churches. More specifically, the survey will ask questions about your migration experience and church experience

절차:

만일 참여하시기로 결정을 하시게되면 다음과 같은 절차로 이루어집니다; 연구자와 한번 90분동안 만나셔서 인터뷰를 하시게 됩니다. 인

Appendix F: Informed Consent Form

터뷰 동안에는 제가 질문을 하게 될 것이며 여러분들은 한어 청년으로 여러분들의 경험을 나누시게 될 것입니다. 구체적으로, 이민경험, 이민교회 경험, 한국과의 관계 등에 대해서 나누게 될 것입니다.

Procedures:

If you decide to take part in this study here is what will happen: I will meet you for a 90-minute interview. I will ask questions, and we will all discuss together your migration experience, church experience, and ties with Korea. This session will be recorded, and I will take notes during the discussion. After the session, my research team and I will listen to the recording to transcribe and take notes on what we discussed.

위험 혹은 불편 요소:

본 리서치는 최소위험수치의 연구입니다. 모든 질문에 대답은 전적으로 여러분의 자유에 있으며 특정한 질문에 대해 대답하지 않으셔도 됩니다.

Risks or Discomfort:

There is minimal risk with being involved with this research study. Answering questions is completely up to you, and you may skip questions or withdraw at any time.

이 연구의 혜택:

이 포커스 그룹에 참여하심으로서 얻으시는 직접적인 혜택은 없으나, 연구자가 한어 청년 사역을 더 깊이 이해 할 수 있습니다. 또한 이 리서치의 결과는 논문을 통해 집합적으로 발표되게 될 것입니다.

Benefits of This Study:

Although there will be no direct benefit to you for taking part in this study, the researcher may learn more about the current ministry of Korean-speaking emerging adults. Furthermore, the research will share the aggregative results of the survey through the dissertation.

Appendix F: Informed Consent Form

비밀 및 익명보장:

이 리서치에 대한 여러분의 참여는 철저히 비밀이 보장됩니다. 여러분에 대한 어떤 정보도 유출 되지 않을 것입니다. 어떠한 자료도 연구자인 저 외에는 볼 수가 없으며 디지털로 저장된 모든 자료에는 비밀번호가 함께 붙여지게 되어 다른 사람에게 쉽게 노출 되지 않을 것입니다. 손으로 작성된 문서들은 디지털 문서로 곧 변환되며 손으로 작성된 문서는 폐기 될 것입니다. 리서치를 통한 결과를 통해 참석자가 누구인지 드러나지 않게 될 것이며 이름과 장소의 명칭을 변경하여 외부독자로 부터 보호받게 되실 것입니다.

Confidentiality:

Your part in this study is confidential. None of the study information will identify you by name. All records will be available only to the research team and will be saved and backed up digitally and will be password protected. All handwritten documentation will be transcribed digitally, and the hard copies will be disposed of. Only after names and places have been changed will any findings or data be revealed or available to any outside party.

자발적 참여와 참여 취소:

이 리서치의 참여는 자발적으로만 진행됩니다. 여러분에게는 이 리서치를 거절할 권리가 있으십니다. 만일 참여하시기로 결정하셨다가 마음이 바뀌시면, 어떤 시점에서라도 취소하실 수 있습니다. 또한 어떤 질문에도 답하지 않으시고 넘어가실 수 도 있습니다. 무엇을 결정하시던지 개인에게 어떠한 피해가 가지 않습니다.

Voluntary Participation and Withdrawal:

Participation in research is voluntary. You have the right to refuse to be in this study. If you decide to be in the study and change your mind, you have the right to drop out at any time. You may skip questions.

질문, 권리 그리고 항의:

만일 이 리서치 프로젝트에 대해 어떠한 질문이 있으시면 Jinna Jin 진실로 626-584-5596이나 jinnajin@fuller.edu로 연락하실 수 있습니다. 만일 참여자로 이 리서치에 대해 질문이나 걱정이 있으시면 선교연구센터 디렉터 David Scott (626-584-5269, cmr@fuller.edu)으로 연락하시면 됩니다.

Appendix F: Informed Consent Form

Questions, Rights, and Complaints:

If you have any questions about this research project, please call Jinna Jin at 626-584-5596 or email at jinnajin@fuller.edu. If you have any questions or concerns about your rights as a research participant in this study, please direct them to David Scott, CMR Associate Director at the School of Intercultural Studies (626.584.5269, email: cmr@fuller.edu);

동의서:

이 동의서는 여러분이 18세 이상이고 이 동의서를 잘 읽으셨으며 여러분이 가지고 계신 모든 질문이 해결되었음을 동의하는 문서입니다. 또한 여러분께서는 어떤 시점에서라도 참여를 취소하실 수 있으며 그로인해 어떤 피해도 받지 않게 됨을 이해하신다는 것을 동의한다는 문서입니다. 연구자 Jinna Jin, 진실로 에게 답하게 되시는 모든 답은 보안이 유지됩니다. 또한 이 논문이 출판되기 전에 결과를 보실 수 있는 권리가 있습니다.

Consent Statement

This statement certifies the following: that you are 18 years of age or older and you have read the consent and all your questions have been answered. You understand that you may withdraw from the study at any time. All of the answers you provide to Jinna Jin will be kept private. You should know that you have the right to see the results prior to their being published.

I consent to participating in being involved in an interview about Korean-speaking emerging adults being conducted by Jinna Jin. 나는 Jinna Jin 진실로가 진행하는 한어 청년에 대한 연구에 참석함을 동의합니다.

_____   _____
Signature of Participant 참석자 서명   Date 날짜

_____   A copy of the informed consent
Typed/Printed Name 참석자 이름   will be given to you. 동의서 복사본이 여러분께 제공됩니다.

Bibliography

ENGLISH TEXT

Akhtar, Salman. *Listening to Others*. Lanham, MD: Aronson, 2007.
Alba, R. D., and Victor Nee. *Remaking the American Mainstream: Assimilation and Contemporary Immigration*. Cambridge: Harvard University Press, 2003.
Anderson, Ray. *The Shape of Practical Theology: Empowering Ministry with Theological Praxis*. Downers Grove, IL: IVP Academic, 2001.
———. *The Soul of Ministry: Forming Leaders for God's People*. Louisville: Westminster John Knox, 1997.
Arnett, Jeffrey. "Emerging Adulthood: A Theory of Development from the Late Teens through the Twenties." *American Psychologist* 55.5 (2000) 469–80.
———. "Emerging Adulthood: What Is It, and What Is It Good For?" *Society for Research in Child Development* 1.2 (2007) 68–73.
———. *Emerging Adulthood: The Winding Road from the Late Teens through the Twenties* 2nd ed. New York: Oxford University Press, 2014.
Baker, Don. "The Transformation of Confucianism in Contemporary Korea—How It Has Lost Most of Its Metaphysical Underpinnings and Survives Today Primarily as Ethical Rhetoric and Heritage Rituals." *Keimyung Korean Studies Journal* 44 (2011) 425–55.
Barry, Carolyn McNamara, and Mona M. Abo-Zena. "Emerging Adults' Religious and Spiritual Development." In *Emerging Adults' Religiousness and Spirituality: Meaning-Making in an Age of Transition*, edited by Carolyn McNamara Barry and Mona M. Abo-Zena, 21–38. New York: Oxford University Press, 2014.
Bedford, Nancy. "Protestantism in Migration: *Ecclesia Semper Migrada*." In *Theology of Migration in the Abrahamic Religions*, edited by Eliane Padilla and Peter C. Phan, 111–31. New York: Palgrave Macmillan, 2014.
Birman, Dina. "Ethical Issues in Research with Immigrants and Refugees." In *The Handbook of Ethical Research with Ethnocultural Populations & Communities*, edited by Joseph E. Trimble and Celia B. Fisher, 155–77. Thousand Oaks, CA: Sage, 2006.
Bosch, David Jacobus. *Transforming Mission: Paradigm Shifts in Theology of Mission*. Maryknoll, NY: Orbis, 1991.

Bibliography

Branson, Mark Lau. *Memories, Hopes, and Conversations*. 2nd ed. Herndon, VA.: Alban Institute, 2004.

———. "Perspectives from the Missional Conversation." In *Starting Missional Churches: Life with God in the Neighborhood*, edited by Mark Lau Branson and Nicholas Warnes, 28–47. Downers Grove, IL: IVP Books, 2014.

Branson, Mark Lau, and Juan F. Martínez. *Churches, Cultures, and Leadership: A Practical Theology of Congregations and Ethnicities*. Downers Grove, IL: IVP Academic, 2011.

Browning, Don. *A Fundamental Practical Theology: Descriptive and Strategic Proposals*. Minneapolis: Fortress, 1996.

Bryant, Alyssa N., and Helen S. Astin. "The Correlates of Spiritual Struggle during the College Years." *The Journal of Higher Education* 79.1 (2008) 1–27.

Budde, Michael L. *The Borders of Baptism*. Eugene, OR: Cascade, 2011.

Campese, Gioacchino. "But I See That Somebody Is Missing." In *Ecclesiology and Exclusion: Boundaries of Being and Belonging in Postmodern Times*, edited by Dennis M. Doyle et al., 71–92. Maryknoll, NY: Orbis, 2012.

———. "The Irruption of Migrants: Theology of Migration in the 21st Century." *Theological Studies* 73.1 (2012) 3–32.

———. "Theologies of Migration: Present and Future Perspectives." In *Migration als Ort der Theologie*, edited by Tobias Kefller, 167–88. Regensburg: Friedrich Pustet, 2014.

Catterton Allen, Holly, and Christine Lawton Ross. *Intergenerational Christian Formation*. Downers Grove, IL: IVP Academic, 2012.

Cavanauch, William T. *Migration of the Holy*. Grand Rapids: Eerdmans, 2011.

Cha, Peter, et al., eds. *Growing Healthy Asian American Churches: Ministry Insights from Groundbreaking Congregations*. Downers Grove, IL: IVP Books, 2006.

Charmaz, Kathy. *Constructing Grounded Theory: A Practical Guide through Qualitative Analysis*. Thousand Oaks, CA: Sage, 2006.

Choi, Hee An. *A Postcolonial Self*. Albany: State University of New York Press, 2015.

Choi, Karen. "Beyond 'Strictness' to Distinctiveness: Generational Transition in Korean Protestant Churches." In *Korean Americans and Their Religious: Pilgrims and Missionaries*, edited by Ho Young Kwon et al., 157–79. University Park: Pennsylvania State University Press, 2001.

———. "Competing for Second Generation: English-Language Ministry at a Korean Protestant Church." In *Gathering in Diaspora: Religious Communities and the New Immigration*, edited by Stephen Warner and Judith Wittner, 295–332. Philadelphia: Temple University Press, 1998.

Chong, Kelly. *Deliverance and Submission: Evangelical Women and the Negotiation of Patriarchy in South Korea*. Cambridge: Harvard University Press, 2008.

"A Chronicle of the Last 100 Years." http://the.honoluluadvertiser.com/specials/Korean100/timeline/.

Chung, Sinai. "A Review of 'A Postcolonial Self: Korean Immigrant Theology and Church.'" *Religious Education* 111.2 (2016) 223–24.

Clark, Chap, ed. *Adoptive Youth Ministry: Integrating Emerging Generations into the Family of Faith*. Grand Rapids: Baker Academic, 2016.

———. *Hurt 2.0: Inside the World of Today's Teenagers*. Grand Rapids: Baker, 2011.

———. "Youth Ministry as Practical Theology." *Journal of Youth Ministry* 7.1 (2008) 9–38.

Clark, Chap, and Dee Clark. *Disconnected*. Grand Rapids: Baker, 2007.

Commission on Theological Concerns. *Minjung Theology: People as the Subjects of History*. Maryknoll, NY: Orbis, 1983.

Bibliography

Connor, Philip. "6 Facts about South Korea's Growing Christian Population." *Pew Research Center*, August 12, 2014. http://www.pewresearch.org/fact-tank/2014/08/12/6-facts-about-christianity-in-south-korea/.

Côté, James E. "The Dangerous Myth of Emerging Adulthood: An Evidence-Based Critique of a Flawed Developmental Theory." *Applied Developmental Science* 18.4 (2014) 177–88.

Cooperrider, David, and Suresh Srivastva. "Appreciative Inquiry in Organizational Life." *Research in Organizational Change and Development* 1 (1987) 129–69.

Cooperrider, David, et al. *Appreciative Inquiry Handbook*. Brunswick, OH: Crown Custom, 2008.

Creighton, Millie R. "Revisiting Shame and Guilt Cultures: A Forty-Year Pilgrimage." *Ethos* 18.3 (1990) 279–307.

Creswell, John W. *Research Design: Qualitative, Quantitative, and Mixed Methods Approaches*. 3rd ed. Thousand Oaks, CA: Sage, 2009.

Cummings-Bond, Stuart. "The One-Eared Mickey Mouse." *Youth Worker Journal* (1989) 76–78.

Danico, Mary Yu. *The 1.5 Generation: Becoming Korean American in Hawaii*. Honolulu: University of Hawai'i Press, 2004.

De La Torre, Miguel A. *Doing Christian Ethics from the Margins*. 2nd ed. Maryknoll, NY: Orbis, 2014.

Dean, Kenda C. *Almost Christian: What the Faith of Our Teenagers Is Telling the American Church*. New York: Oxford University Press, 2010.

Deck, Allan Figueroa. "A Christian Perspective on the Reality of Illegal Immigration." *Social Thought* 4 (1978) 39–53.

DeVries, Mark. *Family-Based Youth Ministry: Reaching the Been-There, Done-That Generation*. Downers Grove, IL: InterVarsity, 1994.

Diaz, Miguel H. "On Loving Strangers: Encountering the Mystery of God in the Face of Migrants." *Word and World* 29 (2009) 238–39.

Ebaugh, Helen Rose. "Transnationality and Religion in Immigrant Congregations." *Nordic Journal of Religion and Society* 23.2 (2010) 105–19.

Everist, Norma. *The Church as a Learning Community*. Nashville: Abingdon, 2002.

Exline, Julie J., et al. "Guilt, Discord, and Alienation: The Role of Religious Strain in Depression and Suicidality." *Journal of Clinical Psychology* 56.12 (2000) 1481–96.

Faist, Thomas, et al. *Transnational Migration*. Malden, MA: Polity, 2013.

Fifield, Anna. "Young South Koreans Call Their Country 'Hell' and Look for Ways Out." *The Washington Post*, January 31, 2016. https://www.washingtonpost.com/world/asia_pacific/young-south-koreans-call-their-country-hell-and-look-for-ways-out/2016/01/30/34737c06-b967-11e5-85cd-5ad59bc19432_story.html.

Flick, Uwe. *An Introduction to Qualitative Research*. Los Angeles, CA: Sage, 2009.

Garland, Diana S. Richmond. *Family Ministry: A Comprehensive Guide*. 2nd ed. Downers Grove, IL: IVP Academic, 2012.

George, Kondothra M. "Theology of Migration in the Orthodox Tradition." In *Theology of Migration in the Abrahamic Religions*, edited by Eilane Padilla and Peter C. Phan, 63–76. New York: Palgrave Macmillan, 2014.

Gerschutz, Jill Marie, and Donald Kerwin. *And You Welcomed Me: Migration and Catholic Social Teaching*, edited by Donald Kerwin and Jill Marie Gerschutz. Lanham: MD: Lexington, 2009.

Bibliography

Goette, Robert. "The Transformation of a First-Generation Church into a Bilingual Second-Generation Church." In *Korean Americans and Their Religions: Pilgrims and Missionaries*, edited by Ho Young Kwon et al., 125–40. University Park: Pennsylvania State University Press, 2001.

Good, Marie, et al. "Just Another Club? The Distinctiveness of the Relation between Religious Service Attendance and Adolescent Psychosocial Adjustment." *Journal of Youth and Adolescence* 38.9 (2009) 1153–71.

Groody, Daniel G. "Crossing the Divine: Foundations of a Theology of Migration and Refugees." *Theological Studies* 70 (2009) 642–43.

———. "Jesus and the Undocumented Immigrant: A Spiritual Geography of Crucified People." *Theological Studies* 70 (2009) 314–16.

Groome, Thomas H. *Sharing Faith*. San Francisco: HarperSanFrancisco, 1991.

Gordon, Milton M. *Assimilation in American Life: The Role of Race, Religion, and National Origins*. New York: Oxford University Press, 1964.

Guder, Darrell L. *Missional Church: A Vision for the Sending of the Church in North America*. Grand Rapids: Eerdmans, 1998.

Haah, Kevin. "A Beautiful Community of Diversity: New City Church." In *Starting Missional Churches: Life with God in the Neighborhood*, edited by Mark Lau Branson and Nicholas Warnes, 86–105. Downers Grove, IL: IVP Books, 2014.

Hall, Barry L., and Judith C. Kulig. "Kanadier Mennonites: A Case Study Examining Research Challenges among Religious Groups." *Qualitative Health Research* 14.3 (2004) 359–68.

Hanciles, Jehu J. *Beyond Christendom*. Maryknoll, NY: Orbis, 2008.

———. "Migration and Mission: Some Implications for the Twenty-First-Century Church." *International Bulletin of Missionary Research* 27.4 (2003) 146–53.

———. "Transformations within Global Christianity and the Western Missionary Enterprise." *Mission Focus: Annual Review* 14 (2006) 4–27.

Hendry, Leo B., and Marion Kloep. "How Universal Is Emerging Adulthood? An Example." *Journal of Youth Studies* 13.2 (2010) 169–79.

Hersch, Patricia. *A Tribe Apart: A Journey into the Heart of American Adolescence*. New York: Ballantine, 1999.

Hertig, Young Lee. *Cultural Tug of War: The Korean Immigrant Family and Church in Transition*. Nashville: Abingdon, 2001.

Heo, Chun Hoi. *Multicultural Christology*. New York: Lang, 2003.

Hirchman, Charles. "The Role of Religion in the Origins and Adaptation of Immigrant Groups in the United States." *International Migration Review* 38 (2004) 1206–33.

Hoeffel, Elizabeth, et al. "The Asian Population: 2010." https://www.census.gov/prod/cen2010/briefs/c2010br-11.pdf.

Hurh, Won Moo, and Kwang Chung Kim. "Religious Participation of Korean Immigrants in the United States." *Journal for the Scientific Study of Religion* 29.1 (1990) 19–34.

Im, Chandler. "The Korean Diaspora Churches in the USA: Their Concerns and Strengths." In *Global Diasporas and Mission*, edited by Chandler Im and Amos Yong, 130–47. Oxford: Regnum, 2014.

Im, Chandler, and John Jungho Oh. "Trends and Issues from the Korean Diaspora Churches in the USA." In *Scattered and Gathered: A Global Compendium of Diaspora Missiology*, edited by Sadiri Joy Tira and Tetsunao Yamamori, 314–26. Eugene, OR: Wipf and Stock, 2016.

Joh, Wonhee. *Heart of the Cross*. Louisville: Westminster John Knox, 2006.

Joiner, Reggie, et al. *Creating a Lead Small Culture: Make Your Church a Place Where Kids Belong*. Cumming, GA: Orange, 2014.

Kadison, Richard, and Theresa Digernimo. *College of the Overwhelmed: The Campus Mental Health Crisis and What to Do about It*. San Francisco CA: Jossey-Bass, 2004.

Kang, Hyeyoung, and Marcela Raffaelli. "Personalizing Immigrant Sacrifices: Internalization of Sense of Indebtedness toward Parents among Korean American Young Adults." *Journal of Family Issues* 37.10 (2016) 1331–54.

Kang, Hyeyoung, and Reed W. Larson. "Sense of Indebtedness toward Parents: Korean American Emerging Adults' Narratives of Parental Sacrifice." *Journal of Adolescent Research* 29.4 (2014) 561–81.

Keohane, Robert, and Joseph Nye. *Transnational Relations and World Politics*. Cambridge: Harvard University Press, 1972.

Kerwin, Donald, and Jill Marie Gerschutz, eds. *And You Welcomed Me: Migration and Catholic Social Teaching*. Lanham, MD: Lexington, 2009.

Kim, Kwang Chung, and Shin Kim. "The Ethnic Role of Korean Immigrant Churches in the United States." In *Korean Americans and Their Religions: Pilgrims and Missionaries*, edited by Ho Young Kwon et al., 71–94. University Park: Pennsylvania State University Press, 2001.

Kim, Sharon. *A Faith of Our Own: Second-Generation Spirituality in Korean American Churches*. New Brunswick, NJ: Rutgers University Press, 2010.

———. "Hybrid Spiritualities: The Development of Second Generation Korean American Spirituality." *Human Architecture: The Journal of the Sociology of Self Knowledge* 4.2 (2006) 225–38.

Kirk, Daphne. *Heirs Together: Establishing Intergenerational Church*. Rev. ed. Suffold: Mayhew, 2003.

Kirk, Donald. "What 'Korean Miracle'? 'Hell Joseon' Is More Like It Is as Economy Flounders." *Forbes*, February 27, 2016. https://www.forbes.com/sites/donaldkirk/2016/02/27/what-korean-miracle-hell-joseon-is-more-like-it-as-economy-flounders/?sh=3aa8cd214dba.

Kwon, Victoria Hyonchu. "Houston Korean Ethnic Church: An Ethnic Enclave." In *Religion and the New Immigrants*, edited by Helen Rose Ebaugh and Janet Saltzman Chafetz, 109–24. Walnut Creek, CA: AltaMira, 2000.

Lee, Helen. "Silent Exodus." *Christianity Today*, August 12, 1996. http://www.christianitytoday.com/ct/1996/august12/6t9o50.html.

Lee, Jung Young. *Marginality: The Key to Multicultural Theology*. Minneapolis: Fortress, 1995.

Lee, Sang Hyun. "Called to Be Pilgrims." In *Korean American Ministry*, edited by Sang Hyun Lee and John V. Moore, 37–74. Louisville, KY: General Assembly Council, Presbyterian Church U.S.A., 1993.

———. *From a Liminal Place: An Asian American Theology*. Minneapolis: Fortress, 2010.

———. "Pilgrimage and Home in the Wilderness of Marginality." In *Asian Americans and Christian Ministry*, edited by Inn Sook Lee and Timothy D. Son, 75–88. Seoul: Voice, 1999.

Lee, Song-Chong. "Revisiting the Confucian Norms in Korean Church Growth." *International Journal of Humanities and Social Science* 1.13 (2011) 87–103.

Lefkowitz, Eva, et al. "Religiosity, Sexual Behaviors, and Sexual Attitudes during Emerging Adulthood." *The Journal of Sex Research* 41.2 (2004) 150–59.

Levitt, Peggy. *The Transnational Villagers*. Berkeley: University of California Press, 2001.

Bibliography

Levitt, Peggy, and Nadya B. Jaworsky. "Transnational Migration Studies: Past Developments and Future Trends." *Annual Review of Sociology* 33 (2007) 129–56.

Levitt, Peggy, and Nina Glick Schiller. "Conceptualizing Simultaneity: A Transnational Social Field Perspective on Society." *International Migration Review* 38.3 (2004) 1002–39.

Liamputtong, Pranne. "Doing Research in a Cross-Cultural Context: Methodological and Ethical Challenges." In *Doing Cross-Cultural Research*, edited by Pranne Liamputtong, 3–20. Social Indicators Research Series. Dordrecht: Springer, 3–20.

———. *Performing Qualitative Cross-Cultural Research*. New York: Cambridge University Press, 2010.

Lipka, Michael. "Millennials Increasingly Are Driving Growth of 'Nones.'" *Pew Research Center*, May 12, 2015. https://www.pewresearch.org/fact-tank/2015/05/12/millennials-increasingly-are-driving-growth-of-nones/.

Lopez, Hugo. "Toward a Theology of Migration." *Apuntes* 2 (1982) 68–71.

Magyar-Russell, Gina, et al. "Potential Benefits and Detriments of Religiousness and Spirituality to Emerging Adults." In *Emerging Adults' Religiousness and Spirituality: Meaning-Making in an Age of Transition*, edited by Carolyn McNamara Barry and Mona M. Abo-Zena, 39–55. New York: Oxford University Press, 2014.

Mahoney, Annette, et al. "Religious Coping by Children and Adolescents: Unexplored Territory in the Realm of Spiritual Development." In *The Handbook of Spiritual Development in Childhood and Adolescence*, edited by Eugene C. Roehlkepartain et al., 341–54. Thousand Oaks, CA: Sage, 2006.

Martinez, Juan F. *Los Protestantes*. Santa Barbara, CA: Praeger, 2011.

Min, Pyong Gap. "A Comparison of Korean Protestant, Catholic, and Buddhist Religious Institutions in New York." In *Koreans in North America: Their Experiences in the Twenty-First Century*, edited by Pyong Gap Min, 75–102. Lanham, MD: Lexington, 2013.

———. "The Immigration of Koreans to the United States: A Review of a Forty-Five Year (1965–2009) Trend." In *Koreans in North America: Their Experiences in the Twenty-First Century*, edited by Pyong Gap Min, 9–34. Lanham, MD: Lexington, 2013.

———. "Introduction." In *Religions in Asian America: Building Faith Communities*, edited by Pyong Gap Min and Jung Ha Kim, 1–14. Walnut Creek, CA: AltaMira, 2002.

———. *Preserving Ethnicity through Religion in America: Korean Protestant and Indian Hindus across Generations*. New York: New York University Press, 2010.

———. "The Structure and Social Functions of Korean Immigrant Churches in the United States." *International Migration Review* 26.4 (1992) 1381–90.

Min, Pyong Gap, and Sou Hyun Jang. "The Diversity of Asian Immigrants' Participation in Religious Institutions in the United States." *Sociology of Religion* 76.3 (2015) 253–74.

Min, Pyong Gap, and Dae Young Kim. "Intergenerational Transmission of Religion and Culture: Korean Protestants in the U.S." *Sociology of Religion* 66.3 (2005) 263–82.

Naidoo, Marlin. "Spiritual Formation in Protestant Theological Institutions." In *Handbook of Theological Education in World Christianity*, edited by Dietrich Werner et al., 185–95. Oxford: Regnum, 2010.

OECD. "Enrolment Rate." https://data.oecd.org/eduatt/enrolment-rate.htm#indicator-chart.

O'Keefe, Theresa. "Growing Up Alone: The New Normal of Isolation in Adolesecence." *Journal of Youth Ministry* 13.1 (2014) 82.

Osmer, Richard Robert. *Practical Theology: An Introduction.* Grand Rapids: Eerdmans, 2008.
Papadopoulos, Irena, and Shelley Lees. "Developing Culturally Competent Researchers." *Journal of Advanced Nursing* 37.3 (2002) 258–64.
Park, Andrew Sung. *The Wounded Heart of God.* Nashville: Abingdon, 1993.
Park, Joon-Sik. "Korean Protestant Christianity: A Missiological Reflection." In *International Bulletin of Missionary Research* 36.2 (2012) 59–64.
Park, Mijung, and Catherine Chesla. "Revisiting Confucianism as a Conceptual Framework for Asian Family Study." *Journal of Family Nursing* 13.3 (2007) 293–311.
Pak, Su Yon, et al. *Singing the Lord's Song in a New Land: Korean American Practices of Faith.* Louisville: Westminster John Knox, 2005.
Phan, Peter. *Christianity with an Asian Face.* Maryknoll, NY: Orbis, 2003.
———. "Embracing, Protecting, and Loving the Stranger: A Roman Catholic Theology of Migration." In *Theology of Migration in the Abrahamic Religions*, edited by Eliane Padilla and Peter C. Phan, 77–110. New York: Palgrave Macmillan, 2014.
Portes, Alejandro. "Introduction: The Debates and Significance of Immigrant Transnationalism." *Global Networks* 1.3 (2001) 181–93.
Portes, Alejandro, and Ruben G. Rumbaut. *Immigrant America: A Portrait.* Berkeley, CA: University of California Press., 1996.
Proffitt, Anabel C. "Countering Commodification: A Review of Recent Research Writings on Youth, Young Adults, and Religion." https://nanopdf.com/download/countering-commodification-resources-for-american-christianity_pdf.
Rah, Soong-Chan, et al. *Honoring the Generations: Leading with Asian North American Congregations.* Valley Forge, PA: Judson, 2012.
"The Rise of Asian Americans." *Pew Research Center*, June 19, 2012. http://www.pewsocialtrends.org/2012/06/19/the-rise-of-asian-americans/.
Root, Andrew. *Christopraxis: A Practical Theology of the Cross.* Minneapolis: Fortress, 2014.
———. "Practical Theology: What Is It and How Does It Work?" *Journal of Youth Ministry* 7.2 (2009) 55–72.
Roxburgh, Alan. *Joining God, Remaking Church, Changing the World: The New Shape of the Church in Our Time.* New York: Morehouse, 2015.
———. *Missional: Joining God in the Neighborhood.* Grand Rapids: Baker, 2011.
Roxburgh, Alan, and Scott Boren. *Introducing the Missional Church: What It Is, Why It Matters, How to Become One.* Grand Rapids: Baker, 2009.
Rumbaut, Ruben G. "Ages, Life Stages, and Generational Cohorts: Decomposing the Immigrant First and Second Generations in the United States." *International Migration Review* 38.3 (2004) 1160–205.
Schiller, Nina Glick, et al. "Transnationalism: A New Analytic Framework for Understanding Migration." In *Towards a Transnational Perspective on Migration: Race, Class, Ethnicity, and Nationalism Reconsidered*, edited by Nina Glick Schiller et al., 1–24. New York: New York Academy of Sciences, 1992.
Schlegel, Alice. "Adolescent Ties to Adult Communities: The Intersection of Culture and Development." In *Bridging Cultural and Developmental Approaches to Psychology: New Syntheses in Theory, Research, and Policy*, edited by Lene Arnett Jensen, 138–60. New York: Oxford University Press, 2011.

Bibliography

Schoeni, Robert, and Karen Ross. "Material Assistance from Families during the Transition to Adulthood." In *On the Frontiers of Adulthood*, edited by Richard Settersten et al., 396–416. Chicago: University of Chicago Press, 2005.

Schoon, Ingrid, and S. John Schulenberg. "The Assumption of Adult Roles in the UK, the US, and Finland: Antecedents and Associated Levels of Well-Being and Health." In *Youth and Work Transitions in Changing Social Landscapes*, edited by Helena Helve and Karen Evans, 45–57. London: Tufnell, 2013.

Sheringham, Olivia. *Transnational Religious Spaces: Faith and the Brazilian Migration Experience*. Basingstoke: Palgrave Macmillan, 2013.

Śleziak, Tomasz. "The Role of Confucianism in Contemporary South Korean Society." *Rocznik Orientalistyczny* 1 (2013) 27–46.

Smith, Christian, and Melinda Lundquist Denton. *Soul Searching: The Religious and Spiritual Lives of American Teenagers*. New York: Oxford University Press, 2005.

Smith, Christian, and Patricia Snell. *Souls in Transition: The Religious and Spiritual Lives of Emerging Adults*. New York: Oxford University Press, 2009.

Smith, Christian, et al. *Lost in Transition: The Dark Side of Emerging Adulthood*. New York: Oxford University Press, 2011.

Snyder, Susanna. "Introduction: Moving Body." In *Church in an Age of Global Migration: A Moving Body*, edited by Susanna Snyder et al., 1–22. New York: Palgrave Macmillan, 2016.

Swinton, John, and Harriet Mowat. *Practical Theology and Qualitative Research*. 4th ed. London: SCM, 2006.

Tan, Jonathan Y. *Introducing Asian American Theologies*. Maryknoll, NY: Orbis, 2008.

Tanner, J. L., et al. "Emerging Adulthood: Learning and Development during the First Stage of Adulthood." In *Handbook of Research on Adult Learning and Development*, edited by M. Cecil Smith and Nancy DeFrates-Densch, 34–67. London: Routledge, 2009.

Teke, John, and Waleed Navaroo. "Nonimmigrant Admissions to the United States: 2015." https://www.dhs.gov/sites/default/files/publications/Nonimmigrant_Admissions_2015.pdf.

Twenge, Jean. *Generation Me: Why Today's Young Americans Are More Confident, Assertive, Entitled—And More Miserable Than Ever Before*. 2nd ed. New York: Free, 2014.

Underwood, Ralph. *Empathy and Confrontation in Pastoral Counseling*. Philadelphia: Fortress, 1985.

Van Gelder, Craig. *Missional Church in Context*. Grand Rapids: Eerdmans, 2007.

Vertovec, Steven. "Cheap Calls: The Social Glue of Migrant Transnationalism." *Global Networks* 4.2 (2004) 219–24.

Waks, Leonard J. *Listening to Teach*. Albany: State University of New York Press, 2015.

Walsh-Tapiata, Wheturangi. "A Model for Maori Research: Te whakaeke i te ao rangahau o te Maori." In *Making a Difference in Families: Research That Creates Changes*, edited by Robyn Munford and Jackie Sanders, 55–73. Sydney: Allen & Unwin, 2003.

Ward, Graham. "Belonging to the Church." In *Liturgy in Migration: From the Upper Room to Cyberspace*, edited by Teresa Berger, 1–18. Collegeville, MN: Liturgical, 2012.

Warner, W. Lloyd, and Leo Srole. *The Social Systems of American Ethnic Groups*. New Haven: Yale University Press, 1945.

Watkins, Jane Magruder, et al. *Appreciative Inquiry: Change at the Speed of Imagination*. San Francisco: Jossey-Bass, 2001.

Weinfurt, Kevin P., and Fathali M. Maghaddam. "Culture and Social Distance: A Case Study of Methodological Cautions." *The Journal of Social Psychology* 141 (2001) 101–10.

Yong, Amos. "The Im/migrant Spirit: De/constructing a Pentecostal Theology of Migration." In *Theology of Migration in the Abrahamic Religions*, edited by Eliane Padilla and Peter C. Phan, 133–54. New York: Palgrave Macmillan, 2014.

Yonker, Julie, et al. "The Relationship between Spirituality and Religiosity on Psychological Outcomes in Adolescents and Emerging Adults: A Meta-Analytic Review." *Journal of Adolescence* 35.2 (2011) 299–314.

Yoon, Young-mi. "Young People Stuck with 'Passion Wages' and Little Opportunity to Learn." *The Hankyoerh*, June 25, 2015. http://english.hani.co.kr/arti/english_edition/e_business/697517.html.

Zetter, Roger. "Labeling Refugees: The Forming and Transforming of a Bureaucratic Identity." *Journal of Refugee Studies* 4 (1991) 39–62.

Zhou, Min. "Segmented Assimilation: Issues, Controversies, and Recent Research on the New Second Generation." *International Migration Review* 31 (1997) 975–1008.

Zong, Jie, and Jeanne Batalova. "Korean Immigrants in the United States." http://www.migrationpolicy.org/article/Korean immigrants-united-states.

KOREAN TEXT

Amennet. "세월호 사고 관련 성명서: 대한민국이여, 다시 일어나라" [Petition for Sewol Ferry: Rise Up Korea Again]. https://usaamen.net/bbs/board.php?bo_table=data&wr_id=4951&page=154.

An, Sun Young, et al. "청년기에서 성인기로의 이행과정 연구 II: 총괄 보고서 [Transition from Youth to Adulthood II: Comprehensive Report]." *Korean National Youth Policy Institute* 17.3 (2011) 1–221.

The Bank of Korea. "국민계정 2015 [National Accounts 2015]." http://www.bok.or.kr/contents/total/ko/boardView.action?menuNaviId=598&boardBean.brdid=125186&boardBean.menuid=598.

Choi, Jonghun. "도시와 청소년 문제 [Urbanization and Youth Issues]." *Studies on Korean Youth* 23.5 (1995) 5–13.

Choi, Yoon Sik. "2014년 한국교회를 전망한다, [Prospecting Korean Church in 2014]." *Kukmin Ilbo*, January 25, 2014. http://news.kukinews.com/article/view.asp?page=1&gCode=kmi&arcid=0007970748&cp=nv.

Gallup Korea. "한국인의 종교 [The Religion of Koreans]." *Gallup Korea*, May 2, 2014. http://www.gallup.co.kr/gallupdb/reportContent.asp?seqNo=625.

Han, Wan Sang. "한국사회에서의 세대갈등에 대한 한 연구 [A Study of Generational Conflicts in Korean Society]." *Sa Sang* 3 (1991) 248–309.

Hong, Duk Ryul. "한국사회의 세대연구 [Research on Generations in Korean Society]." *History Criticism* 64.8 (2003) 150–91.

Hong, Sung Tae. "세대갈등과 문화정치 [Generational Conflicts and Cultural Politics]." *Cultural Science* 37.3 (2004) 154–72.

Jung, Jae Yong, et al. 한국 교회 제자훈련 미래전망 보고서: 무엇을 위한 누구의 제자인가 *[Report for the Future of Korean Church Discipleship: For Whom and for What Is the Disciple]*. Seoul: InterVarsity, 2016.

Jung, Soo Bok. 한국인의 문화적 문법 *[Korean Cultural Grammar]*. Seoul: Tree of Thought, 2007.

Bibliography

Kim, Ae Soon. 혼돈의 20대, 자신을 말하다 [*Confused Twenties Speak about Themselves*]. Seoul: Sigma, 2010.

Kim, Eun Jung. "새로운 생애 발달 단계로서의 성인모색기(Emerging Adulthood): 20대 전반 여대생을 중심으로, ['Emerging Adulthood' in Korea: Understanding the New Way of Young Korean Women's Coming of Age Experiences]." *Society and Theory* 19.2 (2011) 329–72.

Kim, Jangsub. "한인교회 미래 . . . 2세 목회자 육성에 달려" [The Future of Korean Immigrant Church Depends on Growing 2nd Generation Pastors]." http://kr.christianitydaily.com/articles/85412/20151112/.

Korean Educational Development Institute. "교육통계연보 2015 [Statistical Year Book of Education 2015]." http://kess.kedi.re.kr/eng/publ/view?survSeq=2015&publSeq=2&menuSeq=0&itemCode=02&language=en#.

Lee, Ki Ho. 이것은 왜 청춘이 아니란 말인가 [*Why This Is Not Young Life*]. Prunsoop: Seoul, 2010.

Lee, Ki Hyung. "청년세대의 삶과 소통의 위기 [Life of Younger Generation and Crisis of Communication]." *Korean Society for Journalism and Communication Studies* 5 (2011) 269–97.

Lim, Chang Gi. 임장기 교수 "20년후 한인교회와 이엠의 관계역전" [After 20 Years, the Status of Korean Immigrant Church and EM Would Be Reversed]. https://usaamen.net/bbs/board.php?bo_table=data&wr_id=5341&sca=%EC%9D%B4%EB%AF%BC&page=11.

Ministry of Foreign Affairs. "2015 재외동포정책 및 현황" [Numbers of Korean Diaspora in 2015]. http://www.mofa.go.kr/travel/overseascitizen/index.jsp?mofat=001&menu=m_10_40&sp=/webmodule/htsboard/template/read/korboardread.jsppercent3FtypeID=6percent26boardid=232percent26tableName=TYPE_DATABOARDpercent26seqno=356334.

Park, Hayng Sook. "초기 성인을 위한 기독교신앙교육: 신생 성인기를 중심으로 [Christian Faith Education for Young Adulthood: Focusing on Emerging Adulthood]." PhD diss., Seoul Theological University, 2012.

Park, Jae Heung. "한국 사회의 세대 갈등: 권력, 이념, 문화 갈등을 중심으로 [Generational Conflicts in Korea: Power, Ideological, and Cultural Conflicts]." *Korean Demography* 33.3 (2010) 75–99.

Shin, Kwangyoung, and Soo Yeon Moon. "계급과 스펙경쟁 [Class and Qualification Competition]." *Korean Sociological Association* 12 (2012) 81–96.

Shu, In Sil. "미주 첫교회 후 110년 만에 4,233 교회 됐다 [4,323 Korean churches in America after 110 years of the First Korean Immigrant Church in America]." http://christiantoday.us/sub_read.html?uid=20910&section=section12&section2.

———. "북가주에 282, 남가주에 1,077개 분포. (282 in Northern California and 1,077 in Southern California)." http://christiantoday.us/sub_read.html?uid=23878&section=sc154.

———. "해외한인교회는 5,929개, 미국에 4,323개 [4,323 Korean churches in America out of 5929 Korean Diaspora Churches in the World]." http://christiantoday.us/sub_read.html?uid=21674&section=sc154&section2#.

So, Tae Young. "성인 발현기(Emerging Adulthood) 청년들(20-29세)의 요구분석에 기초한 교회교육과정개발을 위한 제안 [The Study on the Church Curriculum Which Reflects and Responds to the Need Analysis of Korean Twenties in the Emerging Adulthood]." *Christian Education & Information Technology* 9 (2015) 1–34.

Song, Ho Geun, et al. 위기의 청년세대, 출구를 찾다 [*Younger Generation at Crisis, Finding an Exit*]. Seoul: Nanam, 2010.
Song, In Kyu. "Introduction." In 한국 교회 제자훈련 미래전망 보고서: 무엇을 위한 누구의 제자인가 [*Report for Future of Korean Church Discipleship: For Who and for What Is the Disciple*], edited by Jae Yong Jung et al., 9–11. Seoul: InterVarsity, 2016.
Statistics Korea. "2015년 혼인 이혼 통계 [Marriage and Divorce Statistics 2015]." http://kostat.go.kr/portal/korea/kor_nw/3/index.board?bmode=read&aSeq=352515.
Woo, Suk Hoon. *88만원 세대* [*Generation of 880 Dollars*]. Seoul: Redian, 2007.
Yang, Hee Song. 다시프로테스탄트 [*Protestant, Again*]. Seoul: Bokitnuen Saram, 2012.
Yoo, Eun-Hee. "성인모색기의 도덕적 표류현상과 기독교적인 도덕적 성품교육 ["Morally Adrift": Emerging Adulthood and Christian Moral Character Education]." *Christian Education & Information Technology* 9.42 (2014) 283–327.

www.ingramcontent.com/pod-product-compliance
Lightning Source LLC
Chambersburg PA
CBHW070313240426
43663CB00038BA/2223